VEILED FIGURES

Veiled Figures

Women, Modernity, and the Spectres of Orientalism

TERESA HEFFERNAN

UNIVERSITY OF TORONTO PRESS
Toronto Buffalo London

Toronto Buffalo London
www.utppublishing.com

ISBN 978-1-4426-3723-8

Library and Archives Canada Cataloguing in Publication

Heffernan, Teresa, 1962–, author
Veiled figures : women, modernity, and the spectres of Orientalism / Teresa Heffernan.

Includes bibliographical references and index.
ISBN 978-1-4426-3723-8 (cloth)

1. Veils in literature. 2. Veils – Social aspects. 3. Veils – History. 4. Muslim women in literature. 5. Islamic literature – Christian interpretations. I. Title.

PN56.V44H43 2016 809′.933564 C2015-908775-9

University of Toronto Press acknowledges the financial assistance to its publishing program of the Canada Council for the Arts and the Ontario Arts Council, an agency of the Government of Ontario.

Canada Council for the Arts
Conseil des Arts du Canada

Funded by the Government of Canada
Financé par le gouvernement du Canada
Canada

For my siblings

In memory of my dear sister, Shelagh Heffernan (1955–2010)

Contents

Illustrations

Acknowledgments

I would like to thank the many people without whom this book could not have been written. Donald Ross organized one of the first travel writing conferences, "Snapshots from Abroad," at the University of Minnesota, which I was lucky enough to attend. During a research trip at the Huntington Library, Daniel Goffman was incredibly generous and patient as he responded to my early email inquiries about the cosmopolitan nature of Ottoman society. While there, I also came across Nancy Micklewright's work on Lady Annie Brassey's photographs, and she has since shared her expertise with me at conferences and over email. I am grateful to Işil Baş, who invited me to present at "A Century of Women in Turkey" at Boğaziçi University, Istanbul, and who was a wonderful host. I had the very good fortune of meeting Reina Lewis at that conference, and we have since worked together over the years on our "Cultures in Dialogue" series and participated on scores of memorable panels. It has been a real pleasure to work with the many contributors to the "Cultures in Dialogue" series, from whom I have learned a great deal, particularly Carolyn Goffman and Hülya Adak. I am grateful to Zeynep İnankur, Reina Lewis, and Mary Roberts, who invited me to participate in "The Ottoman Empire and British Orientalism Symposium" at the Pera Muzesi in Istanbul. The organizers of "America in the Middle East/The Middle East in America Conference" at the American University of Beirut and the "Women to Watch" series at Hofstra University both graciously invited me to present some of this research. Thanks also to Piers Smith for organizing the "Aesthetic Encounters" conference at the University of Kuwait and for his encouragement; and also to Joyce Goggin for inviting me to give guest lectures on this material at the University of Amsterdam. I have presented this research at numerous conferences and really benefitted from the constructive contributions of colleagues; particularly those at the Middle Eastern Studies Association, the Modernist Studies Association, and the Berkshire Conference on the History of Women. Leslie Pierce and Virginia Aksan both generously responded to email questions; their work has been inspirational. llhan Kaya and Erik Steinskog both read chapters for me. Thank you to Daniel O'Quinn for many stimulating conversations over the years and for editing Lady Mary's *Turkish Embassy Letters* with me; and to my friend and colleague Goran Stanivukovic, who shares my interest in the Ottoman world. Michael Bosson, the archivist at Sandon Hall, and Elaine Wright, the curator of the Islamic Collection at the Chester Beatty Library, have been immensely helpful as have the staff at the British Library, King's College Library, the Huntington Library, and the Atatürk Library. I am indebted to the anonymous readers who offered very insightful suggestions for revisions. Many thanks to my various research assistants who have worked on this project with me over the years – Candice Albright, Jackie Cameron, Erika Pineo, Eda Acara, Kaley Joyes, and Shawna Ferris – for their careful work and enthusiasm for the project; and to Thom Loree for early copy edits. A special thanks to my editor, Richard Ratzlaff, for his early support of this work and for carefully shepherding it to its final stages. I am grateful to the staff at the University of Toronto Press: in particular Gillian Scobie, an outstanding copy editor; and Barb Porter, Associate Managing Editor, whom I have the pleasure of working with for a second time.

This research has been generously supported by Social Sciences and Humanities Research Council grants, a King's College Fellowship, an Andrew W. Mellon Foundation Fellowship, and Saint Mary's University Faculty of Graduate Studies Research Awards. Earlier versions of some this work first appeared as "Feminism Against the East/West Divide: Lady Mary's *Turkish Embassy Letters*," *Eighteenth-Century Studies* 33.2 (2000): 201–15; "'He Who Believes in the Devil Already Belongs to Him': Rescuing Women from Afghanistan to Iraq," *Arab Journal in the Humanities* 89.23 (2005): 175–88; "The Reflexive Orientalist: An American in Istanbul," introduction to *In the Palaces of the Sultan* by Anna Bowman Dodd, Gorgias Press, 2005: v–xxiv; "Travelling East: Veiling, Race, and Nations" in *The Poetics and Politics of Place: Ottoman Istanbul and British Orientalism*, eds. Zeynep İnankur, Reina Lewis, and Mary Roberts, Istanbul: Pera Museum, 2011: 157–65 (Turkish translation, 2012).

Finally I would like to thank my parents for encouraging me to ask questions and inspiring my interest in history and literature; my siblings, nieces, and nephews, who offer up such interesting commentary; Shelagh Heffernan, whom I miss daily, and Peter Sinclair for their support and for hosting me on my many visits to London; and David Vainola for his many years of offering his intelligent and insightful comments on my work.

VEILED FIGURES

Introduction

Consider the portrayals of the veiled woman that have long populated western literature, painting, film, and newspapers. From eighteenth-century travel narratives to nineteenth-century orientalist painters to twentieth-century Hollywood films to the media coverage of the wars in Afghanistan and the Middle East that began this century, this figure has been consistently cast as some combination of imprisoned, erotic, backward. Juxtapose these portrayals with the recent outpourings of Muslim extremists who argue that the education of women is a western import and that girls should not go to school, most famously and brutally expressed in the 2012 shooting of Malala Yousafzai in Pakistan. Now consider the image that graces the cover of this book. It is titled "Women Reading," and it is from a manuscript produced in the Mughal Empire, c. 1600. A woman in a pink veil reads while a woman in European-inspired dress fans her. Two other women in the harem are also reading and discussing books; a pen box and more books sit between the three women. This early-seventeenth-century depiction of a community of female scholars offers a provocative and simple challenge to both western stereotypes and contemporary extremists' arguments about Muslim women. What various interests have been at work in the production of orientalist depictions of the veiled woman from the eighteenth century onward? Why has the figure of the (un)veiled woman played such a central role in the various constructions of the East/West divide? Could releasing her from this restrictive bind help to undo the clash of civilizations rhetoric fueling contemporary wars fought in her name? Is it possible to bury the spectres of orientalism that hold her captive? These are some of the central questions of this study.

From the Islamic Revolution in 1979 and the rise of Ayatollah Khomeini to the 11 September 2001 terrorist attacks that launched this century, debates about the veil have become increasingly heated, garnering international attention. The chador became mandatory for women in post-revolutionary Iran, influencing Saudi Arabia to tighten its dress code for women. In 1989, three girls refused to remove their headscarves in a classroom in a school in Creil, France, which erupted into the *l'affaire du voile islamique* (the Islamic veil affair). In the 1990s, under the Taliban, wearing a burqa was made obligatory for women in Afghanistan. In 2001, several employees of the White House and members of the Congress started wearing "burqa swatches" as a symbol of protest; the USA and its allies connected terrorism and burqa wearing, while the invasion of Afghanistan was popularly justified by the logic of needing to liberate its women from this garment.

In 2004, France instituted the "veil law" that banned the wearing of headscarves and other religious articles in schools in the name of keeping the state separate from religion. That same year, the European Court of Human Rights rejected a grievance brought forth by Leyla Şahin, a medical student at the University of Istanbul, who was denied access to exams and classes because she wore a headscarf to the university. In 2008, the Turkish parliament's attempt to revise the constitution and overturn the law against wearing headscarves at educational and state institutions caused mass protests; the country's highest court blocked the AKP's efforts. The Dutch government proposed a complete ban on veiling in public spaces and the veiled woman continues to be a flashpoint after the assassination of the filmmaker Theo Van Gogh, who made *Submission* in 2004 (with Ayaan Hirsi Ali), a sensationalist film about violence against women under Islam. The 2005 tube bombings in London heightened discussions about veiling and security in England, and Jack Straw, Foreign Secretary and Labour MP, revealed in 2006 that he had asked women to remove their face veils during consultations with him, arguing that they hindered communication.

In the 2007 Quebec election, when protestors wanted women who wear niqābs (a veil that covers the face) to unveil or lose the right to cast a ballot, Prime Minister Stephen Harper's government upheld its policy against "veiled voting" even as it was challenged by Elections Canada. Since the divisive debates around the Quebec Charter of Values began, there has been an increase in attacks against veiled women in the province. When tensions began escalating between Iran and the USA, Iran, as part of an attempt "to increase security in society," started cracking down on improperly veiled women. Post the Iraq and Afghanistan invasions, there has been a resurgence of fundamentalisms; from Canada to Iraq to Pakistan, women have been attacked, raped, and killed for not wearing a veil. In 2009, the Muslim Canadian Congress supported the ban on niqābs and burqas in this country.

These are only a few of the hundreds of relatively recent examples where the figure of the (un)veiled woman has ignited controversy and has been made to serve various political, religious, and cultural agendas in the global arena. Why do these headdresses for women consistently inflame debates in ways that men's headdresses rarely do? Why, for instance, are there no special police to enforce the wearing of the keffiyeh, ghutrah, or shemagh or calls to ban them on the grounds that they oppress men? For a host of reasons, ranging from the power and wealth of Gulf countries to multiculturalism in western cities, veiling of all sorts and varieties has become increasingly visible in these past couple of decades, and wearing or not wearing this piece of cloth has provoked wide-ranging discussions on everything from freedom to fashion to rights.

Predating all the Abrahamic religions, the veil has never been unique to a particular gender, class, religion, or culture.[1] Yet the veil has nevertheless become one of the most visible signs of Muslim faith as debates about its many forms – including the headscarf, niqāb, hijab, abaya, burqa, tesettür, turban, jilbab, chador, shayla, yashmak, khimar – have intensified with calls to ban it, market it, police it, embrace it, refashion it, and enforce it. The veil, in this context, has been a much discussed topic, causing Pnina Werbner to remark that "it would seem almost impossible to say anything new" about the subject.[2] This study draws on much of this research, but it is mainly concerned with the metaphorical and semiotic implications of not only veiled – but also unveiled women's bodies – in a global context that spans three centuries. It is not about why or how women do or do not wear veils or whether they should or should not veil – rather, it asks how veiling in any of its forms emerged as an over-determined sign of Islam and how the figure of the (un)veiled woman became key in the divide between Islam and the West.

Anjum Alvi, in her ethnographic study of Malot, Pakistan, discusses veiling as a value system that operates on questions of *sharam* (which includes notions of shame, respect, and dignity) that extends beyond gender and the particularities of women's dress. Including discussions of death, divinity, responsibility, saints, asceticism, and power, she argues that veiling as concealment is a fundamental indigenous value that permeates and shapes all Punjabi social relationships, from architecture to marriage arrangements to wealth. Thus she argues that the veil should not be torn from its context and treated as a symbol that refers to an external referent (i.e., rights, patriarchy, class, sexuality, religion). It is, rather, Alvi argues, a subjective practice, a way of being-in-the-world where the ethical self is oriented towards and responsible for the other. Separating the meaning from the act, or semiotics from practice, she argues, impedes access to the veil's "full meaning" and denies the non-modern other a voice as Islam gets assimilated into a modern "universalizing" frame. She considers this argument in the context of a model of concealment and revealment that operates among the Muslims in her ethnographic study, and she objects to the prevalent discourse in the critical literature that argues veiling "has no meaning" in and of itself.[3]

While I agree with Alvi on the usefulness of expanding discussions of veiling to include concepts beyond the specific sartorial item and on the importance of understanding veiling and unveiling as relational and fluid, the division she makes between a non-modern Islamic culture and a universalizing modernity problematically establishes her as a "transparent" investigator who gives voice to a reified non-modern "other" even as she uses "modern" theory (Levinas, Dumont, Wittgenstein, Said) to frame her research·subject. I argue that, rather than the threat of modernity assimilating the voice of the "other," the dialectic of veiling and unveiling constructs the very division between the non-modern and the modern that structures Alvi's argument. In other words, the moment that veiling as – concealment, religion, the sacred – is pitted against unveiling as – revelation, reason, the secular – there is a refusal to acknowledge the alternative modernity inherent in Islam. It is this moment that inaugurates the divide between the East and the West in the eighteenth century. In the nineteenth century, the understanding of unveiling and veiling shifts again as they come to differently structure competing models of the nation: European versus Islamic. In the late-twentieth and early-twenty-first centuries, the East/West divide – fed by global capitalism – is at its most polarized. At each moment this tension between East and West plays itself out on women's bodies, both veiled and unveiled.

Rather than veiling as static and singular – as having a "meaning in itself" – this study suggests that veiling has always necessarily involved interpretation and thus is open to multiple and dynamic readings that can never be "full." Yet in its everyday performance, the symbol solidifies through repetition – it becomes naturalized as a timeless tradition or a cultural practice or as a way of being in the world or as a code or value. For instance, veiling in some ancient societies was used to create a boundary between free women and slave women, "respectable" and "disreputable" women, sexually protected and sexually vulnerable women, a code that was adopted by various religions, including Islam.[4] Yet the veil as a symbol of class in Muslim cultures is itself in continual flux. A brief survey of even the writers reviewed in this book suggests no consistency. In the early-eighteenth-century Ottoman territories, Lady Mary Wortley Montagu notes that the "wives and daughters" of mostly Greek gardeners go unveiled in the countryside of Adrianople, "a liberty not permitted them in town," whereas the veils that the women wore in Pera (the side of Istanbul inhabited by mostly Franks – people of European descent – in the eighteenth century) "only serve[d] to show their beauty" and were different than the "Turkish veil" that required them, across the Golden Horn in Constantinople, to cover their faces.[5] Over a century later, Lady Annie Brassey writes about the changes in veiling practices in Istanbul where Armenian women had veiled "as carefully as the Turkish women," but ten years later, like Europeans, they were walking the city without veils. In the early part of the twentieth-century in Turkey, Halidé Edib discusses the disguise she adopts so she can escape the attention of the Allies while escaping from Istanbul on her way to Angora: dressed as the wife of a hodja (teacher), she dons an "old-fashioned *charshaf*," but does not veil her face "because a woman of that class never veils her face."[6] It was also at this time that some elite and middle-class urban women in Egypt and Turkey began to unveil as a mark of their modernity.[7] Although post-9/11, the burqa is still considered a sign of social mobility among rural women in Afghanistan, as Nelofer Pazira explains it is a mark of unsophistication in urban centres[8] whereas in contemporary Egypt, some wealthy urban women are adopting face veiling to signal wealth and status as Gulf-inspired fashion hits the runways. The veil as a symbol of class is always shifting – sometimes marking the elite and urban and sometimes marking the rural and poor.

This study draws on scholarship about veiling, unveiling, orientalism, nationalism, Islamism, colonialism, and feminisms, using travel writing, histories, fiction, harem literature, and newspaper accounts as its main source material. Rather than distinguishing "true" accounts and histories from fictional stories, it accepts that both serve to consolidate ideological assumptions.[9] It considers the early liminality of the Ottoman Empire which was displaced by the increasingly rigid borders that developed between the East and West, and tracks the rise of the Republic of Turkey and its accelerated transformation from a cosmopolitan Empire to a racialized nation. It argues that the global debates about religion and secularism, modernity and tradition, nationalism and cosmopolitanism, social justice and market economies, community and individualism, pivot around the figure of the (un)veiled woman, often to women's detriment.

In his groundbreaking work *Orientalism* (1978), which analyses western canonical texts, the literary critic Edward Said makes a persuasive argument about the ways in which the West has defined itself against an Oriental other. The Orient in the western imaginary, he argues, is consistently produced as monolithic, mysterious, and backward. Whereas Europe produces itself as active, vocal, masculine, rational, secular, and free, the Orient is rendered decadent, despotic, silent, passive, queer, feminine, and irrational. Said also asks if – considering the whole complex relationship between knowledge and power, which, he argues, is perfectly illustrated by the simultaneous rise of the British Empire and of orientalist scholarship – there might not be an alternative model of engaging with "the other" that avoids the hostility of the division of "us" in the West and "they" in the East. Rather than engagement or dialogue, he argues, the knowledge produced from this power dynamic has only served "to polarize the distinction – the Oriental becomes more Oriental, the Western more Western – and limit the human encounter between different cultures, traditions, and societies."[10]

Since Said's book, a host of Ottoman and Arab historians, including Virginia Aksan, Daniel Goffman, Nabil Matar, Linda Darling, and Palimira Brummett, and literary scholars such as Bernadette Andrea, Humberto Garcia, and Mohja Kahf, have argued that the history of East/West relations have been far more nuanced. The representation of the Turk as a terrible and fearful figure belies the ways in which early modern England was also deeply dependent on the much more powerful Ottoman Empire and thus needed to cultivate healthy trade and diplomatic relations. As the global power dynamic begins to shift in favour of the West in the eighteenth-century, travel narratives representing Turks as backward and decadent proliferate, but there is also a complicated balance that must be negotiated as the still powerful Ottoman world remained strategically important to western powers. That the Europeans fought against the Ottomans in the Greek War of Independence, but sided with them against Russia in the Crimean War, and then occupied Istanbul after the Great War suggests some of the complexities of this relationship.

The main thesis in *Orientalism* is also further complicated by women's conversations about the Ottoman that interrupt the largely malecentric discourse articulated by Said. Scholars such as Lisa Lowe, Billie Melman, and Reina Lewis suggest that the orientalist/occidentalist dynamic is far more heterogeneous than Said's model allows for and that texts by women involved in emergent feminisms often subvert traditional orientalist tropes. At this historical moment when the polarization between East and West is at its most extreme, I argue that shifting the focus to the figure of the (un)veiled woman points to how this divide is both constructed and maintained at the expense of women, but also to how exchanges between some women begin to unravel it, giving way to the possibility of a dialogue that opens up "the human encounter between different cultures" that Said argued was lacking.

This book charts the changing nature of the East/West divide at three important moments: the "birth" of secularism in the West in the eighteenth century, the racialization of nations in the late-nineteenth and early-twentieth centuries, and the rise of global capitalism and Islamism in the latter half of the twentieth and early-twentieth-first centuries. More specifically, the book focuses on the ways in which the figure of the (un)veiled woman has been used to prop up the East/West divide as it has been differently articulated – Religion versus Reason, the Islamic *umma* versus the European nation, Capitalism versus Islamism. It also considers the narratives of various women who disrupt and subvert the logic of this divide that they have historically been made to secure as it explores other routes to social and cultural interaction.

The story begins in the long eighteenth century, with the rise of western modernity, when the (un)veiled woman first emerged as a contentious figure. As the balance of power slowly shifted from the Ottoman Empire to Europe following the Battle of Lepanto in 1571 (one of the first major defeats for the Turks), despite the similarities in the subordinate positions of women in the East and West, the veiled woman in the western imaginary becomes one of the most powerful symbols of the "irrationality" of Islam. The popularity of tales about Eastern women's oppression, and, given that men had no access to women's quarters, largely imagined, is evident in the burgeoning industry of eighteenth- and nineteenth-century travel literature about the Orient. Early British feminists were quick to import the image of the enslaved Eastern woman in their writing as a means of expressing their own frustration with power inequities at home, and thus contributed to orientalism by casting the East as despotic and backward. These debates about the oppression of the veiled woman and the irrationality of the Orient take place in the context of the emerging narrative about Europe as the birthplace of secularism and universal reason.

However, Lady Mary Wortley Montagu, one of the first female travellers to the Ottoman Empire, not only challenges the voyeuristic tales about Turkish women and their enslavement, in her *Turkish Embassy Letters*, but also disrupts the story of modernity by insisting on the liberty of veiled women. Recognizing the rationalist aspects of Islam and the religious aspects of western reason, Montagu, rather than locating herself on a particular side of the argument (either the one favouring the veil in the name of religion or the one supporting the casting off of the veil in the name of reason), brings each discourse into crisis with the other. Challenging the emergence of the secular/religious divide at its inauguration, she releases the figure of the (un)veiled woman from the burden of her symbolic role in the divide by restoring her agency.

Chapter 2 considers the explosion of western travel writing about the Ottoman Empire in the nineteenth century, which often both mocked the Empire's cosmopolitan populations and encouraged it to adopt the European model of nationalism. It also tracks the shift in the meaning of the term "Turk," from a religious designation to an ethnic/racial marker in this literature. While Europe was obsessed with racial categories, as evident in the works of travellers like Lucy Garnett and Richard Burton, Ottoman accounts, such as those by Melek Hanim, Halidé Edib, and Adalet, were full of descriptions of mixed relationships and interethnic families, challenging the genre of harem literature that depended on "authentic" racial markers of the East/West divide. Western anxieties about miscegenation and class transgressions, this chapter argues, underlie the representations of heterogeneous Ottoman populations as decaying, exhausted, and sick during this century. Further, it suggests, the desire to "liberate" the Ottoman woman from her veil at this time was about policing her body and insisting that it accommodate race and class boundaries.

Chapter 3 engages in a close reading of two travel narratives – one American and one British – in the wider context of western imperialism, comparative cosmopolitanisms, and racialized nationalism. Lady Annie Brassey, a world traveller and well-known writer and photographer in her day, published *Sunshine and Storm in the East, or Cruises to Cyprus and Constantinople* in Britain in 1880. She was known for her efforts to establish branches of the St John Ambulance Association around the globe and this "devotion to the cause of suffering," as her editor put it, is evident in many of her comments about Turkish women and their struggles for freedom. Yet, curiously, Lady Brassey never links these struggles for liberty to the women's suffrage movements in Britain. Nor does she question Britain's relentlessly paternal attitude towards Turkey. Against the backdrop of women agitating for the vote in England, the decline of the Ottoman Empire, and the British involvement in the war between Russia and Turkey, Lady Brassey's narrative exposes the strategic deployment of a feminism that served an imperialist agenda.

Not long after Lady Brassey, the American writer Anna Bowman Dodd travelled to Istanbul with the American ambassador to France, who was there to negotiate the release of the missionary Ellen Stone. Stone had been kidnapped by Bulgarian brigands fighting for Macedonian liberty who were hoping to draw Americans into the "Eastern question." Dodd's *In the Palaces of the Sultan* (1901) records the attempts of Sultan Abdülhamid II to preserve his shrinking cosmopolitan Empire in the face of the numerous internal uprisings, the flames of which were being fanned by Europe, Russia, and America. Riding a new cusp of American orientalism and both fascinated and disturbed by the diversity of men on the streets of Istanbul where the races seemed to be "inextricably mixed" and no one race seemed to "dominate," she exposes America's complicated relationship – given its own policies of racial segregation – to the Empire. Both Dodd's and Brassey's travel narratives highlight the ways in which western women's support for Turkish women unveiling was imbricated with their support for British and American imperialism and racialized nationalism.

Chapter 4 examines the rise of nationalism in Turkey in the aftermath of the Great War. Here the "unveiling" of women is considered in the context of the nineteenth-century "institutionalization" of the female nude in Europe, anti-suffragist literature, militarized nationalism, veiling and the *umma*, European social contract theory, and the gendering of private and public space. A comparative analysis of the models of the Islamic nation and the European nation with respect to the position of women provides the theoretical context for this section.

The British feminist Grace Ellison, one of the first westerners to visit Mustapha Kemal Atatürk behind enemy lines as he was trying to salvage what would become the Republic of Turkey from the remnants of the Empire, witnessed the structuring of this nation. Critical to its "birth" was Atatürk's insistence on the banishment of veils and harems in the name of modernity. Ellison, who had befriended Zeyneb Hanim, an Ottoman woman who had escaped to Europe to flee the gender politics of the Ottoman system, was sympathetic to the plight of Turkish women. Yet while Ellison, in general, supports this new nation, she also, surprisingly, expresses her hesitance about women giving up their veils as Ellison herself was not happy with the terms of gender equality in Britain after women had won the right to vote. In this chapter, I explore the complicated reasons for this hesitance, and the legacy of militarized European nations and armed citizens that is exemplified in the founding moment of the Turkish Republic.

Like Ellison, Demetra Vaka Brown, a Greek Ottoman living in America, visited Istanbul during its occupation by the Allies. She also, but for different reasons, expresses nostalgia for the system of veils and harems in her 1923 travel narrative, *The Unveiled Ladies of Stamboul*. Like many modernist writers, she was opposed to the virulent racialized nationalism that was sweeping Europe and that was infecting the Republic of Turkey at the moment of its founding. The veiling and unveiling of women's bodies take on particular meanings in the context of the construction of militarized and racialized citizens in these two very different works as Ellison and Vaka suggest an alternative course for modernity that was foreclosed by the adoption of the European model of the nation.

Chapter 5 considers how once again the contested figure of the (un) veiled woman has been deployed to prop up an East/West divide at the turn of the twenty-first century.[11] It turns from travel literature to mainstream journalism, which, in many ways, has taken over the function of earlier travel narratives. America and its allies legitimated the war in Afghanistan, over the protests of Afghani feminists, by insisting on liberating "helpless" women from their burqas. Meanwhile, American women were lauded for stripping off their clothes with bravado as a sign of their liberty and Playboy bunnies were celebrated as the "true patriots." A different dynamic unfolded in the war in Iraq, where veiled Iraqi women were portrayed as aggressive and militant, whereas American women in the military were cast as virginal and in need of saving from "lascivious" Arab men. The Jessica Lynch story, patriotic pornography, the Abu Ghraib scandal, Riverbend, and Malalai Joya expose the fallacy at the heart of the East/West divide, the "us and them" rhetoric famously deployed by George Bush.

This chapter concludes with a survey of the many factors that have contributed to the recent global rise in visible veiling. It considers the works of Leila Ahmed, Joan Scott, and Nilüfer Göle, which trace the causes and implications of this confrontation between secularism and religion. It considers Islamic branding and marketing, neoliberalism, state coercion, cosmopolitanism, social justice, and the regulation of women's bodies in the context of contemporary calls to both ban and enforce veiling. For centuries, the figure of the (un)veiled woman has been held hostage in the clash of civilizations argument. This divide between East and West has been strategically constructed to serve varied interests and has shut down the more fluid and nuanced continuities, both progressive and reactionary, between Islam and western modernity. This book is about exposing the spectres of orientalism that continue to haunt the contemporary moment in order to release the figure of the (un)veiled woman and unravel this restrictive bind.

Chapter One

Islam, the Enlightenment, and the Veil

"I want women to be fully included. If you want equality, you have to be in society, not hidden away from it."

(Harriet Harman, British Labour MP, on veiling, in 2006)

"They [Turks] boast a sort of unconfin'd Authority, which makes their *Wives* submissively Obedient; but since it ne'er allows that mutual Confidence, that *generous, free,* and *open familiarity,* so requisite to make a Marriage truly happy, I cannot praise their Policy in robbing Wives of that well tolerated Liberty."

(Aaron Hill, *A full and just account of the present state of the Ottoman Empire,* 1709)

The all-pervasive and overdetermined figure of the (un)veiled woman is central to the rhetoric of clashing civilizations and cultures that feeds the divide between Islamism and western modernity in the early twenty-first century. Yet the long and contentious history of how this figure came to occupy this position is often obscured in these heated debates. This chapter – thus – sets out to track her emergence in the burgeoning field of European travel literature about the Ottoman Empire in the eighteenth century. Produced by merchants, diplomats, ambassadors, and historians, this genre played an important role in the establishment of a divide between East and West. Early modern representations and maps of the polycentric and dominant Ottoman Empire offered no neat boundaries between Islam and Christian Europe, but after the defeat of the Ottoman army at the Battle of Vienna in 1683, western representations became increasingly invested in establishing a firmer boundary that stressed differences rather than similarities. It was during this shift in the balance of power – from East to West – that the figure of the sequestered and veiled Muslim woman emerged as a key symbol in this newly emerging divide.

The Politics of Eighteenth-Century Travel Literature

If premodern travel narratives were largely fabulous tales that drew on classical and biblical sources, by the eighteenth century travel literature had gained a reputation for being objective and credible. Sir James Porter, in his *Observations on the Religion, Law, Government, and Manners of the Turks* (1771), explicitly rejects the premodern tradition and distances himself from earlier stylistic conventions that valued imitative, fantastic, and poetic rhetoric over plain prose, accuracy, and objectivity. He writes of his own contribution: "Had the author wrote merely for reputation, he would have studied elegance of composition, and well-turned periods; he would have aimed at all the refined embellishments of a pure and classical stile. But he freely resigns the ornaments of rhetoric to those who are more solicitous about words than things; who prefer cultivating the talents of imagination to the investigation of truth; who delight more in gathering the flowers of eloquence, than in dispelling the clouds of error, and the enchantments of delusion."[1]

Promoting this new sensibility, with its stress on immediate and unadorned observations, The Royal Society issued specific directives to travellers to help them record their experiences and compile their knowledge about a particular place. Richard Chandler informs us in his *Travels in Asia Minor* (1775) that the Royal Society directed him to "keep a very minute Journal of every Day's occurrences and Observations, representing things exactly in the light they strike [him], in the plainest Manner, and without any regard to Style or Language, except that of being intelligible."[2] In the travel narratives of the period, the declaration of the accuracy of an account is a common convention: other writers' works are read, cited, and dismissed as products of fantasy and imagination while the author declares that his unique position and access to sources guarantee the truth. In 1784, Elias Habesci's *The Present State of the Ottoman Empire* (translated from French) begins with just such a declaration as his editor informs us that the author "had in his possessions materials of a more ample and accurate account of the present state of the Ottoman Empire than any extant: that he had read the different productions of the English and the French press upon the same subject, and found great room for correction and improvement."[3] The author himself promises that his pages contain "nothing but real facts ... which no one, not in a similar situation, could relate as undeniable truths."[4] Thomas Thornton's *The Present State of Turkey* (1807) also offers an opening declaration that dismisses other "imaginative" travel works and promises a more "objective" record as he accuses previous travellers of describing nature "[n]ot from an accurate survey of real life, but from the distorted phantoms of their own imaginations"[5] and insists that almost all other writers on Turkish manners have displayed "partiality, prejudice, or defect."[6]

Part of this transformation in the travel genre has to do with what Ian Watt refers to, more broadly, as the shifting world view of the eighteenth century. Watt argues that the rising faith in science and progress was displacing classical and religious readings of the world as static, fixed, and complete. If, earlier, the belief in abstracts and universals trumped the transitory world of the senses and sense perception, science and philosophy were now encouraging the idea of "reality" as the product of individual sense and cognition. Historical teleology was gradually replacing the view of history as cyclical; and the valuing of plain prose and novel perspectives meant the devaluing of figurative and poetic writing, which had sought to replicate the original – understood as a return to the first or ideal.[7] This shift, in turn, led to the emphasis on "things" as opposed to "words," as Porter declared, even as he and others suppressed the fact that words – be they plain or poetic – are still words and not things.

As trading opportunities and diplomatic postings were beginning to open up the possibility of English travel to the Ottoman Empire, these claims to the superiority of eyewitness accounts should have served as a corrective to one of the first histories of Turkey published in English: Richard Knolles's *The Generall Historie of the Turkes* (1603). Knolles, who had never travelled to the Ottoman Empire, drew on a vast array of sources and accounts for his history, but its explicit overall mission was still part of a religious, as opposed to scientific, world view. His extensive work promised to explain why an "infidel" empire that had expanded into Asia, Europe, and Africa had been far more successful and powerful than Christendom. Working with the early modern understanding that God directs the course of human history, Knolles argued that the triumph of the heretical and dark forces of the Turks was just punishment for Christian failings. Yet while eighteenth-century travel accounts increasingly staked their reputation on the accuracy and truth of their representations by appealing to the immediacy of experience and the impartiality of their investigative approach, these "rational" works still relied heavily on the moral framework and stereotypes (such as the inherently evil, cruel, and despotic Turk) that Knolles's religiously oriented history had put into play.[8]

This discrepancy in the genre that, on the one hand, prided itself on experience and, on the other, relied on the premodern convention of consistent types or stock characters, is explained in part by the Enlightenment and its relationship to imperialism. The new faith in science, objectivity, and empiricism was inseparable from the growth of the British Empire, and this link, in turn, is critical to understanding the new importance and legitimacy granted to travel writing. If travelling, to some degree, involves a disorienting and disruptive encounter with "the other," obsessive repetition of tropes and cultural stereotypes suggests a neurotic reaction to this encounter. Repetition, then, was a way of keeping the foreigner contained and the traveller and the reader of travel narratives stable, confirming the "rightness" of this shift in the balance of power.

Although Edward Said's 1978 *Orientalism* has rightly been criticized for being too monolithic, too masculine, and too binary in its approach, it does persuasively argue that consistency in the citation and repetition of orientalist tropes in British literature worked to consolidate the ideology of empire. The western traveller, often limited by language and the complexities of the Ottoman social structure, relied heavily on previously published accounts of Ottoman society despite claims to observational accuracy. Sir Paul Rycaut's influential 1665 history of the Turks remained a standard reference late into the eighteenth century, as did his updated version of Knolles's *The Generall Historie of the Turkes*, despite changes in social and cultural practices.[9] For instance, Charles Perry, who published his work about his travels in the Levant in 1793, writes about the Devshirme practice of taking Christian children as payment as if it were happening at the time of his travels, when in fact the practice, which was recorded in Rycaut, had died out in the second half of seventeenth century.[10]

Passages in George Sandys's 1610 account of his travels are frequently copied by other writers without acknowledgment; Sandys writes, for instance, that Greek women "for the most part are brown of complexion, but exceedingly well-savoured, and excessively amorous,"[11] while a hundred years later Aaron Hill uses almost the exact wording to describe them: "for the most part, exquisitely shaped, generally of a brown complexion ... and the most amorous."[12] Similarly, some of Hill's illustrations of Istanbul are taken from Sandys's earlier account and almost perfectly replicate his sketches of the buildings, boats, and even clumps of trees, despite the significant time lag.[13] This practice of largely unacknowledged textual citation and repetition promoted a sense of the Ottoman world as timeless and unchanging.

One of the most pervasive of these transhistorical tropes is that of the oppressed Muslim woman, a figure presented as symptomatic of an uncivilized society. While discussions of veils and harems are largely absent from medieval and Renaissance works about Muslim women,[14] from the late seventeenth century onward – with the new gendering of public and private space in the West[15] – they became standard conventions in western travel narratives, often connoting the mistreatment of Turkish women and in turn Ottoman barbarity. Jean de Thevenot states, in his 1687 account, that "the Turks do not believe that Women go to Heaven, and hardly account them Rational Creatures; the truth is, they take them only for their service as they would a Horse."[16] His account differs little in sentiment from that of William Hunter, who travelled to Turkey in 1792 and noted that "the prejudices which the Turks entertain against their women, are, indeed, one of the great causes of their own inflexible barbarism."[17] So, too, Stanley Lane-Poole noted in 1878: "It is quite certain that there is no hope for the Turks as long as Turkish women remain what they are ... they are choked by a pernicious system which destroys the moral force of the women and thereafter the men of the empire."[18] The pervasiveness of the trope continues today in the debates over the veil; in 2006, for example, British Labour MP Harriet Harman went even further than Foreign Secretary Jack Straw's anti-niqāb comments, insisting that the veil in Britain be abolished: "If you want equality, you have to be in society, not hidden away from it."[19] What this sampling of statements from different historical periods confirms is a world view that understands Muslim women as oppressed, obscure, hidden, and lacking agency.

Despite the consistency of this convention across the centuries, the western desire to "unveil" and "liberate" Turkish or Muslim women points not to the truth of an unchanging, all-encompassing oppression (the sweeping together of all Muslim women under this label over a 350-year period foregrounds the absurdity of the claim) but rather to the strategic interests at play that inform different moments in the history of the construction of an East/West divide. What motivates this "rescue" mission and the desire to unveil or veil women at various historical junctures? In the eighteenth century, the East increasingly served as a foil to the rhetoric of enlightenment in the West. The representations of the Ottoman Empire as arbitrary, irrational, despotic, and tyrannical and Europe as enlightened, just, and rational pivoted on the representations of veiled and unveiled women.[20]

Hill, in his 1709 account, reports that Turkish women were denied entry into Paradise and promises to give "British ladies, an enlivening taste of Turkish arrogance" in order that they may see "how little cause [they] have to grieve" whereas British men in contrast "possess a just and mild pre-eminence by nature's laws and those of matrimony."[21] He further states that Turks "boast a sort of unconfined authority, which makes their wives submissively obedient"; again he contrasts this with the British ideal of matrimony, which values a "mutual confidence, that generous, free, and open familiarity, so requisite to make a marriage truly happy" and so finds himself unable to praise the Turkish "policy in robbing wives of that well tolerated liberty." He notes that despite this "severe behaviour," Turkish wives "fawned humbly on their injurers" and complains that "while those [women] in Turkey grow good-natured by a brutish usage, ours in Britain sometimes think it out of fashion to oblige an easy husband."[22] Hill's focus on the confinement and subservience of Turkish women then gives way to several erotic fantasies about Europeans who end up in the embraces of sex-starved harem women and are "forced" to engage in group sex with the "lewd" captives: "So lascivious are their inclinations," he writes, "that if by ingenuity of their contrivances they can procure the company of some stranger in their chamber, they claim unanimously an equal share of his caresses, and proceed by lots to the enjoyment of his person; nor can he be permitted to leave them, till having exerted his utmost Vigour in the embraces of the whole company, he becomes incapable of further service."[23]

Hill himself claims to have penetrated the palace and further indulges in details about the "wanton inclinations" of these harem women bereft of male company. Desperate to attract the attention of the sultan, he reports, they spend their time in "lascivious dances, postures and performances," and if selected by their master must then "creep in from the base of the bed" to receive his embraces. Setting up a contrast between the Eastern and Western woman, he suggests that Englishwomen, "if I know them rightly, think too worthy to bestow in such a mortifying and submissive manner."[24] Only fourteen at the time of his travels to Istanbul, Hill might be forgiven his overcharged adolescent fantasies of sexually starved women. He later dismissed his book as "a puerile sally." Nevertheless his work was well-received in

England and was often cited, suggesting a keen appetite for orientalist representations that focused on the comparative liberty of English women. Lady Mary Wortley Montagu, however, strongly objected to Hill's account and critiqued the invention of an East/West divide that was put into play by setting the "free" Western woman against her "enslaved" sister.

The Letter-Book of Lady Mary Wortley Montagu

In 1717, Lady Mary journeyed overland to the Ottoman Empire with her infant son and her husband, Edward Wortley, who had been appointed as a representative of the Levant Company and as British ambassador to the Sublime Porte. Although they had planned on a longer posting, Wortley was recalled only fifteen months into their sojourn when the Turks were defeated at Belgrade. During his and Lady Mary's stay, he had tried to negotiate peace between the Ottomans and Austrians and thereby safeguard British commercial and naval interests in the Levant. Lady Mary kept a journal, wrote letters on Ottoman culture and habits, gave birth to a daughter, and had her son inoculated against smallpox. On returning to England, she produced an edited and polished epistolary account of her travels which circulated among her friends, and she also promoted the practice of inoculation in England.

Although her daughter, Lady Bute, burnt her journals and writings and tried to prevent the publication of her travel narrative, which Lady Mary had entrusted to Reverend Benjamin Sowden, it did finally appear posthumously. Smuggled out and hurriedly and inaccurately transcribed, this 1763 edition (that included as a preface the 1725 text written by Mary Astell in back pages of the letter-book) circulated a year after Lady Mary's death under the title *Letters of the Right Honourable Lady M[ar]y W[ortle]y M[ontagu]e, written, during her travels in Europe, Asia, and Africa to persons of distinction*. The *Letters* were immediately popular and reprinted often to meet the demand; they also received glowing reviews from, among others, Dr Samuel Johnson, Voltaire, and the historian Edward Gibbon, who wrote of them: "What fire, what ease, what knowledge of Europe and Asia! Her account of the manners of the Turkish women is indeed different from anything we have seen yet."[25] But the complicated production history, the traditional neglect of women writers, the web of historical references, and the global political reach of Lady Mary's letters have meant that this important record of intercultural exchange has only recently received, as part of a renewed interest in Ottoman history and Islam, the attention given to better-known works of the period.

Analysis of the letters has focused largely on the question of whether Lady Mary participated in or resisted the orientalism of her day and on the related issue of whether or to what extent her narrative can be read as feminist. Lisa Lowe, arguing that Said's theory of orientalism does not take into account the heterogeneity of works on the East, reads Lady Mary's work as a specifically gendered text that makes use of an emergent feminist discourse to resist the standard orientalist tropes about Eastern women found in many of the works of male travel writers, such as Robert Withers, George Sandys, John Covel, Jean Dumont, and Aaron Hill. Lowe argues that despite Lady Mary's own lapses into the orientalist "rhetoric of difference," which characterizes male travel writing and which contributes to occidental–oriental divide, she actually dissents from the dominant discourse by deploying a "rhetoric of likeness" that encourages identification with Turkish women. She concludes: "Lady Mary employs the rhetoric of identification between women of Turkish and English courts as a means of intervening in the differentiating rhetoric of orientalism."[26]

Meyda Yegenoglu, however, takes issue with Lowe's reading, suggesting that Lady Mary's work, rather than disrupting the monolithic narrative of orientalism, instead foregrounds the complicity between orientalism and western feminism. In her travels, Yegenoglu argues, Lady Mary assumes a masculine role (a role unavailable to her in the "masculine" West), figuratively "attaches a penis to herself," and penetrates a "feminized" East, thus complementing, as opposed to challenging, the work of the male colonist. Whereas many of the male travellers to the Orient were frustrated by their lack of access to the space of the Eastern woman (the metonymic heart of the Orient), Lady Mary, in good colonial fashion, exposes the harem's inner workings, thus satisfying the desire for the "truth" of "the other" and solidifying the position of the West as knowing subject.[27] Cynthia Lowenthal also argues that Lady Mary replicates orientalist conventions and questions the veracity of her account, suggesting that romance clouds Lady Mary's perspective and "seduces her into believing that the fictional constructs are real. As a result she fails to perceive the violence and pain endured by some women in Turkey because she views female sorrow through the veil of romance."[28]

However, Srinivas Aravamudan suggests that Lady Mary is far too conscious of the performative and playful nature of writing to invest unquestioningly in such an empirical or romantic model in her travel account. It is the very terms of the masquerade Lady Mary valorizes that offers the female subject "a kind of freedom that suspends truth." Neither interested in revealing, "capturing," or possessing the Turkish woman nor in indulging the other colonialist narrative of "going native," Lady Mary maintains a "partial identification" with aristocratic Turkish women which allows for the possibility of a "positive orientalist ideal" that is both "progressive and inclusionary."[29]

As these debates in the scholarship suggest, it would be reductive either to dismiss Lady Mary's text as irredeemably orientalist or herald it as unquestionably feminist. The elaborate nexus of her personal life, her blue-blood allegiances, the intellectual circles in which she travelled, and her notoriety as a "gender outlaw"[30] complicate any attempt to endorse her as a "perfect" cultural ambassador.[31] In several letters, for instance, she celebrates the superior beauty of Turkish women, a description that leads Anita Desai to comment enthusiastically on her "extraordinary" attitude to an alien culture, and yet at least part of this description involves a fetishization of white skin.[32] Surrounded by naked women in the Turkish bathhouse, Lady Mary observes: "There were many amongst them as exactly proportioned as ever any Goddess was drawn by the pencil of Guido or Titian, and most of their *skins shineingly white*, only adorn'd by their Beautiful Hair divided into many tresses, hanging on their shoulders, braided either with pearl or riband, perfectly representing the figures of the Graces" (emphasis mine).[33] While attending the ceremonies of a Turkish bride, again setting the stage with a classical reference to the Epithalamium of Helen by the Greek pastoral poet Theocritus, Lady Mary writes: "'Tis not easy to represent to you the Beauty of this sight, most of them being well proportion'd and *white skin'd*, all of them perfectly smooth and polish'd by the frequent use of Bathing" (emphasis mine).[34] Rendering the Mediterranean complexion "shineingly white" in one letter and "white skin'd" in another and overlaying the scene with classical allusions, Lady Mary, following the trend of the neoclassical eighteenth-century intellectual, claimed an "idealized" ancient Greek world as the rightful origin of Enlightenment England, effacing the dark-skinned populace that inhabits the landscape.[35]

Further, although aware that British society valued women as little more than chattel – from her early complaints of the marriage contract to her remarks later in life that she would "prefer liberty to a chain of diamonds" – she, nevertheless, in one letter, perhaps due to her resentment over her financial dependence, first on her father and then on Wortley, covets Turkish women's wealth and playfully but problematically equates indulgent husbands and pampering with freedom: "Turkish Ladies, who are (perhaps), freer than any Ladys in the universe ... are the only women to live a life of uninterrupted pleasure, exempt from cares, their whole time being spent in visiting, bathing or the agreeable Amusement of spending Money and inventing new fashions. A Husband would be thought mad that exacted any degree of Economy from his wife, whose expenses are no way limited but by her own fancy. 'Tis his busyness to get Money and hers to spend it, and this noble prerogative extends itselfe to the very meanest of the Sex."[36]

Despite the complex nature of her politics, however, Lady Mary's work crucially intervenes in the debates about Muslim woman, which continue to underlie some of the troubled relationships between feminism and Islam today. By exposing the foundational rhetoric of the social contract that co-opts and unveils women's bodies in support of a religion/reason binary, Lady Mary's letters dismantle the East/West divide just as it is emerging.

The Emergence of the (Un)Veiled Woman as Placeholder in the East/West Divide

In an episode titled "The Captive's Tale" in Cervantes's *Don Quixote de la Mancha* (1604), a veiled Moorish woman and a Spaniard arrive at an inn where Quixote and various other guests are lodged. After reassuring the guests, who are disturbed by the presence of the veiled woman, that although his companion is "Moorish ... in body and dress," she is "in her soul ... a very good Christian," the Spaniard tells of his adventures while she is persuaded to remove her veil.[37] He recounts how he fought for "his God and king," defeated the Turks at the Battle of Lepanto (1571), then was captured and imprisoned in Algeria (much like Cervantes, who spent five years as a slave there). Coming to his rescue, a wealthy Moorish woman promises to free and marry him in return for his taking her to Christian lands. This veiled woman, "the most beautiful princess in the whole kingdom," according to the Spaniard, betrayed her father, denounced her people, and changed her name from Zoraida to Maria, warning her Spanish saviour, "Do not trust any Moor; they are all deceitful."[38]

As the balance of power shifts and Islam begins to lose ground, the West asserts its dominance by speaking for and producing a silenced

Orient, much as the Spaniard speaks for his silent Moorish companion.[39] Moreover, this tale of conquest and domination, which involves the emasculation of the Eastern father and the "rescue" of the daughter, underscores the seminal change in the relations of East and West. No longer is this story only about Christians against the Infidels as in the Crusades. Rather, Zoraida's father, on discovering his daughter's complicity in the betrayal, accuses her of joining the captive not for reasons of faith but in order to indulge in the "immorality" of the West and satiate "her wicked desires": "Do not imagine that she has been moved to change her faith out of a belief that your religion is better than ours. No, it is because she knows that immorality is more freely practised in your country than in ours."[40] Caught between the captive's reading of her in terms of a sexual conquest and her father's reading of her in terms of sexual perversion, Zoraida – the (un)veiled woman – is doubly silenced. This tale, ostensibly about religious difference (the daughter wants to convert to Christianity), undergoes an important shift in this narrative as the religious tension between West and East is recast into its modern form. Depending on which side articulates the dispute, unveiling signals the West's moral decay and spiritual bankruptcy whereas veiling marks the East's sense of faith and belief; alternately, unveiling implies the West's investment in freedom and reason whereas veiling connotes the East's commitment to religiosity and backwardness.

The Christian victory at the Battle of Lepanto was, according to the Spaniard, "when the insolent pride of the Ottoman's was broken forever," proving to "all the nations" that the Ottoman empire was penetrable. This story of the veiled woman's unveiling enacts this victory.[41] Although Cervantes's triumphant announcement was a little premature (the Ottomans continued as a dominant force for more than a hundred years), his tale of saving the Muslim woman from her oppressive culture and religion came to dominate the western imaginary in the ensuing centuries.[42] Despite the power of the Muslim Empire, where the "English were very much the supplicants,"[43] and despite the commercial and diplomatic alliances between Britain and Turkey and between Britain and the Kingdom of Morocco (which encouraged Queen Elizabeth to solicit the help of the sultan against the idol-worshiping Spanish and encouraged the Moroccan ruler, Ahmad al-Mansur, to suggest a joint English-Moroccan assault on Spain), like the Captive's tale, many of the earliest travel narratives about the Orient written by the merchants of the Levant Company, established in 1581, stressed the cultural divide between East and West, keeping "intact the separateness of the Orient, its eccentricity, its backwardness."[44]

In the seventeenth century, a burgeoning publishing industry began to develop around these tales of the "exotic" East, and the construction of the un(veiled) woman was central to the depiction of the Levant as barbaric. These scandalous stories testified to the essentially uncivilized behaviour of distant neighbours. In his diary detailing his travels in the Levant (1599), Thomas Dallam writes of catching a glimpse of the Seignior's concubines through a grate in a "very thick wall" surrounded by "very strong iron." He lingers, on pain of death, over the spectacle of these bejewelled captive women, perversely commenting that the sight "did please me wondrous well."[45] In John Covel's diary, in an entry dated 23 May 1676, we are told a sordid tale about a slave of great beauty who is ravished by an admirer. The sultan, overcome "with madnesse that he lost one so sweet," beheads the man and takes the girl for his harem.[46] Ottaviano Bon, in his 1625 account of the Ottoman Court, writes of the eleven or twelve hundred virgins who make up the sultan's harem. He further gives details of the brutality these women faced at the hands of the Grand Seignior, claiming that in some cases the punishment consisted of their being bound hand and foot, put into a sack, and thrown into the sea in the dark of night. He adds that these "young, lusty, lascivious wenches" are allowed radishes, cucumbers, and gourds only in slices, to prevent them from engaging in any unnatural or unclean acts.[47]

In *A New Voyage to the Levant* (1696), Jean Dumont reports that the sultan's wives are guarded by white and black eunuchs "who never permit 'em to enjoy the least Shadow of liberty,"[48] while Habesci, objecting to, but also titillated by, same-sex love, writes in *The Present State of the Ottoman Empire* (1784) that "the abominable vices against nature reign there [in the Sergalio] to excess, not only amongst pages, but likewise amongst the girls."[49] Jean-Baptiste Tavernier corrects the rumour of the cucumbers, informing us that these earlier writers "have forg'd the story not knowing that it is custome in the Levant to cut the Fruit a-cross, into great thick slices" and yet preserves the homophobic tone in his protest against same-sex love, writing that in all the provinces of the Empire "the wicked Example of the Men, who, slighting the natural use of Women-kind, are mutually inflam'd with a detestable love for one another, unfortunately inclines the Women to imitate them."[50]

Two hundred years after Cervantes's tale, F.C.H.L. Pouqueville, in his *Travels Through Morea, Albania, and Several Other Parts of the Ottoman*

Empire to Constantinople (translated from the French and published in London in 1806), similarly represents the veiled woman as awaiting rescue from her western saviour. He writes that Turkish women "who feel the oppression to which they are subjected" would readily put themselves "under the protection of the conqueror" in order to escape their fate.[51] Looking back over the life of the Levant Company in 1893 and paying homage to its "heroic" imperial past, Theodore Bent writes in his introduction to an edition of the diaries of two early merchants (Dallam and Covel) that the Company, "besides the amount of wealth it accumulated for this country, did infinite service in the development of art and research, geography and travel, the suppression of slavery, and the spread of civilization in countries which would still have been unapproachable had not the continued efforts of the 244 years [the life of the Company] been towards civilization and humanity."[52] As I suggested at the opening of this chapter, the image of veiled women as oppressed is persistent. As the recent war in Afghanistan (2001) demonstrates, although the stakes have changed, the West is still in the business of rescuing this figure.

These early accounts of the abusive and perverse treatment of the veiled woman are largely imagined given that male travellers had no access to women's quarters, and yet these fantastical accounts of the treatment of the veiled woman are standard tropes of travel narratives to the Levant. At once voyeuristic and indignant, these works distracted attention from gender inequities at home, presented the Orient as a place in need of rescue, and secured the idea of Europe as being free, fair, and civilized. They also allowed the male reader, in the vein of Cervantes or Pouqueville, to cast himself in the role of heroic saviour. To rephrase Gayatri Spivak: they allowed white men to save veiled women from Muslim men while satisfying fantasies of penetration and domination of the East.[53] Furthermore, despite the similarities in the subordinate positions of women in the East and West, the veiled woman, as portrayed in these narratives, becomes one of the most powerful symbols of the "irrationality" and "backwardness" of Islam. Dumont, claiming there is "no slavery equal to that of the Turkish Woman," suggests that these customs are the product of a mind that "is at the bottom nothing else but a pure Insensibility and a Weakness that is altogether inexcusable in any reasonable creature."[54]

This seventeenth- and eighteenth-century orientalist literature that foregrounds the trials of the (un)veiled woman is already part of the story of the West's shift to modernity. Whereas the West was preoccupied with the struggle of liberating itself from the tyranny of the father and articulating itself as secular, a story in which paternal rule is replaced by a fraternal order and reason displaces faith, Islam was represented as arrested, irrational, backward, and at the mercy of despots. The modern understanding of the opposition between, on the one hand, a traditional, religious, and conservative Islam that values community, faith, and spirituality and, on the other, a secular society founded on liberty, reason, and materialism – in short, the contemporary East/West divide – is already evident in these tales. Like Zoraida, the (un)veiled woman who is captive in this narrative can only be "saved" from her culture or "submit" to it.

Feminism and Orientalism

Early British feminists were quick to import the image of the enslaved Eastern woman into their writings as a means of expressing their own frustrations with power inequities. Mary Wollstonecraft, for instance, employs the analogy of the East as a way of discussing the subjugation of British women. She writes in her introduction to *A Vindication of the Rights of Woman* (1792) that in the books written by Western men, "in the true style of Mahometanism, [women] are treated as a kind of subordinate beings, and not as a part of the human species, when improvable reason is allowed to be the dignified distinction which raises men above the brute creation, and puts a natural scepter in a feeble hand."[55] Not only is it "the true style of Mahometanism" to oppress women, Wollstonecraft argues, but while reason is claimed as continuous and compatible with Christianity, the teachings of Islam are understood to be "irrational" and brutish.

Many works have focused on this complicity between feminism and colonialism. Joyce Zonana argues in her essay on *Jane Eyre* that the metaphors used to discuss women's oppression in the writings of western feminists, from Wollstonecraft to Florence Nightingale, are frequently the stereotypical orientalist images of the Eastern woman veiled and imprisoned in the harem or seraglio. She further argues that the reading of masculine tyranny as foreign and eastern only serves to reinforce the notion of western superiority: "If the lives of women in England or France or the United States can be compared to the lives of women in 'Arabia,' then the Western feminist's desire to change the status quo can be represented not as a radical attempt to restructure the West but as a conservative effort to make the West more like itself."[56]

A number of western feminists have used the example of Eastern women as "enslaved" and oppressed by an irrational East as a means of discussing their own lack of freedom, and in so doing have encouraged, directly or indirectly, western imperialism.[57] The legacy of orientalist feminism has persisted through much of the modern era, as evidenced in the Republic of Turkey, Iran, Afghanistan, and Egypt, countries that early on adopted a project of modernization that included the forceful unveiling of women. Mustapha Kemal Atatürk, the leader of the Turkish nationalists, for instance, wanted to transform Turkey from a "backward" nation into a "modern" one; he encouraged the "emancipation of women" and strongly discouraged veiling: "I see women covering their faces with their head scarves ... Do you really think that the mothers and daughters of a civilised nation would behave so oddly or be so backward?"[58]

Yet while "western" feminism has aided imperialism and colonialism by accepting the "barbarism" of the East, conservatives in Islamic countries have in turn denounced gender struggles as "western." Women interested in raising issues about gender in Muslim countries are countered by claims that feminism is inseparable from colonialism and that, in order to rid Islam of this legacy, these countries must in equal measure abandon "feminist" rhetoric. Marie-Aimée Hélie-Lucas, a founding member of the international feminist network Women Living Under Muslim Law, articulates this dilemma: "We have been accused in our own countries of being brain-washed by 'foreign ideologies,' as if our reality was not enough of a reason to protest." Similarly, Ayşe Düzkan writes in her discussion of feminism in Turkey in the 1980s that "we have such an atmosphere in Turkey that if you defend ideas of freedom, of liberation, it sounds like you are adopting a Western attitude; and to defend the opposite of this is considered something Eastern."[59]

Thus, women, trapped in this East/West divide, are veiled in the name of religion or unveiled in the name of reason. In order for feminisms to be viable in a transnational frame, they must be read against this divide that is secured by the figure of the (un)veiled woman, and they must begin by challenging the story of the West's shift to reason against which the East was positioned as irrational. This shift, of course, already takes place within what Spivak refers to as "the story [in the West] of Christianity to secularism ... the only story around," which also claims "in praise or dispraise of reason, *that reason is European*" (emphasis mine).[60] In the next section, I suggest that an analysis of the birth of this East/West divide also works to undo it.

(Un)Building the Divide

For most of the modern era, Islam, whether condemned or celebrated, has been increasingly associated with the other of reason and secularism. Feminism is too often caught in this schism, having to choose between materialism or spirituality, individual rights or community allegiance, reason or religion. However, Lady Mary, one of the first female travellers to record her travels in the Ottoman Empire, began to question this divide, even as it was emerging, by challenging the voyeuristic tales about Turkish women and their enslavement. In her letter-book, she writes to one of her correspondents: "Your whole Letter is so full of mistakes from one end to t'other. I see you have taken your Ideas of Turkey from that worthy author Dumont, who has writ with equal ignorance and confidence. 'Tis a particular pleasure to me here to read the voyages to the Levant, which are generally so far remov'd from Truth and so full of Absurdities I am very well diverted with 'em. They never fail to give you an Account of the Women, which 'tis certain they never saw, and talking very wisely of the Genius of the Men, into whose Company they are never admitted, and very often describe Mosques, which they dare not peep into."[61] Lady Mary frequently berates earlier travellers for their exaggerated accounts of the abuse of Oriental women; in another letter, she remarks: "'Tis also very pleasant to observe how tenderly he [Aaaron Hill] and all his Brethren Voyage-writers lament the miserable confinement of the Turkish Ladys, who are, perhaps freer than any ladies in the universe."[62]

While these criticisms of other travellers' work certainly accommodate the convention of "bettering" previous accounts, a trope of the genre, Lady Mary also begins to break up the orientalist equation of the Turkish woman's "slavery" and the "pure Insensibility" and "Weakness" of the eastern mind – an equation that keeps the (un)veiled woman captive in the logic of an East/West divide. Thus she provides an alternative reading of the (un)veiled woman – one in which she neither has to be "saved from" nor "submit to" her culture. Countering the prevailing representation of the East as irrational and alluding to its long tradition of science and rational philosophy, Lady Mary suggests, in one letter, that Dr Samuel Clarke, who wrote about rational theology, and Mr William Whiston, who held the Chair of mathematics at Cambridge, would both find receptive audiences in the Ottoman Empire.[63] In another letter, she discusses the shunning of virgins by Islam and the worship of them by Christians, concluding: "[w]hich divinity is more rational I leave you to determine."[64]

Figure 1.1. *Rayhana, Daughter of Ka'b ibn Malik, Neglected by Her Husband*; Life of the Prophet (Siyar-i nabi); Turkish and Arabic text; AD 1594–5 (dated AH 1003); Istanbul, Turkey (CBL T 419, f. 435b).

Neither is the intellectual work she describes limited to men. When Lady Mary visits the Turkish bath, she compares it to a London coffee house (the latter having been introduced into London from Istanbul),[65] where men engaged in intellectual and artistic pursuits. The Ottoman Empire, unlike the post-feudal West that had newly gendered the private sphere as female and domestic and the public sphere as masculine and political, continued to understand the private sphere as a sacred place of power and learning. Lady Mary, in this comparison, not only points to the privileges that segregated spaces afforded but also acknowledges the tradition of female scholarship in Islamic cultures, which was largely ignored by Europe. Images from early manuscripts confirm Lady Mary's view. In a manuscript printed in Istanbul in 1594–5, an image titled "Rayhana, Daughter of Ka'b ibn Malik, Neglected by her Husband" depicts a woman in a room with a writing desk and an inkpot (see fig. 1.1). Another, titled "Women Reading," from the Mughal Empire in India (c. 1600), portrays women as book collectors, writers, and readers (see cover image). Both images (now part of the Chester Beatty Library in Dublin) demonstrate the rich tradition of Muslim women's scholarship. In striking contrast, western depictions of the *hammam* and the harem have generally focused on the eroticism of the "captive" female body.[66] Jean-Auguste-Dominique Ingres copied a passage from Lady Mary's letter on the *hammam* in one of his journals, which later inspired his 1862 orientalist painting "The Turkish Bath," but his passive, languid, naked women have little in common with Lady Mary's description of the active women she encounters: "some conversing, others at their work, others drinking coffee or tasting a sorbet" (see fig. 1.2).[67]

Not only do these letters suggest, as Billie Melman points out, Lady Mary's awareness of the "relativeness of belief and values"; they also show her refuting claims about the irrationality of Islam, questioning Europe as the birthplace of reason, and foregrounding the continuity between reason and religion under both systems.[68] However, to fully understand the radical implications of Lady Mary's reading of Islam as rational, we have to turn to the writings of some of her contemporaries, for, as Katherine Turner notes, "Montagu's *Letters* are uncharacteristic of the eighteenth century of which they are so often claimed to be paradigmatic."[69]

John Locke, following and building on the tradition of both Aquinas and Descartes and their insistence on the compatibility of reason and religion, was preoccupied with proving the superiority of Christianity on the grounds that it is a religion that defers to reason.[70] Reason, and

Figure 1.2. *Le Bain Turc* (1862); Jean-Auguste-Dominique Ingres (Art Resource).

not faith, he argued, was the means to knowledge: "*Reason* must be our last Judge and Guide in every Thing."[71] In Locke's analysis, however, reason mimics rather than replaces religion as the divine light becomes continuous with the light of reason. Locke does not leave behind the language of revelation, that is, of revealed religions; he only removes that aspect of doubt or indeterminacy that is inherent in religious faith: "*Reason* is natural *Revelation*" and "*Revelation* is natural *Reason* enlarged by a new set of Discoveries communicated by GOD immediately, which *Reason* vouches the Truth of, by the Testimony and Proofs it gives that they come from GOD."[72] The otherness of revelation is reinscribed as "natural" while the prophet, of divine origins, merges with modern man: "God when he makes the Prophet does not unmake the Man. He leaves all his Faculties in their natural State, to enable him to judge of his Inspirations, whether they be of divine Original or no. When he illuminates the Mind with supernatural Light, he does not extinguish that which is natural."[73] At every point, Locke is set on closing the gap between man and God, between the natural and supernatural, between Truth and reason. The knowledge acquired through the application of reason is presumed to originate with the divine, trumping the "leap" required for faith, and hence becomes the grounds for establishing universal values in the world as reason becomes the "last Judge."

The Enlightenment's understanding of divinity as translated through reason, where the divine becomes readable, establishes the ground for the imposition of "universal" values. Thus Locke can ask, rhetorically, "Can those be the certain and infallible Oracles and Standards of Truth which teach one thing in *Christendom*, and another in *Turkey*?"[74] He argues that there can only be one true standard and it is poor judgment or lack of reasoning that leads to error.[75] Locke prepares the groundwork for later rationalist philosophers, such as Hume and Kant, who suggest that difference can only be understood as deviance; a defective mind or inadequate education underlies "unenlightened" views.[76] Obscuring the founding of western reason in divine knowledge, Hume, in his essay "Of the Standard of Taste," cites the "Alcoran" as an example of the problem of founding "morality on sentiment, more than on reason," which results in the "pretended prophet" bestowing praise "on such instances of treachery, inhumanity, cruelty, revenge, bigotry, as are utterly incompatible with civilised society."[77] Hume's construction of a bigoted religious East pitted against a rational West is frequently echoed in the travel literature of the period: Paul Rycaut, for instance, devotes a chapter to outlining the ways in which deference and obedience to the Sultan are taught in Turkey as a matter of "religion rather than of state."[78]

Islam had also produced a narrative very similar to that of the Enlightenment about revolution and the struggle for justice, in which the "barbaric" and tyrannical *jahiliya* (the pre-Islamic era) was overcome by the civilizing influence of Islam in 622. As Fatima Mernissi writes, "Beyond its spiritual dimension, Islam was first and foremost a promise of power, unity, and triumph for marginalized people, divided and occupied, who wasted their energy in inter-tribal wars."[79] Moreover, Islam saw itself as continuous with Judaism and Christianity, rather than in opposition to these religions. The Qur'an instructs its followers to respect these religions: "Believers, Jews, Christians, and Sabians – whoever believes in God and the Last Day and does what is right – shall be rewarded by their Lord; they have nothing to fear or regret" (2:62). Because Islam presented itself as the final instalment and the restorer of these monotheistic religions, it shared their prophets, and the Qu'ran refers to many of the same events and people that are found in the Torah and the Bible. If Christian Europe viewed Islam as false, threatening, and the product of a "pretended prophet"; and Judaism refuted the divinity of Christ and the prophecy of Muhammad, Islam saw Christians and Jews as "People of the Book" and as sharing one God. Islam thus had a tradition of being more accommodating and tolerant of these religions, which led Paul Rycaut, among others, to point to Islam's "unfair" advantage as Ottoman populations were increasing. In places like Spain and Portugal, what with the expulsion of Jews and Muslims, the burning of suspect Christians in the Inquisition, and the practice of discriminating against new converts, the populations of Christian lands were declining.[80]

While Islam, which literally means "submission to God," is about universal faith, the Qur'an forbids compulsion of religion and forced conversion (2:256). Revealed to the human Muhammad, God's Word, where ambiguous, cannot be understood, explained, or claimed in any absolute way as "no one knows its meaning except God" (3:9). Further, the Hadith (the prophet's saying) that "Allah will never make my community concur upon misguidance" also prevents man from displacing God as absolute Judge. It is only when the entire community of Muslims is in complete agreement that a position can be considered true – as long as there is disagreement among this community, no one can claim the absolute authority or rightness of his or her position. If Muslims, unlike Christians, hold that both Muhammad and Christ were human, Locke overlooks this important difference when he argues that "Christians, as well as Turks, have had whole Sects owning, and contending earnestly for it, *That the Deity was corporal and of human shape*" (emphasis mine).[81] The Deity is not corporal in Islam and man does not share in the divinity of God – there is an impassable gulf, a lacuna, between the divine and the secular. However, Edward Gibbon recognized this incommensurability between God and man that is at the heart of Islam: "The Mahometans have uniformly withstood the temptation of reducing the object of their faith and devotion to a level with the senses and imagination of man."[82]

Thus, as Islam encountered and conquered other cultures, it was able to tolerate differences in its social order because its followers were forbidden to assume absolute knowledge: the eternal could not be translated in the temporal world, man was distinct from God, and reason could not mimic divinity. The Christian West, however, which had a long history of forced religious conversion, continued, in its transition to secularism, to assume access to a divine or universal knowledge: now through reason rather than faith. While Europe carried out its colonial exploits confident of its own superiority, the East employed a non-hegemonic reason in its negotiation of the social body.[83] The heterogeneity that flourished under the Ottoman Empire's different approach to expansion – its multilingual, multireligious, interracial, and transnational makeup – was often heavily criticized by western travellers, though some acknowledged the acceptance it implied. John MacDonald Kinneir, whose account of his travels appeared in London in 1818, wrote of Wallachia (then under the suzerainty of the Ottoman Empire; now southern Romania): "The inhabitants are composed of a mixture of all nations and religions, who have distinct places of worship, and, under the government of the sultan, enjoy a degree of toleration unknown in many of the more civilized states of Europe."[84]

Yet this narrative of change and social progress has been, to varying degrees, suppressed in both the West and East, and this suppression in turn has contributed to the misreading of the West as modern and secular and Islam as rooted in tradition and religion. From its inception, the *umma* (Islamic nation) has combined secularism with religion, its caliphs attending to religious, criminal, and civil law. As Rycaut complains: "The civil laws appertaining to religion amongst the Turks, are so confounded into one Body, that we can scarce treat of one without the other."[85] The Islamic world is widely understood, in the narrative of western progress, as having not yet embraced reason, and yet as a religion that attends to the secular, that is not based on miracles or saints, and that is revealed to a prophet who does not claim divine origin, Islam, with its "calm and rational precepts," as Gibbon was to describe them, predates John Locke's humanising and "naturalizing" of the divine.[86] Secularism and religion are intermixed in both the East and the West, yet western modernity grounded "universal" reason in the divine even as it claimed to separate the secular from religion; Islam, on the other hand, acknowledged both the secular and the divine but resisted collapsing the temporal with the absolute.

The two very different approaches to imperialism exemplify the seminal difference in the understanding of reason in the East and West. During the period of Islamic conquest, Jews, Christians, and Muslims coexisted under Moorish rule whereas the Christian conquest involved the forced conversion, expulsion, and finally extermination of Muslims and Jews. The *jihād*, whether by pen or by sword, refers only to the establishment of Islamic rule and does not involve forced conversion; the multiethnic, multireligious domains of the Ottoman Empire thus stood in direct contrast to European powers, which invested in the religious and, later, the racial homogeneity of the populace. The cosmopolitan world that Lady Mary and others encountered in the Ottoman Empire reflected this tolerance.

In the course of modernity, the divine origins of reason in the West were increasingly suppressed – so that reason itself is claimed as both foundational and western – and the story of the break with religion and the separation of church and state came to dominate. The secular and rational aspects of Islam were also suppressed in both the East and the West, and, for most of the modern era, Islam has been overwhelmingly associated with the "other" in the West. Citing Ernest Renan's 1883 talk at the Sorbonne titled "L'Islamisme et la science," Edward Said writes that the French theorist insisted that "Islam and its Arabic language represent hatred to reason, the end of rational philosophy, unremitting enmity to progress."[87] There is no trace left of Gibbon's and Lady Mary's earlier understanding of Islam as valuing reason. The Muslim world will increasingly adopt this view of itself as living under a translation of God's law, a trend that finds its most extreme expression in the rise of Wahhabism, a marginal and relatively recent sect that emerged in the eighteenth century and that began by wanting to "purify" itself of western influences. Dominant today in Saudi Arabia and the Arab peninsula, this school, a branch of Sunni Islam, positions itself as anti-western, countering the tradition of an inclusive and tolerant Islam. This sect claims absolute and foundational knowledge based on literal readings, contrary to the Qur'an and the teachings of Muhammad, and dismisses all Muslims who do not adhere to its dogma and the "true" path. Although they make up only a small percentage of Muslims and are viewed by many as heretical, Wahhabis, well-funded from the mid-1970s by petrodollars in the Gulf, have spread a destructive and brutal religion that, despite its claims, has little to do with the origins of Islam.

Shi'ism produced its own version of fundamentalist Islam with the rise of Ayatollah Khomeini in Iran, who also subscribed to an East/West divide, and in the 1970s turned away from secularism and set himself up as the government of God, violently suppressing alternative interpretations and dissent. As if fulfilling the role of the radical and irrational "other" perpetuated in the West, Khomeini became a "monolithic face, defending an unchanging world," as Spivak, in her reading of the Salman Rushdie affair, describes him.[88] The 1979 Iranian Revolution and the rise of Khomeini, of course, cannot be understood outside the decades of British, Soviet, and American imperialism. From the British and Soviet invasion of Iran in 1941 to the foreign control of Iranian oil resources in 1942 to the British- and American-backed coup of Mohammad Mossadegh (who had been democratically elected and had nationalized oil) and the reinstatement of Mohammad Reza Pahlavi as the shah in 1953 to the shah's increasingly autocratic rule, brutality, and material excess, the conditions in Iran, by the late 1970s, were ripe for an anti-western backlash. Playing into the already well-established division of East and West, Khomeini matched the hegemony of reason with the hegemony of religion.

While I cannot do justice to the complexities of the history of Iran and Shi'ism in this brief overview, I want merely to point to the long legacy of orientalism and imperialism that served to slowly solidify the formerly porous boundaries between East and West, religion and secularism. The critic Hussein Ahmad Amin has argued that hegemonic versions of Islam are one of the major problems with the modern *umma* as the religious establishment abandoned its commitment to individual reasoning (*ijtihād*) and embraced absolute doctrines (*taqlīd*). He writes: "This [abandonment] caused the *ulamā* [class of legal scholars] in the Muslim world to neglect one of their most fundamental duties, that is, to concentrate on developing the doctrinal and intellectual basis of Islam so as to meet the changing needs, problems and circumstances of their contemporaries."[89] *Ijtihād* translates as to "struggle with oneself" in thought and involves an interpretative practice based on informed and critical thinking and independent reasoning. The differences between Shi'a and Sunni Muslims and progressives and Islamists on the possibilities and limits of *ijtihad*, and the question of who is best situated to practise it is a discussion that lies outside the parameters of this chapter.[90] Yet at the very least, with its stress on hermeneutics (as opposed to literalism), the practice of *ijtihād* confirms Lady Mary's early and astute observation about the rationality of Islam, despite the prevalent eighteenth-century orientalist tendency that read this religion as irrational.

Reading and Writing against the Divide

In an increasingly "global" world dominated by transnational elites, multinational corporations, and neoliberalism, "staying at home" in local or identity politics is problematic, and yet "travelling" or coalition politics often elide sexual, cultural, racial, and economic privileges. How can feminisms function in a transnational frame without imposing a universal subject that suppresses or collapses differences? Gayatri Spivak argues that the cultural critic should not presume to "speak for" the other, a posture that assumes shared interests, universal values, and a common subject – a standard against which the other can only be understood as deviant. Nor should the cultural critic "listen to" the other, a posture that assumes some authentic, original, representative that can be translated, commodified, and put into circulation on the market by a "transparent" investigator.[91]

Before a space can be provided for feminisms, there must be an understanding of how western feminists, in "speaking for" and "listening to the other," have contributed to and participated in orientalism. At the same time, it is important to be cognizant of the gaps in this tradition and of those historical moments when gendered readings have not repeated but rather resisted the binary of the divide. Lady Mary challenged this divide just as it was gaining currency. Her invitation to consider Islam as rational derails the orientalist project as the hegemony of "western" reason, which assumes universal standards, is recast as reason as a universal practice subject to the particulars of culture. In her reading, Europe can no longer claim to be the birthplace of reason but neither can Islam overlook its rational and secular roots.

Yet, in arguing her case for Islam, she is careful not to "listen to" the other. Although she praises the Qur'an, which she maintains has been corrupted by Greek priests, she complicates the idea of any authoritative translation of God's word.[92] The impossibility of a definitive translation is playfully alluded to in her account of the Arnounts, highly prized foot soldiers in the Ottoman army who practised both Islam and Christianity. She reported that they attended mosques on Friday and churches on Sunday because they were "utterly unable to judge which religion is best" and "are not able to determine in this world" the "true prophet."[93] In the translation of God's word, as in that of culture in general, Lady Mary understands that the translator is not transparent and that the translation can never be fully secured. Declarations of cultural authenticity cannot be offered up as an alternative to western imperialism.

In Lady Mary's famous description of her trip to the *hammam,* she further challenges the logic of the desire to "unveil" and liberate the Eastern woman in the name of western reason. In learning to "speak to the other," Lady Mary must "unlearn female privilege." Donning Turkish dress and dissimulated enough by her encounter with the "other" that near the end of her voyage she fears losing her language, she responds to this engagement not by condemning the foreign and propping up the familiar, but by investigating and reflecting on the "grounds" of her position as an English woman. Surrounded by naked Turkish women who encouraged her to join them, she strips off just enough clothes to reveal her own constricted body: "The Lady that seem'd the most considerable amongst them entreated me to sit by her and would fain have undress'd me for the bath," she writes. "I excus'd my selfe with some difficulty, they being all so earnest in perswading me. I was at last forc'd to open my skirt and shew them my stays, which satisfy'd 'em very well, for I saw they believ'd I was so lock'd up in that machine that it was not in my own power to open it, which contrivance they attributed to my Husband."[94]

In this description, Lady Mary invokes the tradition of eighteenth-century travel narratives, such as those of Aaron Hill and Jean Dumont, that misread veiling and the harem and "lament the miserable confinement of the Turkish Ladys."[95] But, as Lady Mary shifts the gaze to her own "imprisoned" body, teasingly opening her shirt to reveal her restrictive underclothes and inviting rescue, she forces attention on the English social order and complicates the role of the colonialist writer/reader who imagines himself as the rescuer of veiled women. Instead, Lady Mary sets herself up as in need of rescue from her own culture. Critical of the exchange of women as property in marriage deals in Europe, she flips the western convention of harem literature, using her own "misinterpreted" clothing to suggest her lack of liberty. Lady Mary's performance of unveiling does not suggest a naive unfettered freedom but rather exposes a gendered social order that underlies the very rhetoric of western reason. Furthermore, in her travels, she appreciates the benefits of wearing a veil, which afforded her an anonymity, freedom, and mobility she could never have enjoyed as a heavily surveilled elite English woman. These gestures interrupt the binary of veiled and unveiled – the enslaved woman and the free woman – that characterizes the travel accounts of her predecessors.

Subsequent travellers were quick to shut down Lady Mary's praise of Muslim women's learning, agency, and power. Although her letters were, in general, celebrated, many male critics forcefully dismissed Lady Mary's account of Turkish women as "free" and insisted that English women were much better off. Pouqueville claimed Lady Mary's letters were the product of a "brilliant imagination" and proved that "Lady Montagu had never been in a harem."[96] James Dallaway, who edited the first five volumes of Lady Mary's works, remarked that "we are forced . . . to pause, and to discriminate the glow of the imagination from the sober colours of truth and nature."[97] Rejecting Lady Mary's observations on the subject of gender and liberty, he wrote that while women in Turkey are poorly treated, women in England "may rest assured that in no other country are the moral duties and *rational liberty* so justly appreciated" (emphasis mine).[98] William Eton likewise dismissed Lady Mary's account as the work of a "warm imagination" and wrote that a Turkish man regards women as no more than "instruments of his pleasures,"[99] while Thomas Thornton was adamant that it was an "inconvertible truth" that "Western Europe owes its high refinement to the liberty of women."[100] But why is Lady Mary so consistently and vociferously "corrected" on the subject of the comparative freedom of women, a topic into which, given men's exclusion from female spaces in Turkey, she might be assumed to have some insight? These rebuttals to Lady Mary's account, which insist men are better authorities on women's freedom, foreground the relationship between the unveiling of women and the rhetoric of liberty and reason that underlies the narrative of western modernity.

Throwing off the bounds of feudalism and paternal authority, the fraternity constructed by social contract theorists established itself as free. But free from what? How could the "free social body" be secured? At least one of the strategies involved reconfiguring the old religious battle of Christians against Infidels as a battle of the enlightened against a traditional and "emasculated" paternal culture that abused women. The Muslim Empire offered the perfect foil: casting its light on the dark shadows of this "backward" culture and exposing it as irrational, Europe wanted to "unveil" and liberate Turkish women in order to disguise its own contentious relationship with European women, who had been excluded from the social body. Lady Mary's letters expose this gender inequity that her critics are trying to cover up again with their accusations about her misguided notions of Muslim women's freedom. The European enlightenment's desire to "unveil" women in the name of "truth" was not limited to Muslim women. In the eighteenth century, writer Charles Pinot Duclos, elected a Fellow of the Royal Society in 1764, remarked:

> I don't know why men have accused women of falsity, and have made Truth [*la Verité*] female. A problem to be resolved. They also say that she is naked, and that could well be. It is no doubt from a secret love for Truth that we pursue women with such ardour; we seek to strip them of everything that we think hides Truth; and when we have satisfied our curiosity on one, we lose our illusions, and we run after another, to be happier. Love, pleasure, and inconstancy are perhaps only a consequence of the desire to know Truth.

Peter Brooks elaborates on this passage: "[w]e have only to think of representations in painting and sculpture to acknowledge that Truth, in our culture, is indeed a woman. She may be naked, or she may be veiled, in which case the veils must be stripped, in a gesture which is repeated in countless symbolizations of discovery, which will often give a narrative similar to Duclos 'pursuit.' In a patriarchal culture, uncovering the woman's body is a gesture of revealing what stands for ultimate mystery."[101] Woman, like the "emasculated" Orient, is first constructed as mysterious and irrational; stripped, pursued, conquered, she is then encouraged to surrender to the force of masculine reason.

Lady Mary, in presenting her imprisoned body in the *hammam,* not only frustrates the orientalist urge to rescue the Eastern woman in the name of freedom but also demonstrates her cognizance of the gender inequity that underlies the very articulation of freedom in the social contract. This document, though it is supposed to protect individual freedom, assumes, as does Locke, the "natural" right of the husband over his wife: "But the husband and wife," Locke writes, "though they have but one common concern, yet having different understandings, will unavoidably sometimes have different wills too; it therefore being necessary that the last determination, i.e., the rule, should be placed somewhere; it naturally falls to the man's share."[102]

Lady Mary was born in the same year (1689) as the withdrawal of the Divine Right of Kings, which required the unquestioned submission of male and female subjects to the monarch, and she had no desire to see its return. She suggests in one letter that Parliament send over its "passive obedient men" – that is, those in favour of the absolute supremacy of the Crown – to witness the brutalities of arbitrary rule under the sultan.[103] Yet, she was also well aware that women did not share the same freedom to consent, the basis of the social contract theory, but remained subjects of despotic rule. Thus she writes to Edward Wortley in response to his marriage proposal: "As for the rest, my Father may do some things disagreeable to my Inclinations, but *passive Obedience* is a doctrine should allwaies be receiv'd among wives and daughters. That principle makes me cautious who I set for my Master" (emphasis mine).[104] Here the doctrine of passive obedience is intentionally invoked in reference to gender in order to politicize the position of women. To her future husband's inquiries about her dowry, she responds sarcastically: "People in my way are sold like slaves, and I cannot tell what price my Master will put on me."[105]

This paternal order depends, as Spivak argues, on the appropriation of the womb and the "effacement of the clitoris," the woman as desiring subject.[106] The autogenic civil society, miraculously giving birth to itself, both excludes women from the public sphere and claims the right to the "private" bodies of women, calming any anxiety about the question of paternity that might arise in lieu of the overthrow of the father. The subsequent separation of public rights (contract) and private ones (natural) ensures that a woman's body, where the question of origin is always at stake, does not disturb the hegemony of western reason, which makes claim to an original and founding truth.[107]

Lady Mary's letter insisting that veiled women are the most free of women disturbs the logic of both orientalism and paternalism. She writes: "This perpetual Masquerade gives them entire Liberty of following their Inclinations without danger of Discovery,"[108] concluding that "[u]pon the Whole, I look upon the Turkish Women as the only free people in the Empire."[109] On the most obvious level, this freedom, on which many subsequent female travellers to the Ottoman Empire also commented, relates to married Muslim women's rights to own property, their financial autonomy, and their right to divorce. In contrast, British women were subject to the doctrine of "coverture," where wives and all their assets were the property of and under the control of, first, their fathers and then their husbands. Lady Mary's reading of the veil also emphasizes Turkish women as desiring subjects, subverting the image of the docile, powerless veiled women awaiting her saviour that fuels European fantasies of the harem and orientalist feminism. The representation of Muslim woman, exemplified by Zoraida in "The Captive's Tale," is thus released from the restrictive colonial script which values her only as an object of conquest and confirms in turn the inferiority/

irrationality of the East. Lady Mary, by equating freedom with disguise, veils, and masquerades, disturbs the Enlightenment equation of reason, revelation, and liberation. Freedom cannot define itself against the veil. Beneath the veil are only more veils, and in this "perpetual masquerade," the logic of origins comes back to haunt the public sphere, disturbing the foundational truth claims of western reason that underwrite the desire to unveil and save the Eastern woman.

Also interrupted is the logic of foundational/fundamentalist versions of Islam, which equally hold the (un)veiled woman captive. Like Zoraida, who is silenced by her father's reading of her as sexually perverted and "wicked," Muslim feminists have been accused of "betraying" their culture and of being seduced and colonized by the West. The only possibility of "return" to Islam, in this scenario, requires submission to a paternal order and a renunciation of sexual agency. As Mernissi has argued, the sexual homogeneity of the *umma* is an abstraction that depends on the veiling of women: "the law of paternity was instituted to screen off the uterus and woman's will within the secular domain."[110] Lady Mary, by suggesting that women's sexual agency is not inhibited but enhanced by veils and seclusion, disturbs the very basis of this paternal social order. The scenario of women, who, enabled by their disguise, meet lovers who cannot identify them, leads Lady Mary to suspect that "the number of faithfull Wives [is] very small in a country where they have nothing to fear from their Lovers' indiscretion."[111] Yet this same custom of veiling also grants the husband the right of private revenge if his wife's actions are discovered. Her account of the anonymous ("no woman's face being known") young female whose body was found in Istanbul naked and bleeding from stab wounds – a case that sparked no enquiry – suggests the violent end a transgressive woman might meet. Nevertheless, the elaborate checks put in place to guarantee paternity can be thwarted, she suggests, albeit sometimes at great cost.

Lady Mary thus opens up a critical space for feminism by complicating the rhetoric of reason and religion. She resists the East/West divide of modernity – already evident in the "The Captive's Tale" and that comes to define seventeenth- and eighteenth-century European travel narratives – by releasing the (un)veiled woman from her position as placeholder. However, feminisms, in order to be useful in a transnational frame, must both check the impulse to universalize and must continue to read for the limits of its discourse. That Lady Mary's critique and her "unlearning" of female privilege are limited is evident in her unwillingness to "speak to" the rural country women of North Africa. The inclusive cosmopolitan and heterogeneous world of Istanbul and Adrianople (modern Edirne) that Lady Mary embraces is bordered by a poor, rural population that she views as inalienably other: "We saw under the Trees in many places Companys of the country people, eating, singing, and danceing to their wild music. They are not quite black, but all mullattos, and the most frightful Creatures that can appear in a Human figure." While Lady Mary writes from Adrianople that "the Manners of Mankind do not differ so widely as our voyage Writers would make us believe,"[112] her description of these "frightful creatures" and later likening of the country women in Tunisia to "baboons" suggests that she considers the gap between herself and this "other" to be immense.[113] Outside the wealthy, elite, "civilized" circles, she falls back into the very conventions of the colonialist traveller that she cautions against.

Lady Mary's Legacy

Even though subsequent travel accounts reiterate Lady Mary's reading of the "freedom" of veiled women, they generally neglect any larger social critique and instead continue to explicitly perpetuate orientalist attitudes. After she was caught in a compromised state with the French ambassador, shunned by English society, and denied custody of her children, Lady Elizabeth Craven travelled to Constantinople in 1785. Her husband, though no more faithful than she, had her followed to a masquerade, where the door of the room to which she had retired with her lover was forced open. It is not surprising, then, to find her celebrating the social, sexual, and economic autonomy of Muslim women as she writes: "I think I never saw a country [Turkey] where women may enjoy so much freedom and liberty as here, free from all reproach."[114] She then informs her readers that if a Turkish husband sees a pair of slippers outside the door of the harem, he is forbidden to enter out of "respect for the sex," adding how "easy it is for men to pass and visit as women!"[115] Like Lady Mary, she also comments on Muslim women's right to own property, as established in the Qur'an. The mahr, which was granted to the bride on her marriage to protect her in the event of a divorce, bore no resemblance to the English dowry that was transferred to the husband. Lady Craven, echoing Lady Mary's observations, notes the "liberty of Turkish women," which renders them "the happiest creatures breathing."[116]

Both Lady Mary and Lady Craven exposed the hypocrisy of the English system, which allowed men to live with their mistresses openly whereas women often lost custody of their children and their wealth if they took a lover. Both had been victims of laws that rendered them as little more than chattel or "slaves" and both had suffered from the social/sexual surveillance of women in "free" Europe. Thus it is not at all surprising to find them celebrating the greater freedom and privacy that the female-only spaces and veiling afforded Turkish women. Yet Craven joins Lady Bute in dismissing Lady Mary's letters, suggesting most of them were composed by men. Moreover, unlike Lady Mary, she is scathing about Turkish women's dress and appearance and thoroughly orientalist and colonialist in tone: she confesses her desire – as a "rational being" – to see "a colony of honest English families" and the establishment of manufacturers "returning the produce of this country to ours" while "waking the Turk from his gilded slumbers" and carrying "fair Liberty" to the Mediterranean.[117] Her letters are limited to a self-interested critique of gender inequity in England. Praising the greater freedom of Turkish women, she does nothing to disrupt the emerging divide that pits a rational and industrious West against an irrational and slothful East.

Lady Mary's son, Edward Wortley Montagu, followed in the footsteps of his mother. Having been inoculated at age four in Turkey against smallpox, he later claimed the process "infused something of Turkish blood into [his] English veins."[118] According to Jonathan Curling's biography, Edward also insisted on his imperial lineage, suggesting that his mother had been impregnated by the sultan. This claim, as he was already four when they arrived in Istanbul, was one of his many deceits. He studied Arabic, Persian, and Turkish, lived in Egypt and Turkey, was a bigamist, adopted or fathered a son with one of his wives (an Egyptian woman), and converted to Catholicism from Protestantism, and then to Islam. Sometimes he declared he was a "universal believer," but he claimed to have died a "Mussulman."[119] Unfortunately, much of his writing, like his mother's before him, was destroyed by his sister, Lady Bute. But his "going native" – another colonial convention – did nothing to dispel orientalist attitudes. According to Curling, he set himself up on display in Venice: he sported a long beard and a turban and sat cross-legged on a carpet in a room decorated in a "Turkish" manner while black mutes wearing silver bracelets and ankle rings and a net of metallic mesh over their groins fanned their master with peacock feathers. Wanting to impress his frequent visitors with his knowledge of the

East, Edward disseminated all sorts of misinformation that fed his audiences' prejudices. He claimed, for instance, that Islam held that women had no souls (a claim his mother had rightly refuted in her letter-book) and that they were "created merely to comfort and amuse men during their journey through this vain world."[120] Having been disinherited as a young man, he continually craved authority and legitimacy. Edward certainly valued performance and masquerade, but instead of using them to question truth claims, as his mother did, he used them to assert truth claims.

I offer this brief discussion of Lady Craven and Edward Montagu by way of comparison in order to make a case for the innovation of Lady Mary's letters, which continue to interrogate and challenge even current political models. Her writing challenges the prevalent "clash of civilization" argument that so often plays itself out at the expense of women – veiled or unveiled – and it resists the religion/reason divide that continues to haunt contemporary debates. With Lady Mary's letters continuing to serve as a backdrop, the next chapters work through the nuances of, and changes in, the East/West divide and its relationship to the veiling and unveiling of women's bodies.

Chapter Two

The Great Whore of Babylon: Cosmopolitanism and Racialized Nationalism

"It is quite certain that there is no hope for the Turks as long as Turkish women remain what they are ... they are choked by a pernicious system which destroys the moral force of the women and thereafter the men of the empire."

(Stanley Lane-Poole, *The People of Turkey*, 1878)

The rhetoric of clashing civilizations takes a new turn with the rise of racialized nationalism in Europe and America, but the (un)veiled woman remains key to its figuration. If eighteenth-century western travel literature argued that the irrationality and barbarism of the still powerful Ottoman Empire were on display in its enslavement of women, against which the West presented itself as refined and rational as evidenced by the "liberty" its women enjoyed, by the nineteenth century the Ottoman world was portrayed as sick and dying, as a result, in part, of its heterogeneous populations. As I will argue in this chapter, the veiling of women was seen as complicit in the cosmopolitanism of the Ottoman world, which both fascinated and disturbed Europeans and Americans. The call for unveiling at this point in the history of the East/West divide was not only about inviting Turkey to become "progressive" and "modern" like the West but also about the policing and shoring up of race and class boundaries.

Nineteenth-Century Travel Literature

Early eighteenth-century accounts of travel to Ottoman lands were likely to be prefaced with statements that announced the uniqueness and novelty of the adventure. In his 1688 account, Jean-Baptiste

Tavernier claimed he was crossing territory "where no European had been before."[1] Lady Mary herself remarked in a letter from Adrianople in 1717: "I dare say you expect at least something very new in this letter, after I have gone a journey not undertaken by any Christian of some hundred years."[2] As early as 1686, however, Jean de Thevenot, a French traveller in the Levant, noted the growing market for travel literature, commenting on the increase in travellers and "the many printed relations of their observations which have been made Publick within these twenty years";[3] by the nineteenth century, the market was saturated.

The rise of middle-class travel, facilitated by steam engines, railways, guide books, and tourist packages (Thomas Cook organized the first Egyptian tour in 1869), found the western travel writer increasingly trying to separate herself/himself from crowds of tourists. Charles Macfarlane, in his account of his travels in Istanbul, distinguished his "mature examination" of the city from "the generality of tourists, who pass hurriedly from place to place."[4] Although the building of the railway from Western Europe to Central Asia was celebrated, an editor at the *Levant Herald* noted that though the "love of travel" was important for "social education" and the "removal of prejudice," it was also the "fashion to sneer at tourists."[5] By the end of the century, even accounts by women were no longer seen as unique. The increase in the social mobility of middle-class British women, many of whom now travelled as nurses, teachers, nannies, and missionaries, combined with an expanding market for harem literature, had generated an impressive number of nineteenth-century women's travel narratives about the Ottoman world. W.H. Davenport Adams, in his 1883 review of nineteenth-century women travellers, praised Lady Annie Brassey, who had travelled around the world in her steam-powered yacht, as "one of the most adventurous and agreeable lady-voyagers,"[6] but he singles out her account of Constantinople and criticizes it for going over "the familiar – nay, over hackneyed – ground," which he insists pales in comparison with the works of earlier travellers.[7]

A sense of belatedness and cynicism began to replace the earlier tone of adventure and novelty. En route to the Suez in the 1830s, the narrator of Kinglake's *Eothen* glories in the "loneliness of the Desert"[8] and exults in his heroic "self-sufficiency" which allows him "to stand thus alone in the wideness of Asia."[9] But his subsequent descriptions of his tent, filled with books, maps, and carpets, and the retinue of servants and guides that travelled with him undercut this mock-triumphant tone and offer a satiric take on an Englishman's search for isolation, which had spawned an entire tourist industry eager to serve it. Nor does he "stand alone" for long; he soon meets another Englishman in the desert. They try hard to ignore each other so as not to disturb the illusion of romantic isolation, but as their respective servants rush to engage, they are finally forced to exchange greetings as if they had never escaped central London: "We lifted our hands to our caps and waved our arms in courtesy, we passed each other as if we had passed in Pall Mall."[10]

Jaded modern travellers, who were disappointed that the East had failed to provide the fantastical spectacle and respite from modernity they had imagined and read about, represented the Ottoman Empire as exhausted. Kinglake described his arrival in Constantinople, "the familiar home of the plague," in terms of disease and death. Adopting a superior tone from the outset, the narrator revels in the power of England: "You go out from your queenly London – the center of the greatest and strongest amongst all earthly dominions – you go out thence, and travel on to the capital of an Eastern Prince, you find but a waning power, and a faded splendour, that inclines you to laugh and mock."[11] Laugh, ridicule, and mock he does: the "East" is never anything more than a caricature in his work as nothing – from the plague to pashas – disturbs the narrator's smug attitude.

So too, Frances Elliot, in her *Diary of an Idle Woman in Constantinople*, laments: "So little remains of the past in this much destroyed city; and of that so little that is outwardly attractive."[12] In this desolate state, the "barbaric" Turk has no option but to embrace "modernity," she suggests: "At least the tram and the cabs are significant of progress. Much as he may desire to cling to Asiatic barbarism, the Turk, like Falstaff, is now forced, in a degree, 'to purge and live like a gentleman,' whether he will or no."[13] Yet when Elliot encounters just such westernization, she is equally dismissive: "I found the saloons painfully European. All nationality seems utterly to have died out in Turkey. Here are papered walls, heavy gilding, and cumbersome chairs. There was not an article, I am sure, that did not come from Vienna."[14] Indulging in a familiar colonialist strategy, she both invites the Turk to be European but then denies him the possibility of ever attaining this title: "Had they remained in their native Asia, the Ottoman Turks might have been respected as a conservative race clinging to their own religion, manner, and habits; but as transplanted into Europe, and taking place in civilized nations, one comes absolutely to detest them, as mere political necessities maintained in a position they fail to fill."[15] In a similar vein, the orientalist Stanley Lane-Poole wrote: "Old Turkey, with its pomp, its power, its gorgeous ceremony, is gone forever; and the time has not yet come for the new Turkey to feel comfortable in its tight European clothes."[16] No longer even a worthy opponent, Turkey was viewed as, at best, a shabby imitator of the West.

The annexation of the Crimea by the Russians in 1783 and the increase in Russian trade through the Dardanelles and Bosphorus; the execution of the French monarch, Louis XVI, who had sided with the Ottomans, and the subsequent invasion of Syria and Egypt by Napoleon in 1798; war with Austria and the partitioning of the Polish commonwealth between Austria, Prussia, and Russia in 1795; the Greek War of Independence (1821–32); the occupation of Algeria by the French; the Serbian revolts against the Ottoman sultan in the early nineteenth century, among other uprisings in the region – all exerted enormous pressure on the Ottoman Empire. The 1867 protests in Crete elicited this cynical response in the *Levant Herald*: "Will this be the beginning of the end for the Ottoman Government? Those folks who amuse themselves by predicting the death of Turkey appear to us very simple. Turkey has no longer death to meet, for she died long ago. What remains of her is like the old trunk of a tree lying stretched upon the ground; and what gives her still a stir of life is only the parasite vegetation and the mosses which have grown over the huge skeleton."[17]

Although Turkey was never formally under British rule, Britain pondered the question of what to do with this failing power in much the same way as it discussed its colonies: the Ottoman Empire was perceived to be both in need of civilizing and as strategically and economically important to Britain. The "Eastern question" was the subject of heated debates. Liberals such as the Duke of Argyll, who advocated for the Christian populations in Turkey, felt that the "great civilized Power of Britain ... had a heavy responsibility" towards a "semi-barbarous Government."[18] Lord Salisbury thought Turkey should either become a protectorate of Europe with Englishmen at the helm or else be partitioned among the European powers. Wilfrid Scawen Blunt also challenged British support for Ottoman integrity and instead advocated for the establishment of a "pure" Arab caliphate. To counter western materialism and capitalism, he argued, the Arabs should be liberated from the corrupting influence of the Turks and allowed to recover their "origins" in order to provide a "spiritual" alternative. The nineteenth-century Tanzimat reforms in the Ottoman Empire (1839–76), the foundations of which were laid earlier in the century under the guidance of Stratford Canning, the British ambassador at Constantinople (1825–9;

1831; 1841–6; 1848–51; 1853–8), were already heavily influenced by British interests and the model of European nationalism.

"Necessary to be kept where she is, but perfectly hopeless in herself, and incapable of development or reform," Lane-Poole argued, Britain needed to prop up Turkey for strategic reasons: to ensure the balance of power in Europe, to serve as a buffer between Europe and Russia, to protect the overland route to India, and to safeguard Britain's economic investment in Turkey, which provided both a supply of cheap raw material and a market for British manufactured goods.[19] "The 'Sick Man' of the morbid mind of Nicholas [the Czar of Russia who had labelled Turkey such in 1844] must be galvanized into sufficient vitality to sit up and pretend to be well."[20] This "propping up" involved remaking the Ottoman world along the lines of a western nation, encouraging both homogeneity and centralized rule, in the hopes that it would emerge from the process strong enough to resist foreign takeover. Yet it is this very attempt, not, as is commonly argued, corruption or rot or inefficiency alone that killed Turkey. As Elie Kedourie put it: "The Ottoman died of Europe."[21]

Re-imagining the "Turk": From Infidel to Racially Corrupt

The cosmopolitan nature of the Turkish Empire, which was facilitated by the acceptance, equality, and social mobility Islam offered converts, was decried by European writers from the outset as it seemed to offer a perverse advantage to Muslims in the battle for souls. While welcoming the benefits of trade with the Ottoman Empire, Paul Rycaut, like Knolles, attributed the success and power of the growing Muslim populations to the displeasure of God for "the sins and vices of Christians."[22] Constantinople was full of "a strange race, mixture, and medley of different sorts of blood,"[23] Rycaut wrote, referring to Turkey as the "great Babylon" (the mother of all harlots). He proposed that one way of ruining the Empire would be to interrupt the flow of captives and slaves into the port, which would not only diminish the number of servants but also masters, given that the converted Turks received all the privileges and preferment of "the ancient Mahometan Race."[24] Rycaut contrasts this inclusive policy to that of Spain and Portugal where Christian populations, he noted with dismay, are scarcer because newer Christians were discriminated against by "ancient" ones and also because the Inquisition was enthusiastically burning suspected heretics.

Throughout the long eighteenth century, European travellers used the term "Turk" to refer to Muslims (hence the expression "to turn Turk") and often to all inhabitants of the Ottoman Empire, which was unconcerned with bloodlines or racial or ethnic coherence. Leslie Pierce notes that in the Imperial Harem "the sultans' alliances were both ethnically and religiously exogamous ... all royal consorts after the first two Ottoman generations (with one exception) were neither Muslim nor Turkish by birth."[25] Many British travellers (including Lady Mary's son), soldiers, and traders converted to Islam, often attracted by the opportunity for social and economic advancement, which was impossible in the rigid British class structure. Christian female captives were also integrated into the Empire. Lady Mary notes that her beautiful friend Fatima, whom she first met in Adrianople (modern Edirne), was the product of a mother who was captured at the Siege of Camieniec, a Polish fortress. Lady Mary also encountered a "Christian woman of quality" who chose to marry a Turk, lived happily with him, and inherited a huge fortune on his death. Travelling from Naples, the Spanish woman was "ravished" and captured, along with her brothers, by a Turkish admiral. The admiral then freed her brothers and when they then sent a ransom for their sister, the Turk offered her both her liberty and the money in order to alleviate his captive's suffering. Yet, in weighing her options, the Christian decided she was better off marrying the Turk than returning home to her Catholic relations "as the kindest thing they could do for her in her present circumstances, would certainly confine her to a nunnery for the rest of her days. Her infidel lover was very handsome, very tender, fond of her, and lavished at her feet all the Turkish magnificence."[26]

As these conversions and forays, facilitated by porous borders, suggest, there was a great deal of exchange between Europe and Turkey. While it was the convention for Christian writers in Europe to denounce Islam as a false religion started by a fraudulent prophet and to emphasize difference, Islam saw itself as the culmination of both the Jewish and Christian traditions and thus was inclusive of these populations. The Ottoman world was so linguistically, religiously, culturally, and ethnically diverse and intermixed that the border between Muslim/Turkish and Christian/European – that was so carefully defended by the western powers – made little sense in the East. Lady Mary commented on this mix, writing that "I do live in a place that very well represents the Tower of Babel; in Pera they speak Turkish, Hebrew, Armenian, Arabic, Persian, Russian, Slovenian, Wallachian, German, Dutch, French, English, Italian, Hungarian."[27]

Rycaut's and Knolles's early concern about the cosmopolitanism of Turkey intensifies with the rise of racialized nationalism in the nineteenth century, and the very term "Turk" begins to shift in meaning. Thevenot, in his work about his travels in the Levant (1687), wrote: "Where I speak here of Turks, I understand *Natural Turks,* as no such as turn to their religion from another who are very numerous in *Turkie,* and are certainly capable of all sorts of Wickedness and Vice, as is known by Experience, and commonly as unfaithful to Men, as they have been to God; but the *native Turks* are honest people. And love honest people, be they Turks, Christians, or Jews" (emphasis mine).[28] Thevenot, threatened by the idea of conversion, thinks of the world as divided by religious categories that are "natural" or God-given. As problematic as the idea of a "Natural Turk" or a "native Turk" – as a religious designation – is, given that this population only began to convert to Islam in large numbers in the tenth century, the division between the wicked convert and the honest Turk foregrounds the European concern about the power and allure of the Ottoman world. Thevenot's comments, however, also anticipate the shift in emphasis from religion to race.

Almost a hundred years later, in 1771, James Porter also wanted "to enquire as diligently as [he] could, whether the Turks, living in separate hamlets, *unconnected and unmixed* with Greeks, Armenians, and Jews, were more virtuous and honest than those in cities and villages, where all these religions are processed, and the *different sects herding indiscriminately* together make, as it were, but one people"[29] (emphasis mine). Porter voices his concern for what he understands to be the problematic ethnic and religious mixture – the "one people" – that leads to dishonesty and vice. Thevenot's, Knolles's and Rycaut's privileging of the idea of the "natural Turk" and Porter's fear of "different sects herding indiscriminately together" points to the European anxiety about the fluid boundaries and hybrid populations in the Ottoman Empire, which grow even more intense in the nineteenth century. European travellers, no longer focused on the threat of religious conversion, were now uneasy about the Ottoman Empire's cosmopolitan racial mix. Murray's 1900 guidebook to the region advised travellers to the Empire not to expect any national coherence or single dominant "people," quoting the historian Lord Bryce: "Constantinople is 'a city not of one nation but of many, and hardly more than one than of another. You cannot talk of Constantinopolitans as you talk of Londoners or Parishioners, for there are none.'"[30] Charles Eliot referred to the city's inhabitants as "one of the most mixed breeds in the world."[31]

By the middle of the nineteenth century, "Turk," which, as mentioned, had long been used by the Europeans to refer not just to Muslims but, at times, any inhabitant of the Empire, was beginning to displace the term Ottoman, and increasingly referred to a racialized national and/or ethnic designation. But this focus on race, ethnicity, and nations needs to be considered in the larger context of their invention and solidification in the nineteenth century. Although nations were born in Europe at the dusk of the religious age, nationalism is more than a rational construct. The mythic dimension of the nation provides a sense of continuity, destiny, and meaning that fills the void left by the belief in a divinely ordered universe. Hence, while, as Benedict Anderson has argued, "nation-states are widely conceded to be 'new' and 'historical,' the nations to which they give political expression always loom out of an immemorial past."[32] Race or the idea of a people as a "natural" grouping contributes to this invention of a past and comes to serve as the basis for the governance of the modern nation. This idea of a natural people also displaces the classical notion of the citizen as the product of a complex political nexus, where the subject was obliged to consider the broad category of belonging in the world (as a kosmopolitês, or "citizen of the world"). A number of contemporary critics have pointed to the strategic invention of national populations along race lines. Michael Hardt and Antonio Negri write in *Empire*: "Many contemporary analyses of nations and nationalism from a wide variety of perspectives go wrong precisely because they rely unquestioningly on the naturalness of the concept and identity of the people," arguing that the idea of a "people" as a homogenous group overlaps with the concept of race.[33] So, too, Vasant Kaiwar and Sucheta Mazumdar write in "Race, Orient, Nation" that "racism, as a system of social classification, is not passive, that is, simply recording difference already 'objectively' in existence in the world, but one that actively creates subjects ... turning mutable identities into fixed ones" and that, further, the creation of racialized subjects and the emergence of the nation are closely affiliated.[34] In *The Racial State*, David Theo Goldberg similarly argues that the social contract was also a racial contract and that: "Race qua otherness is as necessary and 'natural' to the logic and historical development of modern state formation as modern technologies of state governmentality are to racial formation."[35]

Turkey, in its rapid transformation from a multireligious, multilingual, interracial, and interethnic cosmopolitan empire into a racialized nation, proves an exemplary case of this invention of a "people," exposing the mechanics of the modern nation. The remaking of the Ottoman Empire into the Republic of Turkey required that the conception of community be radically transformed from the Islamic understanding of the nation, the *umma*, to the modern western model. Whereas the former was based on a trans-historical, trans-geographical membership, the latter was based on borders, teleology, and the accident of birth. The Turkish reforms, which involved the adoption of a western style of governance, meant having to deal with the difficulties of a mutable diverse population that did not operate along the same lines as the "imagined communities" of Europe, which were able to foster the illusion of homogeneity through a strict policing of borders, both internally and externally.

The seeds of this change were already evident, for instance, in the Turkish millet system, which had long designated various religious communities that were intercommunal, dynamic, and constantly shifting.[36] Under the British-influenced Tanzimat reforms in the nineteenth century, however, millets begin to operate much more like European nations.[37] Both the millet system and the Islamic nation had operated outside the categories of ethnicity and race, and, thus, a Muslim, regardless of creed (Sunni, Shi'a, Alevis), whether born in France or Morocco, enjoyed, at least theoretically, equal rights under the Empire. The Greek Orthodox millet included Christians, from Albanians to Serbians, despite linguistic and regional differences. All the Ottoman millets – the main ones being Orthodox, Jewish, Muslim, and Armenian – enjoyed an impressive amount of power and autonomy, collecting their own taxes and setting their own laws.

Yet when Russia, England, and France began to vie to act as "protectors" of these various religious communities and to subsidize them, and as the legacy of the French Revolution fueled nationalist causes, religion became increasingly conflated with racialized nationalism in the Ottoman Empire, and the intercommunal make-up of the millets was abandoned as their borders grew more rigid. Sixteen years before Greek independence, John Cam Hobhouse, Baron Broughton's *A Journey Through Albania* was published in London; it dismissed the idea of Greeks as a "proper" people: "The Greeks taken collectively, cannot, in fact, be so properly called an individual people as a religious sect dissenting from the established church of the Ottoman Empire."[38] But if, in this instance, "Greeks" are refused the label of an "individual people," Britain later comes to side with Greece during the War of Independence, recognizing it as a "nation" in 1823. This importation of the model of racialized nationalism further stirred up ethnic tensions in the region among Armenians, Kurds, Bulgarians, and Albanians; and in the divide-and-conquer logic of imperialism, Europe, and then America, actively fostered and disseminated the understanding of a people as organic, homogenous, and racially and linguistically coherent, provoking catastrophic tensions in the Ottoman world – which continue to plague the Middle Eastern nations that emerged after its dissolution. The violent side of national independence movements – in other words, the purging, reviling, and expulsion of those who fall outside what is understood as the official members of the community – was dramatically exposed in the first decades of the Turkish Republic, most notably in the discrimination against the Armenian, Jewish, and Kurdish populations. The early-twentieth-century Turkish historian Yusuf Akçura rightly argued that both the Ottoman and Islamic imaginings of alternative versions of the nation were quickly displaced by the triumph in Germany and the rest of Europe of race-based nationalisms.[39]

Heterogeneity and Fears of Miscegenation

Nineteenth-century newspapers, travel literature, and memoirs from Turkish sources are full of accounts of the porous borders that had long constituted the empire. Halidé Edib, a leading feminist and nationalist, adopted a complicated internalized racism as a child growing up in Istanbul in the 1880s. Her anglophile father's second wife was blonde with blue eyes, and Halidé writes in her memoir that in her first encounter with her stepmother and new "fair" relatives, who mocked her, she was made aware that her own "skin is not pink and her eyes are not blue."[40] "Having acquired an impression from [her] stepmother's relations that it is only fair people with blue eyes who are beautiful," she felt, at a very early age, inadequate.[41] She thus befriended a dark little girl as she admitted to enjoying the contrast in their skin colour, which made her feel superior even as she herself was tutored by an English governess who made it clear "that the Turks were some sort of natives, inferior to the English." Yet despite being brought up with this sense of racial hierarchy and the "English-made" frocks, English diet, English novels, and general "English ways," which her father so strongly admired, Edib's memoir also serves as a record of the interracial and interethnic society, where ever-shifting boundaries countered strict racial hierarchies.[42] Her black Nubian "milk-mother," Nevres Badji, was married to a "blond giant" from Trebizond, Ahmet

Aga. Her sister's father was Kurdish and had both a Syrian and an Abyssinian wife and "three white and three colored children."[43] Two Abyssinian girls are bought for Halidé and her sister, and while at first both sets of girls were terrified that the other came from a culture of cannibalism, they all grew up together, and the slaves were treated as part of the family as was typical of Ottoman households. On a boat to Egypt, Halidé met an African-American from Pera, who had a "white" daughter with a Frenchman (now dead) and was on the verge of marrying another Frenchman.[44] In the second part of her memoir, which is about Turkey's struggle to carve out a republic in the midst of the rising national tensions, she recounts the story of an adopted Arab girl who was seized by the Armenians on account of her dark skin, which her captors read as Armenian. Edib reluctantly approaches the British, who were occupying Istanbul, to request their help in recovering the child. But even as she is explaining the tensions, the colonel announces that the Armenian and Turkish children are so intertwined that, painful as the process might be, the British could only separate them by "cutting straight through the middle." Edib reflects on leaving the Colonel's office that the British were actively encouraging divisions between Turkish and Christians so that they could continue to occupy Istanbul "in the name of peace."

Melek Hanim's memoir, *Thirty Years in the Harem* (1872), which covers the first half of the nineteenth century, also documents this unrestricted mixing of cultural and ethnic identities in Ottoman society. Granddaughter of a woman from the island of Chios who had married an Armenian, daughter of a French father and Greek mother, wife of, first, a London-born Protestant and then a Cypriot-born Muslim, Maire converted to Islam in 1860 and changed her name to Melek. If Edib's anglophile upbringing and nationalist leanings encouraged a hypersensitivity to skin colour and a privileging of fair hair and blue eyes, Melek's earlier narrative rarely comments on colouring, except in passing. At one point, she tries to find a bride for a choosey Pasha who says he wants his future mate to have "black hair and eyes," refuting Edib's belief that there is a universal preference for blue-eyed women;[45] and at another point in her memoir, Melek comments on an Abyssinian of "great beauty."[46]

The newspapers of the period also recorded the equitable treatment of mixed-race marriages. For instance, the *Levant Herald*, an English-language paper that circulated in Istanbul, posted a story in 1871 about the eccentric but wealthy Mahmoud Bey, who died, leaving, apparently, no heirs; his estate was thus passed on to the state and a grand-nephew. A "negress" and her young son came forward, however, and after an investigation that proved she was his lawful wife, the estate was redistributed and Mollah Bey, like "an upright judge, awarded the whole succession, in pursuance of the Ottoman law of the *Sheri*, to the delighted negress and her child."[47] Although Ottoman social structures were hierarchical, rigid, and formal, Islamic respect for equality and difference combined with the relative lack of concern with blood, family name, and birth allowed for a great deal of individual mobility within these structures and facilitated these mixed households. Western travellers were as disturbed by this social mobility and the power accorded to slaves, blacks, and eunuchs as they were by the disregard for national identities and the fluidity of race and ethnicity. Comments like those of Thomas Thornton, a long-term resident in Constantinople at the turn of the nineteenth century, are prevalent in the works of the period: "What would become of the other nations in Europe," he asked, "if, in imitation of the Turkish government, the highest offices in the state were filled by men from the lowest ranks in society."[48]

If the Ottoman world seemed relatively unperturbed by interracial and interethnic mixing, England had long been obsessed with the hybridity of the Ottoman populace By the nineteenth century, the scientific world, increasingly concerned with unions that transgressed these boundaries, was trying to measure, quantify, and place them on a hierarchical scale. This preoccupation with miscegenation was further intensified by the American Civil War and debates about abolition, which in turn led to a plethora of articles and books in Europe that spoke to fears of both racial contamination and transracial desire. I will briefly mention three of the more influential of these works. In 1843, Josiah Nott's "The Mulatto a Hybrid – Probable Extermination of the Two Races if the Whites and Blacks are Allowed to Intermarry" argued, as the title suggests, that the intermingling of these two different races could only result in sterility.[49] In *The Races of Man: A Philosophical Enquiry into the Influence of Race over the Destinies of Nations* (1862), Robert Knox also made a case for races as distinct species, with Anglo-Saxons at the top of the racial hierarchy.[50] In *The Inequality of Races*, Arthur de Gobineau argued in the 1850s that the mixing of superior races with inferior ones could not but result in the decline of civilizations and that race and ethnicity were the most pressing issues of the day.[51] The mixed and mobile populations of the Ottoman could not be anything but deeply disturbing to the western traveller, whose entire perspective was shaped by the distorting lens of racial science; by the nineteenth century, virtually all western travel narratives reflected this obsession to varying degrees. Both the frequent complaints about hybrid populations and the attempts to organize, categorize, encourage, and invent racial and ethnic differences distinguish nineteenth-century travel narratives from earlier ones, which focused primarily on religious differences and the threat of conversion.

England's confrontation with the fluidity of Ottoman identity and its own investment in "authentic" and fixed racialized national identities are evident, for instance, in Julia Pardoe's *The City of the Sultans, and the Domestic Manners of Turks* (1837). Pardoe is quick to distinguish between "faux" Europeans who inhabit Pera (an area of Istanbul) and "real" ones who are born within the national borders of England or France. She writes: "I must not omit to mention that Perotes, or natives of Pera, consider themselves as much Franks as though they had been born and nurtured on the banks of the Thames or the Seine; and your expression of amusement at this very original notion would inevitably give great offense."[52] Pardoe then suggests that you can always tell a Perote from a "genuine European" based on his or her outward appearance, but the fact that all that distinguishes the "faux" from the "genuine" European is make-up and dress also points to the tenuousness of this boundary, undercutting the mythic dimension of modern nationalism and its emphasis on a "natural" and homogenous people by inadvertently exposing it as no more than a new inflection on arbitrary geographical borders.

This tenuousness, which is part of the liminal place Turkey occupies between East and West, is made explicit in Charles Macfarlane's 1829 account of the Franks in Izmir, whom he describes as having "a strange hybridous nature, something neither Christian nor Turk, Asiatic nor European ... A turban and a caftan would make the Frank a Turk; a hat and coat, the Turk a Frank."[53] While the racialized modern nation organizes itself around the idea of a "natural" population, Macfarlane, like Pardoe, unintentionally seems to beg the question, unsettled as he is by this "hybrid" population, about whether race/ethnicity is nothing more than a sartorial performance. In this place where Europe and Asia met, the rigid boundaries of modern nations were dramatically challenged.

In her *Turkey of the Ottomans* (1911), Lucy Garnett, thoroughly educated in the racial sciences that dominated nineteenth-century England, "white-washed" the Ottoman Empire by arguing that the Turks had become "civilized" by mixing with white blood and that this mixture could only happen because Turks were not "coloured" but Aryan. She wrote: "The Osmanli race cannot, however, according to modern ethnologists, correctly be said to be 'Turks' in the sense in which that term, in common with 'Turanian,' is ordinarily used, namely, to designate not only a non-Aryan, but a coloured race, and appear rather to have belonged originally to a branch of that white race of Western Asia variously termed Circassian, Alarodian, or Archaian. But whatever may have been the original stock from which they sprang, the Osmanlis have developed into the great nation they now constitute by admixture during more than six centuries with the best white blood both of Western Asia and Eastern Europe."[54]

She had already erased the "coloured" element from Turkey in her 1890 ethnographic study, which carefully categorized Ottoman women according to national/ethnic "types." If mixing with the "best white blood" had resulted in a great nation, Garnett insisted, in the same vein as Nott, that the "bad" hybrid – the mixing of the "higher races" with the "lower races" – had failed to bear fruit: "The thousand upon thousands of negroes and negresses that have been imported into the country since the Turkish conquest might lead us to expect to find a considerable mixture of black blood in the lower classes especially of the population. This, however, is not the case. Though negresses and Abyssinians are often married, either to men of their own race or to the whites, the climate does not seem favourable to the propagation of the coloured races, and the few negro or mulatto children who come into the world generally die in infancy."[55]

Garnett's ethnography is thoroughly saturated by the many debates about nations, hybridity, mulattos, and race that filled the pages of European and American scientific journals and informed the cultural production in the nineteenth century.[56] Her work cannot be properly unpacked without this context. Although she suggests, rather vaguely, that "climate" is the reason for the supposed decline of the black or mixed-race population in Ottoman society, Garnett's thesis favours the view that humans are the product of polygenesis (multiple species), so that intermixture between two different "species" – the "Ayran" and "coloured races" – could not but end in sterility, just as the biological hybrid – the crossing of horse and donkey – produced the infertile mule. In other words, the true hybrid could not produce viable offspring whereas Turks and Europeans, as they were of the same "white" species, interbred successfully. This thesis was, in turn, used to explain the sophistication of the Ottoman civilization: Osmanlis, as "white," were of the highest race and thus capable of building a great civilization. Garnett's argument about Osmanlis paralleled the one made about ancient Egyptians. They must also have been white, racial theorists insisted, as that was the only way to explain their achievements: "Ancient Egyptians were Caucasians," argued Nott.[57] The greatness of this ancient world in Africa, like that of the Ottoman Empire, could then be explained in a way that did not disturb European theories about the hierarchy of races.

The monogenesis view – humans as one species – which held that successful sexual unions between races could only produce "negative" consequences, was also circulating and was equally informing readings of mixed Ottoman populations as corrupt and dissolute. The intermixing of races and ethnicities, de Gobineau declared, inevitably led to degeneration and heralded the decline of civilization. A correspondent for *The Near East*, voicing this theory, described Constantinople as a "medley": "Turks, Greeks, Armenians, Circassians, Kurds, figure in it, all equally bad, mean, dishonest, and treacherous ... The failure of Turkey is the failure of Rome. Rome fell because there remained no Romans, and Turkey will fall because in Constantinople there remain no Turks. They have become 'Levantine-y.' A Turk will trace in his family, perhaps, a Circassian mother, an Egyptian grandfather, here a rich Greek, always an Albanian or a Jew ... Throughout the centuries many people have come to the city. The city of the Great Whore has sucked most of them in and spit most of them out Levantines – a people who are not a people, without patriotism, without honour, talking myriad tongues in jargon, the sole people in the world without one virtue."[58] The writer concludes his piece with the suggestion that the troubles in Turkey are not about religions divisions but about the tensions between pure races and mixed breeds: "Turkey is represented in England as divided cleanly into the Turk and the Christian, eternally antagonistic. It is not. It is divided into Anatolian and Levantine, native inhabitant and bastard ruling race."[59] Replacing the older insistence on the tensions between Christians and Muslims, the cosmopolitan populace is now set up against the myth of the "authentic" native, who is offered up as the rightful race.

This reimagining of communities along racial lines and the necessity of redrawing national borders were hotly debated in the papers of the day as "multitudes" needed to be converted and reallocated. Indian Muslims who were opposed to the proposed dismemberment of the Ottoman Empire provoked this dismissive response in the *The Near East*:

"We have accepted the principle that the new political boundaries must be so drawn that the world shall be free from the more obvious seeds of future wars. This involves making them accord with racial distribution, and that task in itself is sufficiently difficult."[60] The model of the racially homogenous version of nationalism, paradoxically, spawned both national liberation movements, by populations anxious to escape the yoke of colonialism and empire, and simultaneously proved untenable as the twentieth century witnessed genocide, gender violence, and "ethnic cleansing." These new "political boundaries" organized around race blossomed into some of the worst wars in history instead of preventing "the more obvious seeds" of them from taking root.[61]

The collapse of the Ottoman Empire and the emergence of modern Turkey have traditionally been read as a story of progress, with the "sick man" crumbling and the republic emerging from its ruins as strong and coherent. Yet "the city of the Great Whore," with all its thwarting of naturalized models of the nation and its embrace of a "Levantine" populace, suggests an alternative modernity that is foreclosed by this reading.[62] The Ottoman world's progressive understanding of the nation as cosmopolitan as opposed to racially or ethnically coherent mirrors the current interest in a "new" cosmopolitanism that is often touted as the product of westernization and globalization; yet it might be more usefully understood instead as a return to the alternative model of modernity that can be gleaned in the Ottoman world.[63]

Racial Fantasies and Translations of *The Thousand and One Nights*

At the heart of this radical reform of the very conception of the community – from the umma to a European nation – is the figure of the veiled woman. The terms "Great Babylon" and "Great Whore," hurled at the Ottoman Empire, suggest the underlying anxiety westerners felt about the unregulated female body that produced racially mixed populations. By the eighteenth century, English imaginings of eastern lands were inevitably framed by The Thousand and One Nights – which became, as Richard Burton noted, "the most familiar of books in England next to the Bible."[64] References to these tales became so frequent and constant in the accounts of western travellers that the mere title often served as shorthand, conjuring up for the reader an erotic oriental fantasy that fed the sexual imagination of Europe. The French orientalist and archaeologist Antoine Galland published his multivolume Les Mille et une nuits from 1704 to 1717, which was quickly translated into English and renowned throughout Europe. Subsequent translations of the tales vary widely, from the tame and polite to Burton's very lewd edition (1885–8) with its obsessive focus on sex and extensive footnotes on "oriental" sexual practices.

All the versions, more or less sexually explicit, open with the same frame narrative: King Shahzaman returns home to find his wife in bed with another man and, horrified by the scene, he pulls out his sword and kills them both. Distraught, he then travels to see his brother, King Shahriyar, only to witness a more extreme act of betrayal when he spies his brother's wife engaging in an orgy in the garden. He and his brother then set off on a journey to contemplate their situations and discover whether their tale of calamity is unique or whether all women are untrustworthy. While the kings are on their journey, they encounter an enormous *Jinni,* who has captured a beautiful woman and jealously carries her around in a locked box. While the *Jinni* is sleeping, the woman calls to the two kings to service her sexually. They are reluctant to heed her command but do so when she threatens them with death. She then displays the 98 rings she has collected from other men like them, all behind the back of the unsuspecting *Jinni,* telling the kings: when a woman desires something, nothing can stop her. She warns them never to trust a woman's vows for women are ruled by their passions and merely feign affection. The kings decide that if the powerful *Jinni* is incapable of preventing or controlling a woman, they have no hope. When they return from their quest, King Shahriyar beheads his wife, the palace women, and the slaves. For the next three years, he takes a virgin to his bed only to behead her at the end of each night until Shahrazad shows up and both seduces and distracts him with her storytelling.

For its Muslim audience, this story confirms the explosive and untamed female sexual desires that were seen as a threat to the Islamic social order. As Fatima Mernissi argues, Islam constructs women as fearful and powerful and responds to this "destructive" feminine energy by veiling and secluding them in an attempt to control their sexuality, much like the *Jinni* imprisons his voracious captive in a box.[65] However, for its Victorian audience, raised on the model of women as passive, sexually naive, and innocent, the representation of these sexually desirous women would have been both titillating and disturbing. Whereas a paternalistic West effaces women as agents, a paternalistic East acknowledges their agency and attempts to control it. Yet the most provoking aspect of this tale for its western audience is not the sexual agency of women but rather the race and class mixing, which activated European and American anxieties about miscegenation and transgression.

A review of some of the major translations of these tales exposes this new fear. In comparison with Galland's earlier translation, Burton's edition, informed as it is by nineteenth-century "science" on Africans, exaggerates and emphasizes the race and class dimensions of the encounter. Whereas Galland's version of King Shahzaman's discovery of his wife's transgression reads: *"il aperçut un homme dans ses bras* [he saw a Man in her arms],"[66] Burton's reads: "he found the Queen, his wife, asleep on his own carpet bed, embracing with both arms a black cook of loathsome aspect and foul with grease and grime."[67] Burton further describes the black lover of King Shahryar's wife as dropping "from one of the trees, a big slobbering blackamoor with rolling eyes which showed the whites" and adds that the queen was in love with one of the "filthiest of filthy slaves."[68] Reading the tales as a sociological record of eastern sexuality (which is rather like taking European fairy-tales as representative of Europe), Burton also added the following footnote to this section: "Debauched women prefer negroes on account of the size of their parts. I measured one man in Somali-land who, when quiescent, numbered nearly six inches. This is a characteristic of the negro race and of African animals; e.g., the horse; whereas the pure Arab, man and beast, is below the average of Europe; one of the best proofs by and by, that the Egyptian is not Asiatic, but a negro partially white-washed."[69] In contrast to Burton's, Edward Lane's translation (1838–40), accused of being "uninspiringly literal," reads:[70] "a black slave came to her, and embraced her; she doing the like."[71]

Bernard Lewis, the contemporary Middle Eastern scholar who supports the clash-of-civilizations thesis of Islam and the West, suggests that *The Thousand and One Nights* casts doubt on the "myth of an interracial utopia" in the Muslim world. He argues that King Shahzaman and King Shahriyar "were clearly southern gentlemen, with sexual fantasies, or rather nightmares of an Alabama-like quality."[72] He notes that he is using Edward Lane's tamer translation, but his reading of the tale seems much more reminiscent of Burton's, as nowhere in the various translations of the stories, with the notable exception of Burton's account, do "blackness," "whiteness" or social status function as anything other than descriptions. Nor does the American South serve at all as an apt parallel as the two systems of slavery are entirely different in structure. The institution of plantation slavery in America was built on the belief that blacks were racially inferior. Ottoman slaves were racially diverse and often treated as members of the household. Some enjoyed a great deal of social mobility: the Valide Sultan (mother of the sultan) and the Kislar Aga (the chief black eunuch) – held the highest ranks of the Empire. This frame narrative bears no resemblance to the fears of "hyper-sexualized" and "animal-like" black men raping helpless and virginal white women that fuelled the fantasies of the American South. The women in *The Thousand and One Nights* initiate the sexual encounters, exhibiting a powerful, uncontrollable, and threatening sexual agency.

That Lewis's late-twentieth-century reading of this tale continues to be informed by this powerful European/American myth of the hierarchy of races – which required a great deal of energy and ink to erect – testifies to its pervasiveness. Lewis, like the nineteenth-century translators, invents racial tensions despite the fact that race is nowhere part of the fabric of the framing tale. So indoctrinated by theories of race and class hierarchies were Americans and Europeans that they could not imagine a world unstructured or uninflected by them, and thus read them as universally applicable. The representation of the hidden worlds of veils and harems as the product of a tyrannical system in the nineteenth century was not so much about challenging patriarchy as it was about eradicating the fluidity that was facilitated by the *umma*, which refused the racialized and territorial bounded versions of the European nation and exposed the myth of a dominant race or a "natural" population.

Harem Literature

Harem literature – with the requisite sections on "eyewitness" accounts of harems, polygamy, and veiling – proliferated in the latter half of the nineteenth century. Despite their lack of access, western men had for centuries speculated wildly about what went on behind harem walls. However, as western women started to gain access to this space, their visits opened up a unique opportunity for social interaction between women on both sides of the East/West divide; this complex cross-cultural exchange in turn spawned this distinct genre. In 1896, a "novel" appeared in London and New York called *Hadjira: A Turkish Love Story*, by Adalet, a work that was popular enough to be reprinted into the early decades of the twentieth century and that explicitly marketed itself as harem literature. Yet this work also exposed the very constructed nature of this genre. Adalet (literally "justice" or "equity" in Turkish) was a pseudonym and the novel claimed to be based on the true story of a Turkish lady living in a harem who had disguised her authorial identity for reasons of safety. A review in *The New York Times* claimed that the author did not "draw on her imagination" for the story and that "all the facts and incidents are true."[73] Between 1890 and 1892, *The Nineteenth Century – A Monthly Review* had published several other articles by Adalet with titles such as "A Voice from a Harem: Some Words about the Turkish Woman of Our Day," "Life in the Harem," "Turkish Marriages Viewed from the Harem," and "Turkey-Slavery and Harem Life." Lucy Garnett, the English travel writer and ethnographer, quickly dismissed these articles as fakes, suggesting that they were more likely the product of a European governess than a "genuine 'Voice from the Harem.'"[74] But while Garnett was dismissing Adalet, *The New York Times* was describing her as the "first literary young lady the harem ha[d] produced," vouching for her productions as being "absolutely genuine" and referring to her as a "10 year inmate of the harem."[75]

If we turn to the texts themselves, it seems impossible to determine whether or not they are "authentic" as the author is adept at playing with the orientalist conventions and puts no great stake in consistency. In August 1890, Adalet writes: "So many English ladies have lately visited the Turkish harems, and learning our language have been able to write the truth about us, that it is really difficult to say something new about a country whose customs are as well known to everyone as to ourselves."[76] But a few months later she notes that "The silence kept by Christians about us has always seemed surprising to me, for nowhere could be found better tools for any author in search of novelty … none have written about us, and we are as little known with thousands of Europeans visiting us daily as we were when no Christian could pass the sacred threshold of a harem."[77] Here Adalet plays with two of the standard conventions of nineteenth-century harem literature: travel writing and orientalism. The first article invokes a sense of ennui, decadence, and exhaustion. The Ottoman Empire, the "sick man of Europe, itself emblematic of the fin-de-siecle," is portrayed as being in its death throes. "The veil being literally lifted," the once-mysterious Orient is now found to be wanting and, writes Adalet, "very little remains" of its customs. Modernity and imitation of European ways have done away with the days when "the Turkish woman was spoken of as a mystery which it was dangerous to unravel"; now she walks without shame in public "in habiliments which would hardly be considered decent with the lowest dregs of European society."[78] The second article, however, plays with the convention of the Orient as a mystery waiting to be penetrated, as virgin territory, different, exotic, and absolutely other. The harem, writes Adalet, with its "strange superstition" and "childlike faith," needs to be revealed to Europeans who are largely ignorant of its workings, understanding neither the position of the wife nor that of the Circassian slave residing in it. Adalet's articles are consistently contradictory and indicative of the debates of the day. In the August article, she invites "kind-hearted" European women to participate in the education of Turkish girls[79] whereas in the December article she suggests that no "outside" intervention will be helpful and that Turks must bring about changes on their own.[80]

Adalet's *Hadjira* further complicates the question of "authenticity" on which the market for harem literature in the West depended as it reads like an English realist novel set in an Ottoman harem. In the introductory note, the publisher declares that it is "the original work of a young Turkish lady," adding: "The manuscript was written by her in English in her own handwriting, and neither the MS. nor the proofs have been subjected to any more correction than if the writer had been an Englishwoman. It is unfortunately impossible to reveal the identity of the Author, for her personal safety would be seriously imperiled by doing so; but the Publisher is authorized to vouch for the truth of the above statement."[81] Is this, then, a true story? Or does this work employ the same nineteenth-century realist conventions that Daniel Defoe, for instance, used in his novel *Robinson Crusoe*, where the preface, supposedly penned by the editor, claims to present an unadulterated unedited manuscript of a shipwrecked sailor? Whatever the case, *The New York Times*'s editor, referring to its "excellent" literary style, accepted it as a true account even as it is listed in "Mr. Edward Arnold's List" under "new works of fiction."

In the novel, love potions, witches, and poison are interspersed with witty parlour dialogue, noble acts, wealth disparities, and thwarted romances. The Turkish heroine is described as "beautiful" with "golden hair," "blue eyes," and a "milk-white complexion." The daughter of a poor village blacksmith, she is orphaned and taken in by her grandmother, Fetnè Hanim, nurse to the family of Pasha Nasrullah. When the grandmother dies, Hadjira is adopted by the wealthy family and establishes a close friendship with the youngest son, Nazif Bey, with whom she falls in love. He has bought a voluptuous, sensual, dark Circassian beauty and is expected to marry her, but he prefers the demure but proud and free blonde orphan. Proving herself an honorable woman, Hadjira deflects her lover's attentions as the family adamantly opposes their union. Full of both passion and virtue, she is given to fainting spells, blushing, and tears as she tries to repress her love for Nazif Bey. Despite his marriage proposal, she secretly flees to save him from ruin, taking up a position as a nurse; thus she keeps her promise to her grandmother never to cross Hanem Effendi, Nafiz Bey's mother. Nafiz Bey, resigned, marries another woman, who eventually requests a divorce from him. He goes off to war (likely the Russo-Turkish War, given the reference to his stationing at Plevna), his mother dies, and years later, worn and no longer as handsome, he finds Hadjira and is reunited with his only love.

Like Charlotte Brontë's Jane Eyre, Hadjira, the intelligent and proud orphan, is able to keep her honour intact, rise above her station, and marry the man, now slightly broken, of her dreams. So too, like Jane Austen's *Pride and Prejudice*, this novel documents the changes in women's expectations and rights in the nineteenth century as romantic love comes to challenge the idea of women as objects to be exchanged as part of a marriage contract. Nafiz himself protests to Hadjira, stating his reasons for not wanting to marry his slave:

> A Circassian! A designing, artful hypocrite, like they all are; and is it to such as her that you compare yourself? A woman who has neither principles nor modesty, nor even intellect; who is only intelligent enough to know that by marrying me she would be liberated from her servile condition; and who, if she were sold tomorrow, would lay the same plans to ensnare the first man who went to the slave market. Believe me if you will Hadjira: when I was younger I did think of doing like my countrymen; I thought I might get used to looking at my wife as a chattel, and that anything would be better than to marry a girl I had never seen, and didn't know from Eve; but I pondered it over it much over there, and when I came back, even if I hadn't seen you, I would have preferred death to marrying a Circassian, and breaking thus at a blow all hopes I might have of a congenial home.[82]

As with Darcy in Austen's novel, who decides in the end that he would prefer to marry Elizabeth, his intellectual equal, than a wife who defers to him because of his position and wealth, this Turkish novel challenges traditional marriage arrangements by introducing romantic love. The

Pasha, who forbids the marriage, tells his son: "Love's not a word usually used when Turkish marriages are discussed." Sounding remarkably like Lady Catherine in *Pride and Prejudice,* Hanem Effendi, his mother, refuses to hear of her son's desire to marry Hadjira, exclaiming: "Did you ever dream that I would consent to hear my son's name pronounced in the same breath as a smith's daughter's?"[83]

Yet there are also a couple of notable differences that situate *Hadjira* in a specifically Ottoman, rather than British, context: whereas Elizabeth and her sisters in Austen's novel will be left penniless on their father's death because the law of entailment requires that his estate go to the next male in line (their cousin), making marriage for Elizabeth an economic necessity, Hadjira has inherited her grandmother's wealth, as was the right of Muslim women, and so is financially independent. Many British women, from Lady Mary on, were quick to note that this independence allowed Muslim women far greater freedom than their European counterparts. Furthermore, whereas Nafiz Bey, as was typical of progressive Ottoman men, is the one who makes impassioned speeches about the problem of treating women as chattel, Darcy must be convinced by Elizabeth that women should be treated as intellectual equals rather than as possessions. And while Hanem Effendi's outrage at the transgression of class boundaries reads as suspiciously British, given the class mobility and fluidity in the Ottoman Empire, Nafiz Bey counters his mother's and Hadjira's own protest that she is "inferior" by pointing to the relative lack of concern with heredity and paternal lineage in Ottoman society: "Neither my father nor myself know what my great grandfather was, and he might have been a dustman for all we care." In the end, like that of the Victorian heroines, Hadjira and Nafiz Bey's love conquers all obstacles, and *The New York Times*'s reviewer writes "But for the peculiarities of the names of the personages, their methods of speech and action, they might have been transferred to Paris, St. Peterborough or Vienna," concluding "that when well-bred young people of Constantinople or New York fall in love with one another their conduct is identical."

Adalet refers in her articles to the French and English governesses in the harems and to the prevalence of novel-reading among Turkish girls, who "saw in them the descriptions of happy homes where one wife alone possessed the love of her husband." She also reflexively notes the conventions of love stories in her own novel when she has Nafiz Bey, after he has proposed to his beloved, tell Hadjira: "If you refuse, I won't say I will die of love – no man ever dies of love."[84] Furthermore, she refers to travel narratives such as Thackeray's *Voyage from Cornhill to Grand Cairo,* to well-educated Turkish ladies who have "resided many years in Europe," to Turkish boys brought up "in Paris and Oxford," and to reading English newspapers. Is it possible "Adalet" was a Turkish author influenced by European writers who reworked her tale of the harem to attract British and American markets? Or was Adalet perhaps an English writer well-versed in the expectations of orientalist harem literature, posing as a Turkish woman in order to sell copies and cater to the healthy market for "real" and authentic tales of the harem? Is the reference to "pounds" as currency in the novel, for instance, a Turkish writer's concession to her British readers or a slip by an English writer? What is the purpose of the occasional footnotes that appear in the novel, such as the one that explains "Abbey" as the term by "which the elder son of the family is called by his younger brothers or sisters"; or the one that glosses "mangal," which is described as a tray on which hot coals are placed, in reality a device used as a stove by the lower classes; or the one for "lowta," which translates it as a lute? Are these notes attempts by a Turkish writer to explain Ottoman terms to a western audience or are they the attempts of an English writer to foster the illusion of realism by inserting Turkish terms? And what, in any case, does "genuine" mean in the context of the author's reflexive performance of orientalist and novelistic conventions and what does it mean in the context of the cosmopolitan Ottoman Empire?

Reina Lewis suggests that Garnett – in denouncing Adalet – wanted to police the boundaries of harem literature in order to guarantee the commercial success of the genre: "The appearance of articles such as that by 'Adalet' and the swift response of female authorities in the field highlights the importance of harem literature as an area of cultural activity available to Western women. In defending the integrity of the field, Western authors buoyed up its significance and protected the value of their expertise."[85] Yet in addition to defending themselves as experts, western women, in their dismissal of this liminal work, also revealed an uneasiness about the lack of race and class markers in the Ottoman Empire that was typical of the period. Authenticity depended on these constructions, but Ottoman social fluidity disrupted these comfortable notions, unsettling the neat divide of East and West upon which the market for harem literature depended.

Garnett, interested in racial categories and hierarchies, had meticulously divided the population into autonomous national or ethnic groups, detailing the "natural" characteristics of Greek, Armenian,

Bulgarian, Kurdish, Frank, Gipsy, Albanian, Turkish, and Circassian women in her own two-volume work *Women of Turkey*, published in 1890–1. In her 1911 *Turkey of the Ottomans*, as noted earlier, she refers to the Osmanlis as having "the best *white* blood" of both Western Asia and Eastern Europe (emphasis mine). As I have argued, she was not alone in her desire to divide the world into discrete racial categories even as the very cosmopolitan nature of the Empire refused them.

Her quick labelling of Adalet as a fraud and her desire for an "authentic" voice that would expose the truth of the Turkish woman also speaks to her interest in policing ethnic and racial borders. As Adalet herself notes in her articles, "A Turk rarely married his country-woman" and most Turkish girls were more than "half Circassian."[86] So what would a "genuine voice" from the harem be in the context of the cosmopolitan Ottoman Empire? The genre of harem literature both professed to penetrate the secrets of the Orient and at the same time worked to construct and ensure a strict cultural and racial divide. An author wanting to break into this market then must perform authenticity – must play the "native" or the "expert" that has access to her – to shore up an East/West divide that was, in reality, much more fluid, to allay western anxieties about miscegenation. The playful, liminal work of Adalet was swiftly denounced for pointing to the fallacy on which the genre was based.

Chapter Three

Two Western Women Venture East: Lady Annie Brassey and Anna Bowman Dodd

"The faces behind the veils might have been black, white, or yellow; none among those hundred onlookers would ever know their color ... Within these silken mantles the secret shape or outline, even to the very color of the skin of the favorite wife, daughter, or Khadine, were secrets as closely guarded as though these ladies had never emerged from harem walls."

(Anna Bowman Dodd, *In the Palaces of the Sultan*, 1902; 2005)

"The commitment to an organic ordering of humankind was important also because it endorsed the claims of racial science to observe, organize and regulate the social body."

(Paul Gilroy, *Against Race: Imagining Political Culture Beyond the Color Line*, 2000)

First Case Study: Lady Annie Brassey Orders the World

In the latter part of the nineteenth century, Lady Annie Brassey, a prolific travel writer, collector, and photographer "awoke and found herself famous," following the publication of her *Around the World in the Yacht "Sunbeam."* Enormously popular in her own day, this work, which appeared in 1878 in London and New York, was in its sixth edition by the end of that year. It was adapted for school use and translated into French, Italian, Swedish, German, and Hungarian. Around the World was followed by, among others, the also popular *Sunshine and Storm in the East, or Cruises to Cyprus and Constantinople,* which recounts two trips to Turkey. The first voyage took place in 1874, during the reign of Sultan Abdülaziz; the second in 1878, during the reign of Sultan Abdülhamid II, when the more impoverished city of Istanbul was trying to cope with the flood of refugees displaced by the Russo-Turkish war. In addition to her five travel books, Lady Brassey also displayed the archaeological, botanical, and ethnographical curiosities she collected on her global voyages at various exhibitions at Hastings and South Kensington, and she was working on establishing a private museum at the time of her death. Further, she produced, from both her own amateur attempts and from works of prominent photographers of the day, seventy large gold-embossed photo albums, made up of over 6,000 photos.

Lady Brassey spent a great deal of time and energy shaping and ordering the world she encountered in her travels for her adoring public. She was admired for the fact that she "describes only what she has seen" and "invents nothing ... her narrative is as plain and unvarnished as a ship's log-book," and this plain prose style is complemented by a photographic record.[1] If travel writing from the eighteenth century onward put a new emphasis on the objectivity and credibility of an account, nineteenth-century photography, even more than "plain" prose, extended this logic because it was assumed that the photograph did not lie.[2] Yet, despite the legitimacy granted to her travel writing and photography, Lady Annie's obsessive "fact" collecting and cataloguing, at its core, does not seem to be have been overly motivated by a concern for accuracy. Volume 20 of her photo collection, for instance – labelled "Newfoundland and St. John's" – opens with a photo of a dark-skinned man standing under a palm tree, while another photo appears to be of a Greek island.

Neither does her travel writing display a concern for nor interest in correct details. In *Sunshine and Storm in the East*, referring to a visit by the highly educated Princess Nazli, Lady Annie comments critically that she "smoked all the time, but did not seem to approve of either our coffee or our tea."[3] Yet in the next paragraph, she mentions that it is the last day of Ramadan, without acknowledging this period of religious fasting as the likely reason for the princess's refusal of beverages. In other passages, demonstrating what Said refers to as the consistency and repetition in the citation of orientalist tropes, Lady Brassey recounts two tales that had long been in circulation as recent fact. In the first, she reports on the violent practice of drowning women in the Bosporus: "Not so very long ago," she writes, "six hundred women of the Imperial harem actually suffered this fate ... their bodies [were] sunk in sacks in the Gulf of Ismid, close to where our fleet has been lying recently."[4] This apocryphal tale dates from the seventeenth century, when the mad Sultan Ibrahim I (1615–48) reportedly drowned all 280 women in his harem in the Bosporus. Versions of this story were frequently referenced in early western travel accounts. In the second tale, also lifted from much earlier travel narratives, Lady Brassey recounts the sultan's supposed penchant for watching women get dumped out of boats: "The Sultan sometimes amuses himself by sitting on the bank, while some of the ladies of the harem are rowed about and purposely upset for his amusement. They are all dressed very smartly for the occasion, and he always gives them new dresses afterwards."[5]

The discrepancy between this casual attitude to "facts" and Lady Brassey's "scientific" style, which was enhanced by documentary photography, is partially explained by her commitment to the British imperial project. Travelling around the world in a steam-powered sailing yacht with her husband Thomas Brassey, who was a member of Parliament and later Civil Lord of the Admiralty and responsible for ensuring that colonial rule was facilitating English commerce and trade abroad, Lady Brassey complemented her husband's activities and reinforced the view of England as the dominant world power. In his introduction to William Greswell's book *Outlines of British Colonisation*, Lord Brassey surveys the economic health of the empire and discusses the racial traits of its inhabitants, while accessing their various contributions. From the sugar industry in the West Indies, where the climate, he maintains, will not allow for extensive European colonization but where the growing fruit trade "seems," as he puts it, "specially adapted to the limited resources and aptitudes of a negro peasantry";[6] to the fisheries, forests, and granaries in Canada; to the gold in Australia; to the minerals in South Africa where, he writes, the "Caffres" (a derogatory name for black Africans) are "willing and stable labourers ... lending invaluable support in opening of the resources of their country,"[7] Thomas Brassey assumes proprietorship, as does his wife with her collections and her writings, over the wealth and populations of the world.

Lady Brassey dutifully follows her husband's lead. Speaking of a visit to a Greek island, Lady Brassey informs her reader, in her chatty familiar tone, that her daughter, Muñie, "is as happy as possible at a picnic, or in charge of the ruffianly-looking Turk or Greek to whom her donkey may happen to belong."[8] The arrogance of the Empire is perfectly summed up in this description, where even the English child is presumed to outrank and command the local men. Lady Brassey also indulges in the same racial stereotyping as her husband, scattering remarks through her narrative like: "Armenians are, as a rule, a money getting race, and will do anything for the love of gain, even to the sacrifice of their personal pride" or the Turks are "not a money-making people."[9]

Displaying her knowledge of the inequities of colonial trade, which involved the harvesting of inexpensive raw materials from the colonies, which were then exchanged for expensive manufactured British goods, she writes: "The islands of the Archipelago send their produce in small boats to Syria, there to be reshipped in steamers for ports in England and elsewhere, bringing back various kinds of cotton goods and iron tools, as well as money, in exchange."[10] However, she then refuses to acknowledge the logic of national liberation movements and the resistance to British imperialism, and she instead perpetuates the myth of grateful and welcoming colonial subjects: "Scarcely anyone in England, perhaps, knows," she writes, "how bitterly these poor islanders lament the loss of British rule [the Ionian Islands were under British rule from 1815–64], under which at one time they used to complain that they were only slaves."[11] Making frequent references to the fact that she does not speak the languages of the places she travels, Lady Brassey can, at best, have had only limited engagement with the "islanders" and their laments, but for her British audience these remarks act as a reassurance of both the strength and benevolence of colonial rule.

In the same vein, commenting on Cyprus – the Ottoman Empire had ceded control of this island to Britain in 1878 – and again voicing her oft-mentioned frustration over Greek independence and uppity colonials, she writes about the relative merits of the plan to populate Cyprus with Turkish refugees: "If the Greek element should once prevail, it would be a perpetual thorn in our side, and the end would probably be that we should be requested to move out when we had done everything possible in the way of administrative reforms, the construction of harbours, railways, and improvements of all kinds, just as in the case of the Ionian Islands. The Turks, on the other hand, would suit the climate as well as the natives, and would always be contented with our rule."[12] Like the nineteenth-century British parliamentarians debating the "Eastern question," Lady Brassey tends to treat Ottoman populations as colonial subjects.

An implicit validation of racial hierarchies is also evident in Lady Brassey's description of the slave trade in Santa Ana, Brazil. She and her husband posed as Yanks in order to observe the buying and selling of slaves in the market as the English were forbidden from participating in it, but she shows no disdain for the practice. She writes of this viewing that "the children all seemed to be on very good terms with their masters."[13] Later she remarks, without any criticism and as a matter of course, that the daily Brazilian newspapers were "full of advertisements of slaves for sale, and descriptions of men, pigs, children, cows, pianos, women, houses."[14] Unlike slaves in the Americas, slaves in the Ottoman Empire could rise to very powerful positions, yet Lady Brassey, displaying a contempt for slaves themselves rather than the system of slavery, is disturbed by this mobility. She writes that she cannot "fathom any reason" why the Ottoman sultan would be so proud of his title "Son of a Slave" and describes the Valide Sultan (the Queen Mother) as "a slave of the very lowest description" and as such "*naturally* bigoted and ignorant."[15]

In keeping with her expectations of colonial subjects' deference to British paternalism and of the obedience of slaves to their masters, Lady Brassey herself submits to her husband's rule. Tom Brassey is clearly in charge of the voyages. While she occasionally grumbles about travel plans, she always bows to his authority. Mentioning the prospect of a disembarkment, which everyone on board was looking forward to, but which Tom cancels at the last minute, she recounts: "I tried hard to persuade Tom to remain even a few hours, if only just to let us run ashore, but he was determined."[16] Even when they have to cope with a severe storm that they have sailed into after one of Tom's sudden departures, all for naught, she does not openly challenge him: "It is provoking to have endured so much discomfort for forty-five hours, only to find ourselves back at the place we started. Tom, however, was glad to have thoroughly tried the yacht, and found what a fine sea-boat she is."[17] Her greater sacrifice, however, is in agreeing to sail with him in the first place. Although they ostensibly travelled for the sake of her "weak chest," it was clearly her husband who loved sailing while Lady Brassey, already ill, spent most of her time seasick, died at sea at the age of 47, and was "buried" en route from India to Australia in 1887. Although she rarely complained, the magnitude of her discomfort can be glimpsed in a comment about her brief respite from sea sickness. After many days of enduring terrible storms following their departure from Istanbul, she records: "I think that at last the battle of eighteen years is accomplished, and that the bad weather we have so continuously experienced since we left Constantinople, comprising five gales in eleven days, has ended by making me a good sailor. For the last two days I have really known what it is to feel well at sea, even when it is very rough, and have been able to eat my meals in comfort, and even to read and write without feeling that my head belonged to somebody else."[18] A few days later, however, she writes: "At night I found, to my great disappointment, that all my recent experience had been to no avail, and that I was as ill as if I had never been to sea before in my life."[19]

Lady Brassey, as an acclaimed travel writer and world traveller, lived a remarkable life for a Victorian woman. Yet, despite her adventurous life, she never challenged the paternalism of the British system. She expected colonial subjects to passively submit, she was seemingly unperturbed by slavery, and she herself bowed to her husband's authority. I have gone to such lengths to demonstrate the extent of her rather predictable investment in a paternalistic hierarchical model to highlight her *exceptional* support of Turkish women in their desire for liberty: "It is a great mistake of the Turks," she writes, "to think they can educate their wives and daughters, and still keep them in confinement and subjection ... you would think the revolution must come soon. The children of the present day Turkey are brought up to think the system of yashmaks and confinement a most tyrannical custom and not to be endured."[20] Lady Brassey was clearly more invested in the lingering vestiges of feudal England – evident in her attitude towards colonials, slaves, and women – than in revolting against paternalistic systems, so why does she sympathize with the revolutionary aspirations of Muslim women? Moreover, despite this apparent solidarity with Turkish women's emancipation, she also remained firmly opposed to English women getting the vote even as the "confinement" of Turkish women that barred them from the public sphere (albeit differently conceived) paralleled anti-suffrage policies in England.

At least part of her contradictory view on women can be explained by the Brasseys' enthusiasm for colonialism. Thomas Brassey remained a staunch supporter of the Empire and its "beneficence," which he saw manifesting itself "in the feelings of the people of the colonies towards that old but not exhausted land which it delights them to regard as the common home of the race."[21] Adding that it was "the last importance to the future of our race to prevent our noble Empire from falling asunder," he quoted in support of his view the "statesmanlike wisdom" of Lord Rosebery: "'It is a part of our responsibility and heritage to take care that the world, so far as it can be moulded by us, shall receive the Anglo-Saxon, and not another character.'"[22] In this assessment, Brassey gives an explicit and familiar summation of one of the main tenets of imperialism: England was the norm by which other cultures and countries were to be measured, and it bore the responsibility for shaping colonial populations into its likeness. Lady Annie fully supported her husband in his goal of remaking the world and this required Ottoman women to unveil so that they would more fully resemble their western counterparts: "Ten years ago the Armenian women were veiled as carefully as the Turkish women" she wrote, "and it was difficult to tell them apart. Now it is equally difficult to tell the former from the Europeans, either in dress or manner."[23] The abandonment of the veil seemingly transformed even the Turkish Muslim woman into an English one: "A few months ago Princess Nazli went to Egypt, and was not allowed to return to Constantinople. She put on a thick yashmak and feridjee, borrowed a thousand francs, and travelled back with her English maid, who has now been with her for five years. As soon as they made a clear start they threw off yashmak and feridjee and travelled as two *English ladies*, until they reached Constantinople, when they again assumed the Oriental costume" (emphasis mine).[24]

Reminiscent of travellers in the last chapter, Lady Brassey unwittingly reveals the sartorial performance underlying racialized nationalism, and, at the same time, is quick to assert a strict divide between the English and the other that can never be bridged, so that "natives" are both encouraged to aspire to be European and then mocked for their attempt. Describing a market in Istanbul, she commented: "The crowd was very amusing – such numbers of Turkish ladies, attended by negroes, eunuchs, or old women, making purchases of all sorts, but mostly buying articles of European manufacture. It was amusing to see them admiring and bargaining for second-hand European dresses, all very smart in trimming and of the most gorgeous colours, though somewhat soiled. I have often wondered what became of old ball and dinner dresses, but now that I have seen the enormous quarter of the bazaar devoted to the sale of these articles of apparel, I cease to do so."[25] Like the discarded dresses they buy, Turkish women who adopt European customs can only ever be slightly "soiled" secondhand versions of the original. In the same vein and also recalling the belatedness that characterized travel literature of this period, Lady Brassey waxes nostalgically about a fantastical and fading Orient while making it clear that the East must adopt western forms even as it will inevitably fail: "Cairo as a beautiful and ancient oriental city has ceased to exist, and is being rapidly transformed into a bad imitation of a modern Paris ... Only a few narrow streets and old houses are still left ... where you can yet dream that the 'Arabian Nights' are true."[26]

The representation of women from other parts of the world as oppressed and the characterization of foreign men as despotic provided a justification for the interference of British men, allowing the familiar logic of the "white man's burden" as an alibi for economic exploitation and imperialism. Following suit, Lady Brassey refers to Muslim women as "penned up like sheep " and "muffled up to the eyes" and suggests the sultan treats women as he treats his horses; hence she encourages Ottoman women to unveil and become "English" ladies. Yet as Homi Bhabha has pointed out, even when the native perfectly mimics the Englishman in religion, language, dress, and education – as Friday does Crusoe in *Robinson Crusoe,* the native is never accepted as English so as not to threaten the hierarchical relationship between the subject and the subjected.[27]

One of the means of policing the boundaries between those who are British and in charge and those "natives" who merely adopted European ways was by appealing to a racialized nationalism. Commenting on the heterogeneous and hybrid populations of Adrianople, Lady Brassey reveals an underlying anxiety about just such a mix as she invokes a hierarchy based on place of birth as a default sorting mechanism: "There are representatives of every nation under the sun here ... Some are fine, handsome, intelligent-looking men, while others appear fitted to hold a position in the social scale but a little higher than the inhabitants of Tierra del Fuego." Her endorsement of Disraeli's 1847 novel *Tancred; or the New Crusade* is also telling as Disraeli, for different reasons, was also committed to reimagining the East in terms of racialized nations, writing: "Nationality, without race as a plea, is like the smoke of this nagrilly, a fragrant puff";[28] while another passage in the novel insists: "All is race; there is no other truth, and every race must fall which carelessly suffers its blood to become mixed."[29] In the passage that Lady Brassey quotes from the novel, the Queen of England is invited to "transfer the seat of her Empire from London to Delhi" and rule over the different races as the "supreme power" in the East affirming once again racialized hierarchies, with the English at the helm.[30]

The majority of her seventy photo albums in the Huntington Collection at San Marino, which serve as a visual ethnography and are carefully organized by nation, open with pictures of a representative "native." However, the album on Turkey suggests the cosmopolitan Ottoman Empire cannot readily accommodate this model which assumes a correlation between a nation and a dominant ethnic or racial population. It does open with the category of the national "native," but the representative photographs raise a number of questions. On display are two images of the same woman in different poses, and the caption reads "Arab Types"; below are two photos of another woman, shot in a slightly different pose, and the caption reads – again in the plural – "Turkish Women" (see fig. 3.1). Does "Turkish" here refer to Ottoman, Muslim, or is it an ethnic designation? Does it include other populations named in her narrative – Greeks, Armenians, and Jews – for instance? Are "Arabs" Ottomans, Muslims, or an ethnic group? Are these rival nations: do the "Turks" dominate the "Arabs"? Or are the Turks, as converts to Islam, part of the "Arab" *umma*?

The rest of the photos of Turkey, unlike many of her other national albums, are almost entirely void of people, and this visual representation, supported by textual descriptions, constructs the Empire as a barren and lifeless place.[31] There are no fewer than six photos of graveyards; and the English cemetery (full of the fallen of the Crimean War) is described as in "marked contrast with the desolate, uncared-for Turkish graves."[32] In her travel narrative, Lady Brassey frequently refers to the mud, garbage, and dirt in the streets: "We paddled about in the mud, looking at the shops, but we were hardly rewarded for our trouble. Constantinople has lost much of its glitter and glory, but the mud, squalor, and misery remain, and are increased tenfold."[33] So too Cyprus, which the British are in the process of occupying, is presented as diseased and decayed. Like the women, the land, grown sick under Turkish rule, is also in need of saving: "Every house in Nikosia possesses a luxuriant garden, and the bazaars are festooned with vines; but the whole place wears, notwithstanding, an air of desolation, ruin, and dirt ... We passed through a narrow dirty street, with ruined houses and wasted gardens."[34] Even Sultan Abdülhamid is described as "thin" and "cadaverous."[35] Already sick, diseased, and in ruins, the Ottoman Empire awaits reinvention and reordering by the West.

In comparison to this single volume of photos on Turkey, there are six volumes on Egypt. Several photos that document the bombing of Alexandria make it clear that many of the photos in this collection date from the British occupation of Egypt in 1882. In marked contrast to the representation of the Ottoman Empire, the Egyptian albums are full of studio shots that confidently catalogue "native types," and the street scenes are bustling with people. So why are these two places so recently linked in history (Egypt was almost continuously part of the Ottoman

Figure 3.1 Lady Brassey album, "Natives of Turkey," Huntington Collection, San Marino.

Empire from 1517 to 1914) so differently represented? In the Egypt that Lady Brassey represents, the British clearly dominate. In one photo, the British military cover the Sphinx, and, in another, a lady in Victorian dress (possibly Lady Brassey herself) is captured descending the pyramids in her long black dress surrounded by "enabling" natives (see fig. 3.2).[36] In these albums, unlike the one on Turkey, it is clear that the British are in charge, a racialized national native has been identified, and there are no troubling hybrid populations disturbing boundaries. In other words, Egypt was made to accommodate a racialized nationalism under British rule even as it was developing its own nationalist narrative in response to colonialism.

Lady Brassey's interest in unveiling Turkish women was not about women's emancipation, and her complete lack of interest in "liberation" or rebellion in any other context, including suffrage for English women, reveals her support of Turkish women to be anomalous. Rather, veiled women were a source of anxiety for those invested in European nationalism as this "hidden world" indulged in a "mixing" that refused the policing, ranking, and regulating of raced, classed, and colonial bodies. Emile Bernard's 1898 painting *The Three Races* brings this relationship between race hierarchy and unveiling to the fore (see fig. 3.3). Bernard had left France for Egypt in 1893, looking, as many of the artists of the time were, to escape western modernity and return to a more "primitive" and "pure" culture. Although he married an Egyptian woman (Hanenah Saati) and dressed in "oriental" clothing, he quickly grew disillusioned with the Orient. Despite his own cross-dressing, he objected to the influx of "European" dress and modern technologies that undercut his romantic vision of a timeless place; he lost three of his children to disease, and, by the time he returned to France in 1904, his marriage had dissolved. This painting displays the unveiled bodies of three women working in a brothel in Cairo, which he used to frequent: a white woman is spread out on a bed, naked; below her is a less sexualized black woman who is seated on a cushion off to the side; below both, a lighter-skinned woman sitting on the floor at the foot of the white woman. According to the theory of the three races listed in Meyers Konversations-Lexikon (1885–90), the latter would have been classified as Mongoloid and the other two Caucasoid and Negroid. A fin-de-siècle weariness exudes from the jaded faces of the women in this painting (which inspired Picasso's 1907 *Les Demoiselles d'Avignon*) and the mixture of race and sex, would have suggested both decadence and degeneration to its European audience. The lighter-skinned woman

Figure 3.2. Lady Annie Brassey, *Descending the Pyramids*, photo (Huntington Collection, San Marino).

Figure 3.3. Emile Bernard, *The Three Races* (1898), Art Resource.

would have likely been read as mixed race and ranks below the "pure" white and "black" women, although none of the racialized bodies in this brothel seem fully contained.

In contrast, the Ottoman Empire countered this western penchant for classification and instead presented a commitment to the idea of imagining human beings as part of a racially undifferentiated community. In Fanon's terms, it was engaged in humanizing as opposed to racializing.[37] Sultan Abdülhamid II (1842–1918) collected thousands of photographs of his empire and sent a selection of them as a gift to heads of state in both Britain and America in 1893 in order to prove the technological sophistication of the Ottoman world, but these photos also offered a different version of modernity. Among the close to two thousand photos (housed at the British Museum and the Library of Congress) is a photo of light-skinned and dark-skinned schoolchildren standing together on equal footing (see fig. 3.4). Although seemingly innocuous, this photo would have directly challenged the racially segregated school system that was the norm across the United States until the 1950s, presenting a provocative alternative to the racialized nationalism that infected nineteenth- and twentieth-century Europe and America.

Second Case Study: An American in Istanbul

Shortly after the sultan's gift of the photographs, Anna Bowman Dodd travelled to Istanbul as a guest of the United States Ambassador to France in 1901. She was concerned, as she mentions in her preface, that the foreignness of the language and the limits of a few months' stay might impede her ability to capture an accurate impression of the people and the place. The critics of the day thought she had succeeded in her task, however, and embraced the work. A review of *In the Palaces of the Sultan* in *The New York Times* read: "Mrs. Dodd presents impressions of the things she saw, gives opinions of the moment on the things she experienced, but attempts no final judgment on the eternal enigma of Islam – its society and culture, and its mode of thought. Nevertheless, her opportunities for seeing things, unrevealed to many other travelers, were exceptional ... Open the book where you will, the eye is at once attracted by some incident, description, or pertinent reflection, which at once arrests the attention and arouses curiosity."[38] Although Dodd is credited with suspending judgment on this empire, the review itself more typically presents Islamic society as other and as forever mysterious and foreign – "an eternal enigma."

Dodd's narrative historically situates the tension between East and West as it records the state of relations between the Ottoman Empire and America at the outset of the twentieth century. It sketches the enormous changes that were occurring as the Ottoman world was collapsing: the empire itself was turning away from Europe and towards the East, hoping to increase its Muslim populations and strengthen its role as their leader. Europe and Russia were competing for its resources and territory and internal nationalist movements were erupting as local populations were insisting on their independence. From its ruins, a modern nation would emerge and with it the shift from the cosmopolitan society of the multiethnic empire to the ethnically based one of the new Turkish republic. Dodd's work serves, then, as a record of the last and controversial attempts of Sultan Abdülhamid II, with his Christian confidants and his revival of Islam, to preserve this racially, linguistically, and religiously diverse world which both fascinated and disturbed her, as it had the many nineteenth-century European travellers who had preceded her.

In the Palaces of the Sultan was first published in 1903 and is dedicated to General Horace Porter, the United States ambassador to France, and to the memory of his wife, with whom Dodd and her husband travelled to Turkey. They were entertained by Sultan Abdülhamid at Yildiz court, and shown around the Imperial palaces and parks, and Dodd was allowed to record her impressions of the place. Her work is also lavishly illustrated with photographs, many of which were likely from the sultan's own extensive library of over 30,000 works. At the time of her visit, westerners were less common at Yildiz, as the sultan, abandoning his predecessor's interest in European-style modernization, was attempting to close his empire to western influence even as he courted, resentfully but out of necessity, European and American favour. This intimacy with the sultan, as Dodd describes it diplomatically in her preface, was both a great privilege and a real limitation. In other words, not only did this elite world of the imperial palace necessarily offer a very select view of the city, but, as Abdülhamid was notoriously controlling, censorial, and concerned with representing his declining empire in a positive light, she likely felt pressure to give a favourable report. This may explain the difference in tone between the first section of the narrative that runs for close to 400 hundred pages, which suggests Abdülhamid is still in absolute control of his empire, and the final section, "Notes and Impressions," which attests to the rapid changes and growing discontent with his autocratic rule.

Figure 3.4. *Schoolboys*, Sultan Abdülhamid's photo collection, Library of Congress.

Dodd seems genuinely impressed by the sultan and seduced and charmed by the luxuriousness and wealth of his palace and its grounds as she gives lengthy sensual descriptions of his stables, gardens, the furnishings, the dress, the food and banquet rooms: "Gorgeous is the word, which in a single word, can rightly describe the adornment of the royal table ... With each course the silver plates were quite literally changed, for each service of the beautiful plate was found different in design to the last. Persian arabesques bordered the gleaming silver discs, each design, seemingly, more ingenious than those previously noted."[39] These elaborate descriptions of the excesses and riches of Istanbul are offered up to her western audience, raised on the "magical pages of the 'Thousand and One Nights,'" in order to satisfy their orientalist fantasies of a "dream-city come true."[40]

Dodd reverses the trend of representing the East as in decay and seemingly reverts back to older orientalist models. By the nineteenth century, travel narratives by women had usurped those by men, which had portrayed harems as exotic and sensual: when western women started to visit them, something the male writers could never do, they often mentioned, as Billie Melman notes, how much harems had in common with Victorian domestic spaces.[41] Hence, more "realistic" and desexualized narratives about the harem had flooded the market place. Yet Dodd's work harkens back to the long tradition in harem literature of depicting the East as a fantastical and backward place, rife with intrigue. She was, in fact, riding the cusp of a new wave of American orientalism that was infecting both high and popular culture – in painting, music, film, fashion, travel, advertising, and prints.[42] A highly sexualized Orient was used to market a growing number of commodities, from "Fatima" cigarettes, which featured a "Turkish" woman in a flimsy veil on the package, to the high-fashion designs of the French couturier Paul Poiret, who used "Oriental" styles like his harem pants to "liberate" western women from the corsets of the belle époque. This revival of orientalism in America culminated in Hollywood productions like *The Sheik* (1921), which echo Dodd's very kitschy over-the-top descriptions of a sensual, decadent, and libidinal East. If by the turn of the twentieth-first century, Muslim women in Afghanistan were portrayed as sexless and puritanical in contrast to their sexually free American counterparts, at this earlier historical moment American women's campaign for equal rights and their increasing consumer power combined to produce this version of a fantastical exotic East. In other words, the orientalist representation of sexualized Eastern women, in part, facilitated Western women's struggle for liberation from the confining mores and dress of the Victorian period.

Offering intentionally exaggerated and gaudy descriptions of the harem, which is a key convention of this new American orientalism, Dodd represents Turkish women as beautiful, enslaved, and yearning for rescue: "A nod from the master to his slave," she wrote, "and the curtain of the harem is lifted. The favorite of the night, of a week, of a month, or of years, swings her beauty forward upon her slippered feet. All her being is in palpitant expectancy for the single hour of life in which she is fully permitted to live. The rare, the perfect moment over, the gift of all her being given, back to her cell-like chambers goes the queen-bee Circassian, there to work out in the darkness of seclusion, of sterile pleasures, of petty, embittering jealousies, the labour of maternity appointed her. Who can guess the long succession of revolts among these primitive hot-house bred voluptuaries? Who has registered their stifled longings? Who responded to the wild flutterings amongst these caged birds for a wider, fuller existence?"[43]

Similar passages are sprinkled throughout the work as Dodd wanders through the various palaces. The coup d'état, when Sultan Abdülaziz was overthrown and imprisoned in 1876, is told as a simple harem romance: the sultan searched for a beautiful slave girl to love; her extravagant tastes bankrupted the empire; they met their eventual demise. Dodd's sensationalist account quite pointedly eschews all the more complicated politics of the empire, though they are mentioned elsewhere in her narrative. Fittingly, this tale is framed by yet another fantastical and clichéd description of perfidious harem life: "If the imperial harem has been the walled prison of thousands upon thousands of beauties, whose loveliness was to flower and ripen solely for a single monarch's eye, the harem isolation and seclusion has also offered the seal of a mysterious silence upon many a ghastly deed. Sultans, as well as their treacherous or intriguing wives, have gone smiling to harem alcoves, to smile on still, in distort grimace, as poison, or the supple fingers of African eunuchs, did their hideous work."[44]

However, even as she caters to this new market for orientalism, Dodd is also quick to undercut her own exotic rendering, suggesting a playful and reflexive use of the conventions of the genre. Having shamelessly employed them in her tales of slave girls, sorceresses, and torrid and deadly romances that have ended in the "watery grave of the Bosphorus," she then confronts western readers and asks them to examine the pleasure they derive from these orientalist portrayals and to consider their own hypocrisy: "The Westerner properly shudders over such horrors. I am not over persuaded as to the genuineness of the moral shiver. If we Americans could prove the bed of the Bosphorus to be as empty of dead men, and of murdered women, as is presumably our own unsullied Hudson, since, at least, our period of its ownership, this Turkish stream would, I fear, lose its chief secret of attraction. The barbarian is still alive, and is more or less actively kicking, in the most saintly of us. Only for decency's sake, we prefer it should be the Turk who commits the worst of the modern crimes; it is so gratifyingly picturesque to shudder over them, and him, at a distance of four thousand miles."[45] In another passage, having witnessed Mustafa Bey, without a thought, come to the aid of a "vermin-covered and ragged clothed" blind and ancient "hag," Dodd is impressed with the humanity of "Muslim rules." Even as her own work simultaneously plays to western narrow-mindedness, she admonishes her reader: "It is such traits as these that win you to take fresh views of the Turk as he is at home and among his people, and not as we Westerners accept him – through the snapshot presentments offered us by the hand of ignorance or of prejudice."[46]

She further undercuts the orientalism she plays up elsewhere in the section entitled "Notes and Impressions," which opens with a reference to Lady Mary's progressive views on Turkey in the eighteenth century and contrasts these with the early-twentieth-century climate, where the Turk has "now become the 'unspeakable.' Turkey is the nation above all others at which hands must be uplifted, eyes virtuously rolled, and the political garment withheld from compromising contact."[47] Contradicting her earlier description of the Turkish woman as a "caged bird," pining for her freedom, in this final section, in her discussion on the rights of Muslim women, particularly with respect to divorce and property, she writes: "There has been a vast amount of pity wasted upon the Moslem woman. It may surprise the woman suffragist to learn that the laws of Mahomet confer upon women a greater degree of legal protection than any code of laws since the middle Roman law."[48] She also notes, in contrast to her earlier descriptions of the Orient as a place of unbridled libidinal desire: "A Moslem, in other words can practically have no sexual relations with any woman without assuming full responsibilities for such intimacy."[49] She mocks the stereotypical American woman who has travelled all the way to the Orient to witness a harem and is disappointed to find that most Turkish men marry only one woman: "'Hasn't any one a harem?' The cry was almost tearful. It had the accent of one who felt it to be her right to consider this inconsiderate monogamy of the Turks as a personal grievance."[50]

Thus Dodd plays up the desire to see the Orient as exotic, writing a sensationalist account that will sell copies, while simultaneously challenging this desire, exposing it as fantasy. If the earlier passages render the Eastern woman as absolutely "Other," in this final section Dodd establishes the similarities between the elite women at Yildiz palace and upper-class Western women: "If I should answer that the daily lives of the majority of these ladies correspond more or less to the lives of thousands of well-to-do women throughout Europe and America I should be met by a storm of indignant denial. Yet such is, in the main, the truth."[51]

The Sultan Turns East

Facing increasing internal pressures from ethnically based nationalist movements (including Turkish, Armenian, and Greek uprisings) and external pressures from Europe and Russia, the sultan was trying to hold the empire together, Dodd suggests, with the force of his intellect: "Alone and single-handed, with no European ally to help him, he has fought Europe, and he has also kept this, his throne. With the forces he has had to fight, both at home and abroad, could any other reigning monarch have done as much?"[52] One of the ways in which the Hamidian regime attempted to pump up its image, secure its influence, and encourage favour was to liberally hand out decorations in the hope of garnering the support of the recipients. The ambassador, his wife, Dodd, and her husband were thus all recognized during their visit, although the awards seemed to be not so much about any single achievement as they were about a symbolic display of the sultan's power.[53] Along with the decorations, further symbols of state power include Abdülhamid's investment in elaborate pageants and spectacles. Dinner with the sultan was lavish, according to Dodd, with endless courses: ballotines de cailles en belle vue, asparagus, iced punch, potage, roasts, American corn bread, a national dish of pilaw, and ices and fruits. Following the meal, Abdülhamid, known for his love of opera, and, also famously, for rewriting them to suit his tastes, treated his guests to a performance of acrobats and half-naked wrestlers in the palace theatre. Another display, calculated to impress, as Dodd describes it, was the selamlik, the religious procession (and tourist attraction) that followed the sultan to the Yildiz Hamidiye Mosque and included parades of soldiers in spectacular dress, Arabian horses, eunuchs, and ladies of the harem with their gorgeously attired slaves, and crowds shouting "long live the sultan" as the imperial carriage passed. Dodd describes the selamlik in elaborate detail, convinced that the portrayal of the sultan in western travel books and newspapers as terrified of being assassinated, cowering, and frightened, was false: "The Sultan who had filled the great scene but a few moments before, whose majestic aspect had made his appearance seem the fitting climax of the splendid pageantry, had nothing in common with that pitiful figure."[54]

The Hamidian regime, with its extensive network of spies and its autocratic hardworking sultan at its head, who insisted on overseeing every detail of his empire, took an anti-western stance. Viewing the earlier Tanzimat reforms as too western and incapable of uniting a diverse population, the sultan turned to the East, promoting Islam as the source of education, invention, and modernity. As the Christian territories started to revolt and secede, the empire became more "Muslim" in focus and the sultan adopted a pan-Islamic stance as a way of both preserving power in and beyond his domain and countering the forces of European imperialism. A controversial figure, who was generally hated by western powers, who celebrated his eventual overthrow, he dissolved parliament, suspended the Ottoman constitution in 1878, and set back civil rights and women's rights even as he was committed to modernization, opening schools, introducing postal services, and building railways. Widely condemned by the West for his brutal suppression of Christians, he often secured loyalty, even among Muslim populations, by oppressive means and brute force. The Young Turks, many European-educated, and other elites in Istanbul, who persistently challenged his government and insisted on the reinstatement of the constitution, were often imprisoned or exiled.

Dodd interprets the sultan's iron rule as the product of his supreme position as the "earthly representative of God's holy prophet," arguing that the "soul of the true Turk" is "still the soul of the believer," as she attempts to explain to the "more irreverent Western mind" the unquestioning acceptance of Turks of their ruler. However, the many challenges to the sultan's rule suggest that "Turks" were not at all passive in the face of abuse. Moreover, although the sultan actively addressed the western view of the Orient as static and backward and refuted the West's claim to be the exporter of progress by proposing a competing version of "modernity" in his presentation of Islam as the source of technological inventions, his autocratic rule was a corruption of Islamic precepts. Dodd's characterization of the "Turk," reverting to the earlier use of the term to mean Muslim, as submissive to worldly religious authority plays on the western stereotype of eastern rule as inherently despotic and tyrannical. Dodd's reading of the Turk as the religious "other" feeds the divide between East and West and belies Edward Gibbon's more accurate characterization of Islam a century earlier as a "rational" religion. Further, Gibbon had stressed the dynamic, as opposed to despotic, nature of this religion, which, in its acknowledgment of the temporal nature of existence resisted any human authority as absolute. Islam, Gibbon wrote: "rejected the worship of idols and men, of stars and planets, on the rational principle that whatever rises must set, that whatever is born must die, that whatever is corruptible must decay and perish."[55]

Militant Nationalism

In promoting Islamic faith and employing multi- and intraethnic, cosmopolitan bureaucrats (Turks, Greeks, Arabs, Kurds, Italians), the empire was also trying to stave off the tensions emerging from the racialized nationalism that European and American powers were actively encouraging. Although not involved on an official level, American missionaries in Turkey worked to educate and modernize what they saw as a backward society, as Carolyn Goffman argues in her introduction to Hester Donaldson Jenkins's 1911 book *Behind Turkish Lattices*. Although Jenkins sets out to correct westerners' mistaken readings of Ottoman women, she also "reflects the view that is both Orientalist and missionary, that heathens longed to be taught and converted."[56] These missionaries encouraged a sense of superiority over "infidels" in Ottoman Christian populations and worked against the cosmopolitan nature of the empire in their promotion of national allegiances among their students. Dodd astutely observes that Robert College, an American Protestant Christian College built on the shores of the Bosporus (connected to Bŏgaziçi University), and other foreign mission schools were the source of "two-thirds of all the conspiracies and plots for overturning the hated Turkish yoke in Bulgaria, or Armenia, or other disaffected Turkish provinces" as they graduated "fiery young revolutionaries."[57] So Dodd, noting the hypocrisy of the American position, concludes that the empire, having allowed these schools to open and even fly the American flag in the name of tolerance and openness, was then dismissed as barbaric for responding to the dissent these schools fostered. "If an American missionary can proudly boast before an American audience of the numbers of zealous revolutionaries contributed by Robert College to the Bulgarian outbreak, and if other missionaries throughout Turkey can do their outmost to shield and to help Armenian conspirators, we can scarcely wonder at the mixture of delicate scorn in the Turk's smile when we talk glibly of American standards of honour and fair dealing."[58]

The very reason for the visit of the American ambassador to France, as Dodd notes, had to do with the 1901 kidnapping of Ellen Stone, an American missionary who had been teaching and opening schools in Bulgaria, much like Jenkins was doing in Turkey. "On the person of Miss Ellen Stone ... the eyes of both the diplomatic and religious worlds in America and Turkey, as well as those in the Bulgarian capital, had been focused for some weeks ... this lady's recent capture, in high brigandish fashion, was the burning question upon our own particular square of the diplomatic chessboard," Dodd writes.[59] Captured on Turkish soil by Bulgarian brigands dressed as Turks, Ellen Stone was held for a $65,000 ransom. The Bulgarian-sponsored Macedonian Committee, which was fighting for Macedonian liberty from Turkey, wanted money for arms and also wanted to draw the Americans into the "eastern question" that the European powers had long been debating. Ellen Stone remained committed to supporting the revolutionaries and despite her captivity, after her release she refused to supply the authorities with any information about her kidnappers as she fully endorsed their endeavour. William Eleroy Curtis, a journalist who interviewed Ellen Stone, wrote: "She is intensely sympathetic with the Macedonian cause, notwithstanding her sufferings at the hands of its advocates, and she is evidently under pledges to her captors not to do or say anything that might interfere with their peace of mind or pursuit of happiness, for she has declined, or at least neglected, to furnish the department of state any information concerning them."[60]

Dodd thus offers some much needed context on the Bulgarian and Armenian revolts and the subsequent massacres. Although the western world was quick to condemn Turkey for its persecution of Christians, it failed to admit its own self-interested role in fueling these revolts and conspiracies against the Ottoman world.[61] The sultan's violent response to these uprisings, Dodd suggests, despite the American and European presses claiming a moral high ground in their propagandistic representation of it, was not an attack against Christians in general. Referring to an Armenian uprising in Istanbul, she claims that those who were punished were accurately identified as provocateurs: "Not a single Christian of any other race or sect, not a single Jew, Greek, Persian, or Catholic, suffered hurt or harm."[62] Dodd's report, however, is overly "generous" as, although the violent slaughter of Armenians in the streets of Istanbul was indeed targeted, it did not spare women or children or other innocents caught up in the battle between the revolutionaries and the Hamidian regime. It is also important to note that Dodd's assessment of the Armenian situation occurred before the 1915–16 massacres under the Young Turks. These massacres were far more extensive and differently motivated, being driven by an emerging fervent ethnic and racialized nationalist politics that was to characterize the Republic.[63] Dodd is incisive in her analysis of the ways in which sentiment and moral outrage were stirred up and exploited by politicians and the western press in the interests of a divide and conquer strategy: "American and European sympathy have gone out, within the past two decades, to the Serbian, to the Bulgarian, and to the Armenian. The Turk, their oppressor, has become the synonym to our sensitive, benevolent and philanthropic ears, for all that is cruel, vindictive, and medieval, in point of barbarism ... The thousand and one tales concerning his thirst for human gore, his delight in cruelty for cruelty's sake, his riotous glee in carnage and massacres are discovered to be as disappointingly exaggerated as were the numbers of those who suffered in the 'Bulgarian atrocities.'"[64]

The political exploitation of the massacre of the Armenians continues to bleed into the current century. Hrant Dink, the Armenian journalist who was himself assassinated in 2007 by a Turkish nationalist, continued to fight hard against these divisive politics exposed by Dodd. While persecuted for often and openly referring to the Armenian genocide, a crime in Turkey, Dink nevertheless protested the French law that would persecute genocide deniers because it played into France's strategic resistance to Turkey's bid to join the European Union. He was also critical of those in the Armenian diaspora who remain invested in aggravating as opposed to healing tensions between Turks and Armenians. Dink's dedication to fighting against racialized nationalism and to respecting complicated interconnected identities, the legacy of the Ottoman Empire, was echoed by the thousands of mourners at his funeral who chanted, "We are all Armenians" and "We are all Hrant Dink."

American Fears of Miscegenation

Although Dodd is sensitive to the problematic issue of American missionaries nurturing nationalist revolutionaries, she nevertheless finds the lack of a racialized national coherence on the streets of Istanbul both enchanting and unnerving. She notes on her arrival that: "The streets through which we were presently swept were filled with as strange and wonderful a world of men. The faces of these men were the faces of brown men, of white men, of black men. No two faces seemed to belong to the same race; and no one garb or costume appeared to have been the model chosen for repetition ... Yet the vivid greens, the deep blues, the crimsons, pinks and yellows, melted and fused as only the vats of the Orient yield the secret of such blending."[65] Dodd implies – in foregrounding the "uniqueness" of this "Oriental" city, where the "blending" of various races makes it impossible to assert a dominant race – that America in contrast was homogenous, even though the streets of New York City in her day also would have been racially and ethnically mixed with both the influx of immigrants at the turn of the century (roughly 37 per cent of the population in 1900 was foreign-born) and the arrival of the post-civil-war freed black population that was moving up from the South. But in America, Anglo-Saxons had also asserted their primacy over indigenous populations, African-Americans, and other immigrants in this relatively new country, and its cities were segregated.

Observing the carriage of the daughters and wives of the sultan as they passed in the selamlik procession, Dodd writes: "The faces behind the veils might have been black, white, or yellow; none among those hundred onlookers would ever know their color ... Within these silken mantles the secret shape or outline, even to *the very color of the skin* of the favorite wife, daughter, or Khadine, were secrets as closely guarded as though these ladies had never emerged from harem walls."[66] Writing for a largely American audience, Dodd would have been well aware of the effect that this description of the varied skin colours "hidden" behind the veils of the daughters and wives would have had on her readers. The veil, already eroticized and scandalous, is here explicitly implicated in the miscegenation that was understood to be at the root of eastern decadence.[67] Publishing her work during an era of explicit white supremacy in America when the Jim Crow laws, which enforced the segregation of whites and blacks, were active in many American states, Dodd provocatively describes the streets in Istanbul: "Turk, Greek, Armenian, Khurd, Syrian, Jew, each and all these races, like the rags that draped them, seemed to have been inextricably mixed."[68] In contrast, in America, interracial marriages were outlawed and state laws banning them were not struck down by the Supreme Court until 1970. The "one drop" theory, which held that a single drop of "black blood" in your ancestry made you "black," was circulating; and competing state definitions of race flourished as did shifting census categories, which absurdly attempted to measure "black" blood, inventing categories from black to mulatto to Quadroon to Octoroon to Negro. To simplify things, in 1923 the Census Bureau defined white as "pure-blooded whites" and Negro "a person of mixed blood ... regardless of the amount of white blood."[69] Dodd's travel narrative and her reflections on race, including the passage about the closely guarded "secrets" of veiled women, need to be read in light of the extreme anxiety about miscegenation that structured the America of her day.

Despite this acknowledgment of the racially mixed nature of Ottoman society, Dodd, paradoxically, essentializes and homogenizes the "Turk," pitting him against an equally esssentialized western subject. Reinventing the clash between East and West as racial as opposed to religious, she writes: "[t]here is a deeper racial antagonism existing between the Turk and the European and the American than we willingly concede. Below the chasm separating the religious, political, and civil life of the Turk and that of the American and European, there lies the deepest of divisions – that of race antagonism."[70] She continues with her theory, contrasting the naturally despot-loving nature of the "Turanian" and the "freedom-loving" Aryian, who is set on self-government. Elsewhere she refers to the Turk as the "ruling race ... over the millions of mixed races."[71] But what is the source of this paradox where Dodd wants to claim discrete and hierarchical racial categories even while she is aware of the impossibility of doing this in the "blended" Orient?

America's interest in encouraging racial classification and in fostering nationalist movements based on racial and ethnic identification was motivated by its own desire to confirm white Anglo-Saxons as the ruling race in their adopted land and to forcefully establish their "right" to rule over indigenous peoples, African-Americans, and newer immigrants. Dodd, as a representative of white America, was also invested in the idea of a dominant homogeneous race. In the tradition of European aristocratic families establishing their lineage and status, her mother, Elizabeth Ann Blake, and her father, Stephen Mann Blake, both born in Massachusetts and of Scottish ancestry, were painted by the well-known American portraitist Benjamin Greenleaf; and Anna Bowman

Dodd herself was painted by John Singer Sargent (also an orientalist painter) in 1890. Her investment in establishing a "naturalized" American lineage is also evident in the fund she set up through the American Academy, which was to be used to award a prize every year to the best collection of essays or book of travel writing. One of the conditions for the recipient, however, was that the person be an American-born citizen and of parents who were also born-in-America citizens.

Dodd's description of the crowd awaiting boats around the Galata Bridge in Istanbul exposed the particular racial logic of America: "The close, dense, packed crowd of Turks in loose, ill-fitting coats and scarlet fezes; of negresses with filthy white veils above whose tattered edges the glowing African eyes roamed wide and far, every turn showing the ivory-whites of their setting; of groups of showy Albanians in their blues and gold; of tattered vendors, carrying their wares to inland markets; and the group, above all others, that riveted the eye, the group centering about the correctly attired figure of the American ambassador, whose simple morning coat and black tie, whose collected repose and air of command, were the dress and the bearing of one of the ruling race."[72] In contrast to her earlier descriptions of the ethnically and racially intermixed population, in this scene America is figuratively and literally imposed on Istanbul, the city is reimagined as the various racial and ethnic groups are carefully parsed, and "the American" – highly coded here (not black, Jewish, Native, Asian, Latino, or any of the other possible inhabitants of American cities) – is identified as of the "ruling" race.

The new American empire, based on the same racial logic as that of the fading British one, was preparing to mine the resources of the disintegrating Ottoman world. Predicting a new American/Turkish alliance, Dodd imagines Turkey as a land of undiscovered wealth that is ripe for economic "conquest" as "the coming captains of industry" in the "new world" turn to Asia: "We, in our turn, may fly to the rescue of the weaker power, but with bloodless weapons, with our 'battle-axes turned into pick axes, and our helmets into beehives,' to teach Turkey that her greatest strength, save that which she possesses in the moral qualities of her people, lie in her unworked soil."[73] While Dodd criticizes cultural and religious imperialism, in the last pages of her book she nevertheless looks forward to America's economic imperialism.

There were, however, dissenting voices. Imagining an alternative to this classification and ordering of races, Albert Howe Lybyer, who was admired by Halidé Edib, published his 1913 study of Ottoman governance during the reign of Suleiman I (1520–66). He suggested that the Ottoman Empire might serve as a useful model for America (rather than vice versa), proposing a view of the nation as "much more a body of ideas than a race of men." Lybyer (1876–1949) was a historian who held positions at both Robert's College in Istanbul and Harvard in the first part of the decade. Challenging the American theory that miscegenation could only lead to decline, Lybyer attributed the success of the Ottoman Empire "to the great body of national ideas gathered from men from every direction and every race to unite in a common effort."[74] The Ottomans had descended, he argued, from the Seljuk Turks, who "were already a mixed race, and had no greater objection than their ancestors to the reception of new members."[75] These ancestors, he wrote, had "no race aversions that would hinder inter-mixture, and no race pride that would prevent captives, in the course of time, from attaining full equality in any rank."[76]

That the hybrid and socially mobile populations of the Ottoman Empire went a long way in provoking and disturbing nineteenth-century western theories on race is evident in the fascination with the empire's racial and ethnic mixtures that was the focus of so many of the travel narratives and histories from this period. Lady Anna Bowman Dodd and Lady Annie Brassey lived a type of cosmopolitanism that Marx identified as the product of the exploitation of world markets and the expansive nature of capitalism: available to elite westerners who travelled the world, it depended upon maintaining explicit racial and ethnic boundaries, which rendered other nations both consumable and containable. The very different cosmopolitanism of the Ottoman world, enabled by veiling, interrupted Lady Annie Brassey's attempts to racialize and rank nations in the name of British imperialism and exposed Anna Bowman Dodd's anxiety about miscegenation as rooted in white America's own determined attempt to assert itself as the ruling race.

Chapter Four

The Great War and Its Aftermath: Militarized Citizens, (Un)Veiled Bodies, and the Nation

Mustafa Kemal Pasha, the leader of the Turkish nationalists, in wanting to salvage Turkey from the ruins of the Islamic Ottoman Empire and transform it into a "modern" secular nation, encouraged the "emancipation of women" and strongly discouraged veiling, declaring: "I see women covering their faces with their head scarves ... Do you really think that the mothers and daughters of a civilized nation would behave so oddly or be so backward?"[1] In 1922, Grace Ellison, the English feminist who had spent time in an Ottoman harem and was sympathetic to Turkish women's plight and their desire for greater freedom, travelled to Angora (Ankara), where Atatürk (the "father of the Turks," as Mustafa Kemal Pasha came to be known) was battling for control of this new nation. As Europe and America were engaged in carving up the Ottoman Empire in the aftermath of the Great War and Atatürk was fighting them to save something of Turkey, Ellison, one of the first British journalists to get behind enemy lines, interviewed the leader. She reported on his determination to end fez-wearing for men and face covering for women, and to free every Turkish woman "from this useless tyranny," so that she would have "full freedom in order to take her share of her country's burdens."[2] In *Turkey To-day* (1928), having returned to document Atatürk's remarkable success, Ellison begins what seems to be a fairly Eurocentric and orientalist account about the modernization of Turkey: "Even in the darkest hours of Turkish history, I did not lose faith in this people, knowing full well that if a man would arise strong enough to give Turkey homes instead of harems, she would take her place amongst the great peoples of the West."[3] Yet, curiously, when Atatürk announces again that he is planning to do away with "harems, veils, and lattice-windows," liberating half the population from "bondage," insisting that in "two years' time every woman must have her face uncovered and work side by side with men," Ellison interjects with her "feminine protest" – "'But veils are so picturesque. No more becoming headdress has ever been invented for a woman.'"[4] Ellison's seemingly odd attachment to the veil first finds expression in her introduction to the work of her Turkish friend, Zeyneb Hanim, who in 1913 published, with the help of Ellison, *A Turkish Woman's European Impressions*. In this work, Ellison warned Turkish women about abandoning the veil: "Turkish women are clamoring for a more solid education and freedom. They would cast aside the hated veil; progress demands that they should – but do they know what they are asking? 'Be warned by us, you Turkish women,' I said to them, painting the consequences of our freedom in its blackest colours, 'and do not pull up your anchor until you can safely steer your ship. My own country men have become too callous to the bitter struggles of women; civilization was never meant to be run on these lines; therefore hold fast to the protection of your harems till you can stand alone.'"[5] In the course of this chapter, I explore the reasons both for Ellison's hesitancy about Turkish women abandoning the veil and her own ambivalence about the terms of women's freedom in the West. In other words, what does she mean by the "blackest colours" of "our freedom"? What are the alternative "lines" that civilization should be run on? And what are the repercussions of this "progress" that demands "unveiling"?

Veils and Nations

Although the veil, adopted into Islam from Mediterranean practices, has no fixed cultural or historical meaning, varies widely in both form and name, and signifies different things at different times and places; at the end of the nineteenth century, it becomes key in the debates about competing versions of the nation, as we have seen.[6] Those, like Atatürk, in favour of adopting a western style of governance, advocated for the end of veiling and for equality between the sexes; those reacting to western interference insisted that the Islamic nation, which stressed the difference between the sexes, depended on its continuance. Resistance to the imperialist West was then increasingly seen to require the reveiling of women in the name of Islamic nationalism, while modernization and progress required unveiling women in the name of European nationalism. The ban on veiling in Turkey in the 1980s and the compulsory veiling of women following the Iranian revolution of 1979 are merely the latest manifestations of this legacy as the veiling of women continues to have great (even if relatively recent) symbolic importance in defining both the Islamic and the European nation.

Yet despite this highly visible marker of the different and competing versions of nationalism, veiling of a sort is taking place on both sides of the East/West divide. Under Islam, Nilüfer Göle writes: "the veiling of women maintains the boundaries between the sexes as well as preserving order in the community."[7] Similarly, Fatima Mernissi has argued in *Islam and Democracy* that at least one of the reasons veiling is important to the Islamic nation, the *umma*, is that this act secures it as immutable, eternal, and universal. Both sexual difference and birth, which introduce temporality and mortality, disrupt this reading, necessitating women's separation from and subjugation to a paternal community: "Women's invisibility made it possible to forget difference and create the fiction that the *umma* was unified because it was homogenous."[8]

Both Mernissi and Göle contrast this practice of segregation with civil society in the West, which they argue is founded on the principle of equality between the sexes. However, Carole Pateman, in her study of social contract theory, suggests that the western discourse of individual rights that emerged in the eighteenth century also constructed a private/public divide that was newly gendered. Reminiscent of Lady Mary Wortley Montagu and her complaints about British women being treated as "chattel" and "slaves," Pateman argues that the social contract, the basis of the modern European nation, was dependent on a sexual/marriage contract that subjugated women as it claimed the right to their bodies. While the paternal system of feudalism that assumed the right of men higher in the hierarchy to rule over men lower down the scale was successfully challenged by the social doctrine that claimed "all men are free," women were never extended this right because men had no intention of giving up their "natural" right to be fathers. Instead, women remained subject to the paternal rule of husbands and fathers in the private sphere, and, like women in the Islamic nation, were also excluded from the public sphere. Social/sexual contract theory appropriates the language of birth and generation and thus must separate itself from the complicated "sphere of real birth and the disorder of women," argues Pateman. With women secluded or "veiled" in the private sphere, the fraternity could then "give birth" in public to the artificial body of the modern nation: "Hobbes' 'Artificial Man, we call a Commonwealth,' or Rousseau's 'artificial and collective body,' or the 'one Body' of Locke's 'Body Politik.'"[9] With its gendering of private and public space, the modern nation, like the *umma*, is secured as universal only by segregating and concealing women.

The applicability of the concept of private and public to tribal societies and kinship models and the relation of state formation to religion in the Middle East is, of course, much more complicated than this gendered binary suggests.[10] Moreover, power does not neatly fall on one side or the other: for instance, Nancy Armstrong considers the gendering of private space and the "rise of the domestic woman" during the Enlightenment as itself a major political event that involved the middle class wresting power from the ruling classes by shifting the grounds of the right to rule from property, family name, and title to the moral qualities of the individual, which were modelled on a female ideal.[11] Meanwhile, Alev Çınar argues that visibility and voice in the public sphere in no way guarantees agency for women. Challenging and revising the Habermasian notion, she observes that in Turkey images of "liberated" unveiled women were given public visibility and voice in the early days of the republic in order to promote both a national consciousness and to check western orientalist attitudes even while the state actively controlled women's agency. So too, she argues, Islamicists in the 1990s actively promoted the public visibility of veiled women to bring forth a new national identity while simultaneously denying Muslim women political power.[12] Leslie Peirce has argued, moreover, that the understanding of the public/private divide as it emerged in the post-feudal societies in the West cannot be collapsed with the private/public divide that informed the Ottoman society of the sixteenth and seventeenth centuries, which had more to do with the understanding of the public as profane and common and the private as sacred and privileged, a divide that was not gendered.[13] Meanwhile, Fadwa El Guindi argues that western notions of private and public find no correlative in Arab/Islamic culture: "Evidently, the culture of exclusion of women from the male sphere is rooted in Western European traditions."[14] Both Pierce and Guindi make arguments about women's power in the home/harem, while Pierce argues that the gendered spaces of the imperial harem afforded women immense power and privilege, a point that is not lost on Lady Mary when she compares the female-only Turkish baths to the predominantly male-only London coffee-houses.[15] Nilüfer Göle also considers the historically and culturally specific understandings of the public sphere and the ways in which the new visibility of Islam in the late twentieth century is challenging and confronting western notions of the secular communal sphere.[16]

Notwithstanding the important nuances of these readings, the emergence and explicit gendering of these spheres – domestic, natural, and female versus public, political, and masculine – in the West in the eighteenth century were exported to the Near East and shaped debates about nationalism and veiling at the end of the nineteenth century. Situated as they were in questions about voting, freedom, and women's rights, the debates about the public/private divide, in both the East and West, emerged as gendered constructs that turned on questions of women's power within the confines of marriage.

Thus we find Zeyneb Hanim, whom Ellison befriended during her stay in the imperial harem in 1905, reaching the same conclusion as Pateman as she was quick to observe that despite the tales of universal freedom and equality between the sexes in the West, the marriage contract ensured the subordination of women. Zeyneb, having grown up on tales of the freedom Western women enjoyed, which she contrasted with her own existence of being "veiled," "forever cloistered," " a slave," and "always and always a thing," finally escaped from the harem and travelled to Europe.[17] But on arriving in the West, the dramatic contrast between the imprisoned Eastern women and the liberated Western women, which initially motivated her escape, dissolves as she discovers the "mirage of the West." "The Englishmen," she writes, "remind me of the Turks. They have the same grand demeanor, the same appearance of indifference to our sex, the same look of stubborn determination, and like the Turk, every Englishman is a sultan in his own house."[18] Further, Zeyneb observes that while the veil and the harem are constant reminders of the domination of men over women in the East, making Turkish women wary of marriage, the myth of individual freedom in the West serves to cloak the systemic subjugation of women in the marriage contract, making Western women more gullible: "Marriage, too, is always an interesting subject, and everyone seems eager to get married in spite of the thousand and one living examples there are to warn others of what it really is ... Every bride-elect imagines that it is she who will be the one exception to the general rule. Turkish women do not look forward to matrimony with the same confidence."[19]

The (Un)Veiled Woman

The marriage contract, the paternal claim to women's wombs, and the appropriation of the rhetoric of birth in the social contract are not the only means by which women are subjugated in the European nation. The objectification of women intensifies in the nineteenth century just as men are claiming the right to be political subjects. Noting that the veiled and thus the unveiled male body have no cultural currency in the nineteenth century, Elaine Showalter details the various works concerned with the (un)veiling of women's bodies, from Oscar Wilde's *Salome* to Gustave Courbet's painting of the female genitals, *L'Origine du Monde* (1866), which was exhibited from behind a veil, to Louis Ernest Barrias's statue depicting a woman disrobing, *La Nature se dévoilant devant la Science 1895* (*Nature Unveiling Herself Before Science*).[20] The proliferation of images of the female in various states of undress during the mid- to late-nineteenth century marks it as the era of the "institutionalization" of the female nude.[21] Referring to this nameless or generic nude that flourished at the end of the nineteenth century, Angela Carter writes: "It is a central contradiction of European art that its celebration of the human form should involve subsuming the particularities of its subject in the depersonalizing idea of the nude, rendering her – in the name of humanism – an object."[22] The figure of Woman is "unveiled" only to be reveiled as ornament, object, and artifice.

As men are claiming their right as free subjects, this depiction of women as subjectless gains great currency. In Wilde's *The Picture of Dorian Gray*, Dorian falls madly in love with the actress Sibyl Vane, who performs parts that have been carefully scripted for her (Imogen, Juliet, Ophelia). But when she strays from these parts Dorian rejects her, exclaiming: "'You are shallow and stupid ... Without your art you are nothing.'"[23] After the news of Sybil's suicide, Lord Henry comforts Dorian and convinces him that the parts Sybil played were much more real than she; there is no need to mourn her, Henry tells Dorian, because "[t]he girl never really lived, and so she has never really died." Friedrich Nietzsche, in a similar gesture, values women only as performers: "Reflect on the whole history of women: do they not have to be first of all and above all else actresses?";[24] "her great art is the lie, her highest concern is mere appearance and beauty."[25] Women, he suggests, are only capable of playing roles written by men and cannot themselves write or effect the script. Commenting on this "double displacement" of woman, Gayatri Spivak reads the male philosopher's obsession with woman's performance "[w]ithin the historical understanding of women as incapable of orgasm." Even at the moment of "the greatest self-possession-cum-ecstasy, the woman is self-possessed enough to organize a self-(re)presentation without an actual presence (of sexual pleasure) to re-present."[26] Having no self to lose, she nevertheless simulates loss to enhance the man's enjoyment.

Whereas Pateman argues that women are subsumed in the patriarchal construction of the nation, Spivak further suggests that in "legally defining woman as object of exchange, passage, or possession in terms of reproduction, it is not only the womb that is literally appropriated; it is the clitoris as the signifier of the sexed subject that is effaced."[27] This effacement of the clitoris is the effacement of the "sexed subject," rendering woman an object and ensuring her use (as the analysis of the anti-suffragist literature in the next sections suggests) within the binary logic of the public/private divide that structures the modern nation. Ellison's fondness for the veil in Turkey, a practice that acknowledges women as powerful and disruptive subjects even as it bars them from participating in the *umma* in order to preserve its order,[28] exposes the more insidious metaphorical veiling in the West that strips women of agency. Eastern feminists who favoured retaining the veil until men learned how to behave and how to respect women in public were quick to note that the unveiled woman was subject to the violence of being read only in terms of male desire. Responding to men, like Atatürk in Turkey and Qassim Amin in Egypt, who were calling for the unveiling of women in the name of modernization, Malak Hifni Nassef wrote that the unveiled woman was subject to "foul language," "adulterous glances," and men's "despicableness."[29] As women in the West continue to be exploited as sexual objects, so the (re)adoption of the veil as a resistance to western commodification and objectification of women's bodies continues, as is evident in some of the more recent turns towards veiling and modest dress.[30] Veiling in this case is, at least in part, about an attempt to recover agency and control.

The Modern Citizen I

This violent suppression of women as subjects is an inevitable outcome of the model of the modern citizen as it developed in the West. Anti-suffragist literature circulating in both England and America at the turn of the twentieth century, anxiously responding to the suffragist challenging of borders between private and public spaces, restages, in sometimes extreme or paranoid terms, the birth of this "masculine" citizen. By the end of the nineteenth century, women in England were so utterly associated with the private as distinct from the civil sphere that debates about whether or not women should get the vote turned on the issue of whether they could in any way benefit the public. Albert Dicey, a professor of English law at Oxford and a self-professed advocate of the rights of women in the area of personal freedom and education, argued, in his treatise against giving women the vote, "that the right to a Parliamentary vote ought not to be considered the private right of the individual who possesses it. It is in reality not a right at all; it is rather a power or function given to a citizen for the benefit not primarily of himself, but of the public. This is assuredly the doctrine of English law, no less than of common sense."[31] Dicey continues, it is not a question of whether English women wish for votes "but whether the establishment of woman suffrage will be a benefit to England."[32] His answer is a resounding no. Implicit in his argument is the absolute split between man's membership in a public order as a citizen and woman's confinement in a private domain, the legacy of the Enlightenment, and the gendering of these spheres.

While there are many rationalizations offered as to why women were so incapable of operating in or contributing to public life, from her emotional disposition to her essentially different (and inferior) nature, the most popular reason involved the issue of defence. In the conclusion to his argument against giving women the vote, Dicey argues that, at a time when the defence of the British Empire is crucial, "[w]e are asked [by the advocates of suffrage] to weaken English democracy,"[33] a weakening that threatens to break the "links in a living chain" by which the greatness of the country has been passed on through the ages.[34] Linked together, British men form a barrier that both keeps women out of the public sphere and other foreigners out of the nation in the interests of "democracy." The image of men, not just as defenders of the State, but as metalicized bodies – "a living chain" – recurs in many of the arguments that cite defence as the primary reason against giving women the vote.

In a turn-of-the-century pamphlet entitled *The Blank-Cartridge Ballot*, Rossiter Johnson (1840–1931) is very blunt about this issue. He makes the case that, just as paper money is worth nothing unless it is backed by metal (gold), a ballot is worth nothing unless it is backed by metal (a bullet). He then argues that "when he [a man] wishes to rend a granite rock he does not pry at it with his fingers; he persuades the sledge hammer to do his bidding. Similarly, it would be futile for her [a woman] to go to the ballot-box and with her own fair hand throw in a blank-cartridge ballot; but if through argument or entreaty she can persuade a musket-bearer to throw a right ballot instead of a wrong one, she can accomplish something worthy."[35] In the first instance, paper backed up with gold is made analogous to the ballot backed by the bullet. But man is then abruptly introduced into the equation and becomes continuous with the sledge hammer and then by extension the musket. How did we get from the bullet to man? By the conclusion of the piece, man displaces the bullet altogether. His body is miraculously transformed into metal as he (not the musket or the bullet) proves to be the power behind the ballot: "Wherever we place the ballot, manhood must necessarily be the power behind it to give it effect; and manhood suffrage is therefore the logical suffrage."[36] Not only are citizenship and voting collapsed with defending national borders, but man and metal are so completely melded that the possibility of a musket-bearing woman is never considered.

Performance Anxiety

Johnson concludes his pamphlet, "We have yet but a thin crust of civilization spread over a heated mass of savagery; and organized force is all that saves us from anarchy."[37] Although women, he argues, should acknowledge that they benefit most from the armed men who protect them against anarchy, women also seem to be the very source of chaos: "If an election is carried by a preponderance of votes cast by women … we shall find ourselves in a state of anarchy."[38] In Johnson's analysis, women, lacking agency and ineffective, need to be protected from the enemy, but if they assert agency they become the enemy, plunging the civilized world into anarchy. Why do women as subjects provoke such fear? As modern man, the founder of the western nation, is preoccupied with giving birth to himself, literally from nothing, as rational, omnipotent, and autonomous, he displaces his sense-driven penis and replaces it with a protective armour, a phallus that allows him to claim masculine right. The recurring analogy of male bodies to metal – chains, muskets, bullets, sledge hammers – in the anti-suffragist literature points to this performance.

Susan Buck-Morss writes: "Curiously, it is precisely in this castrated form that the being is gendered male – as if, having nothing so embarrassingly unpredictable or rationally uncontrollable as the sense-sensitive penis, it can then confidently be claimed to be the phallus. Such an asensual, anaesthetic protruberance is this artifact: modern man."[39] Modern man as already castrated does not fear women as castrated (and castrating) but, as the anti-suffragist literature suggests, fears them as subjects who would expose his own performance. The autogenic and autotelic modern man, "doing one better than the virgin birth,"[40] deflects attention from his own fantastical creation and subsequent castration by displacing "lack" onto the figure of Woman, which he is then at liberty to explore at a safe distance. The figure of Woman becomes a convenient vessel for all that is excised in his transformation into the phallus – the body, unreason, emotions, and sensuality. The defence of the modern nation depends on the exclusion of this mutilated modern man masquerading as Woman, while women as subjects expose the masquerade and hence must be violently suppressed.

As the anti-suffragist literature suggests, women are feared as agents and thus rendered as objects. Sigmund Freud's theories of fetishism and narcissism exemplify the logic that naturalizes the performance of modern man. Fetishistic desire in the man, Freud argues, arises from women's supposed castration. The fetish "remains a token of triumph over the threat of castration and a protection against it. It also saves the fetishist from becoming a homosexual by endowing women with the characteristic which makes them tolerable as sexual objects."[41] Traumatized by his early discovery that the mother lacks a penis, the fetishist tries to compensate for her lack. He desires that the woman don objects that stand in for or cover over her lack. Hair, shoes, lingerie, furs, velvet, and veils act as imaginary substitutes for the lost and longed for penis. Further, Freud argues that whereas the man transfers his original childhood narcissism to a sexual object, the "castrated" woman indulges hers and focuses on herself. The woman, donning make-up and veils, preening and pampering her body, seeking compliments and adoration, offsets her genital lack by investing narcissistically in her body. This "self-containment" of the woman then compensates for the "social restrictions that are imposed upon [her]."[42] A woman's need does not manifest itself in loving, but in being loved. She does not desire a love-object as the man does but turns herself into a love-object. Thus, according to Freud, the "normal" woman accepts her subordinate position, her "castration," and becomes an object in order to attract the man and vicariously gain access to phallic power.

Yet, aside from the phallocentric structure of society, there is no logical reason why a boy would see his mother's different sexual organs as absent nor why a women would accept this understanding of themselves as lacking, a reading that effaces both sexual difference, sexual asymmetry, and sexual continuity. However, in light of modern man's miraculous birth, a modified version of Freud's theories begins to make sense. The obsession with Woman as object mimics fetishistic desire. The Woman as object does stand in for the lost penis, but the castration is self-inflicted. It is not, as Freud argued, "castrated" women that produce anxiety and longing, but Modern Man who, donning a phallic sheath, finds himself castrated. Man subsequently longs for his sense-driven penis, which he has displaced onto the figure of Woman. The veil, as fetish, is left intact to "crystallize the moment of undressing, the last moment in which the woman could still be regarded as phallic."[43] The man both knows the woman has no penis and disavows this knowledge. Beneath the metaphorical veil then is not a castrated woman but a mutilated man.

Woman as object allows man the opportunity to reconnect with the senses that he has suppressed in his auto-creation, but the simultaneous hatred of women also suggests the anxiety that his performance might be exposed. Des Esseintes, the hero of J.K. Huysmans's *Against Nature*, reflects, in his fascination with Salome and her dance of the seven veils, the nineteenth-century obsession with Woman as fetishistic object. He is particularly taken with Gustave Moreau's figure of Salome because she rouses the "sleeping sense of the male." He muses on this watercolour: "Here was a true harlot, obedient to her passionate and cruel female temperament; here she came to life, more refined yet more savage, more hateful yet more exquisite than before; here she roused *the sleeping senses of the male* more powerfully, *subjugated his will* more surely with her charms."[44] The "will" of the militarized male is conquered by the figure of the (un)veiled Woman as his excised senses return; the Woman, as inducing this state, is both desired and despised, both "hateful" and "exquisite."

From Huysmans to Freud, from Wilde to Nietzsche, the western interest at the turn of the twentieth century in the veiling and unveiling of Woman both reflects this desire for sense-driven experience and simultaneously protects Man from the knowledge of his self-castration. The objectified female body allows for an erotic dissimulation or loss of the armoured self and the free play of the sensual and the irrational, reviving the castrated man. The suppression of women as "sexed subjects" keeps us from recognizing this figure of Woman as a male creation, a figure that in feminine garb both enables the performance and masks the performance (and performance anxiety) of Modern Man.

The Modern Citizen II

Ellison's "feminine" fondness for the veil, mentioned at the opening of this chapter, can be read as a protest against this militarized version of the citizen, making sense of her declaration: "Civilization was never meant to run on these lines." Thus she counsels Turkish women to hold on to the harem until they "can stand alone." At the same time that Ellison was writing her book on the modernization of Turkey, she published *The Disadvantages of Being a Woman*, which was about the problems plaguing English women following their hard-won right to vote. Ellison's argument centres around the problematic suppression of "femininity" as women enter into the civil contract, complaining that this process renders women "neutral": "It may be convenient for us to ask women to give up their femininity, but the sacrifice is too great. It is marking her with the same gender as a table."[45] This reading of the model of the modern citizen as producing table-like or neutral (as opposed to masculine) individuals suggests the masculine performance that underwrites it; in other words, the militarized citizen is not a manifestation of the essential qualities of either sex. Ellison, who is all in favour of the modernization of Turkey and women's freedom, nevertheless wants to warn Turkish women to retain the veil. This apparent contradiction makes sense in the context of her warning about Europe's mistakes: her favouring of the veil is not to reinforce the exclusion of women from the public sphere but rather to force an acknowledgment of female agency and expose the patriarchal construction of the public space in the West that masquerades as "masculine."

Ellison is also cognizant of the fact that women are as easily coopted into the existing social structures as men. Their entry into public life, though it enabled the social mobility of individuals, did not in itself necessarily effect any social or political change: "There was a time when one supposed women would clear up politics as they cleared up a dirty house. But are they to be trusted in politics any more than men? A woman comes out of labour ranks; as she gets on, she becomes socially ambitious, then she throws her party aside. Men have done it over and over again; they call it 'evolution,' and women no doubt will say the same."[46] Ellison's progressive critique of the gendered nation, however, did not extend to race. A committed Turkophile and enamoured with Atatürk's vision, she embraced his Republic and its new racialized nationalism that expressed itself in many areas, including a new law that required diplomats to marry "Turkish" wives. An early supporter of Turkey's aspirations to be treated as a "European nation,"[47] Ellison bemoans the cosmopolitanism of the former Ottoman Empire evident in such places as its embassy in London, which had been, she writes: "tragic in its lack of nationality. After a Polish Ottoman Ambassador came a Greek who stayed for many years, and finally three Moslem Turks with German, Russian, and Italian wives respectively."[48]

Racialized and classed nationalism underlies many feminist works from this period. For instance, Frances Power Cobbe, the Irish suffragist, in her introduction to *The Woman Question in Europe* (1884), argued that women should get the vote because they would better defend the interests of the nation than racial others and the working class: "The difference – nay, rather the contrast – should likewise be insisted on between proposals to admit the dregs of a population to the franchise, and those to admit the mothers, daughters, and sisters of the men who already exercise it; and again, between proposals to admit aliens of another race, and those to admit women who have the same hereditary tendencies, attachments, creeds, and interests; and who are the inevitable partakers of the nation's prosperity, and the deepest sufferers by its disasters, or misrule."[49] Cobbe readily adapts to Johnson's "musket-bearers" rather than challenging this version of the citizen who is hostile to "alien" races.

So too, Atatürk's adopted daughter, Sabiha Gökçen (1913–2010), was "honoured" with the title "The First Woman War Pilot of the World" and heralded as an icon of the new Turkish Republic and defender of the nation. Gökçen, a military pilot, who participated in the bombing raids on Kurds during the Dersim Massacres (1937–8) in the eastern provinces, where Armenians had also sought refuge after 1915, was celebrated as one of the Republic's most prominent young women, a symbol both of the nation's new independence and the status and equality it accorded to women. Voting rights and the participation of women in the public sphere, in this case, replicated rather than remade the citizen, merely allowing women, like men, to transform themselves into a metalicized body, adding new "links in a living chain." After her death, the journalist Hrant Dink, who, as mentioned in the last chapter, was later assassinated by nationalists, suggested that Gökçen's biological father had been killed during the slaughter of Armenians in 1915. Dink was called a "traitor" for exposing the Armenian ancestry of this Turkish heroine, foregrounding the extent to which the Republic of Turkey had fully and problematically embraced racialized nationalism.[50]

Zeyneb, in the final lines of her book, writes: "[d]ésenchantée I left Turkey, desenchantée, I have left Europe."[51] She did return to Turkey but "willed herself to die" before the age of thirty.[52] In recognizing the gendered construction underlying both the Islamic and the European nation, she was ultimately unwilling to resign herself to life in either place. Ellison's experience in the harem, which led her to support the idea of Turkish women's emancipation and simultaneously to voice a "feminine protest" in favour of the veil as a symbol of female agency, also challenged the patriarchal model of both nations. Western civilization, she suggested, which disguised the gendered nature of the modern nation, was as problematic as the *umma* and its explicit segregation of women. However, Ellison, even as she embraced Atatürk's reinvention of Turkey and despite self-identifying as a "cosmopolitan,"[53] would later come to rewrite Zeyneb's unhappiness as the consequence of her mixed heritage (French and Turkish), asking: "Is a person of dual nationality ever quite an accurate judge?"[54] Her question exposes how fully nationality as a product of race and ethnicity in Turkey had displaced the cosmopolitanism of the Ottoman world.

Virginia Woolf, more vocally, makes the same protest against militarized nationalism that Ellison had made a decade earlier. Insisting that the gendered modern nation was not in any sense her nation as it has historically treated women as chattel, her protest also echoes both Zeyneb's claims of being "always and always a thing" and Lady Mary's of being a "slave." Her "sex instinct," she argued, expressed itself differently, famously declaring on the eve of the Second World War: "If you [Englishmen] insist upon fighting to protect me, or 'our' country, let it be understood, soberly and rationally between us, that you are fighting to gratify a sex instinct which I cannot share; to procure benefits which I have not shared and probably will not share; but not to gratify my instincts, or to protect myself or my country." She continued, "The outsider will say, 'In fact as a woman I have no country. As a woman I want no country. As a woman my country is the whole world.'"[55] As an "outsider," Woolf was not interested in wars that claimed to defend women even as their bodies were claimed as objects of exchange; but nor was she interested in the militarized model of citizenship and the defence of racialized national boundaries that foreclosed the ancient Greek idea of cosmopolitanism as a political stance.

After the War: The Nostalgia of Demetra Vaka Brown

Yet even as racialized nationalism came to dominate the discussions of Turkey, there were still pockets of resistance to this new arrangement of communities. Demetra Vaka Brown (1877–1946), a Greek Ottoman, grew up on Büyükada (one of the Prince Islands in Istanbul). She moved to America when she was eighteen as the governess of the children of the Turkish consul to New York and pursued a career as a journalist, novelist, and critic, positioning herself as an expert on the Orient and marrying an American, Kenneth Brown. In April 1921, Vaka returned to Istanbul, then under occupation by the Allied forces as Turkey had sided with Germany in the Great War. In *The Unveiled Ladies of Stamboul*, she described the city as poor, neglected, and tarnished. Burnt-out sections had been ravished by fire; the Allies were squabbling and brawling and acting as "masters"; the dogs, always respected in the city's streets, had been banished by the Young Turks. Ironclads were floating on the Bosporus, flying alien flags, and the blue and white flag of Greece, hoisted high, was flying right below the Galata Tower. This triumphant Greek flag saddened the narrator despite her Greek heritage. Sordid cabarets played "unholy" music, swarms of young prostitutes filled the narrow streets, and unveiled Turkish women swept the streets and chatted with Turkish men, causing her to think of the old Turkish saying: "When women uncover their faces and wear trousers, the power of the Osmanlis will be broken."[56] Unveiling and occupation are explicitly linked in Vaka's account of Istanbul and the narrator now sought out the city's women in public spaces – rather than behind the walls of the harem, as in her earlier work *Haremlik* – as they attempted to rebuild their lives in the post-war ruins.

Critics have often approached Vaka's work as the staging of an encounter between western modernity and eastern tradition. Reina Lewis points out that while Vaka was nostalgic for Ottoman culture, harem walls, and veils, she herself took advantage of women's comparative freedom in the West. As a journalist originally from Turkey, she was professionally positioned and uniquely qualified to operate in both worlds, but her expertise was dependent on maintaining the border between East and West, which, Lewis argues, "explains her lack of affinity with the emancipated, unveiled women that she observed in the modern Turkey of 1921."[57] While not discounting Vaka's ambitions to establish herself as an authority, an argument Lewis skillfully lays out, I want to position Vaka's work in the wider context of the debates about modernity and nationalism in the early part of the twentieth century.

From Friedrich Nietzsche to E.M. Forster to James Joyce to Virginia Woolf, Vaka joins a number of modernists from the same era who were critical of the racialized versions of nationalism that were sweeping Europe, which culminated in the First World War and precipitated the Second World War. Nietzsche warned of the disease of nationalism that was infecting populations with "race hatred," leading the "nations of Europe to delimit and barricade themselves against each other as if it were a matter of quarantine."[58] Similarly, Forster, in *Passage to India,* which was first published in the aftermath of the First World War, presented the colonial occupation of India as intolerable, even as he remained sceptical about the revolutionary promises of nationalism. He has Fielding taunt Aziz, who is hopeful about the liberation of the Indian nation, with the remark: "India a nation! What an apotheosis! Last comer to the drab nineteenth-century sisterhood!"[59] Edward Said argued that Forster's novel, despite its sympathies with India, maintained that Indians were not yet ready for "self-rule."[60] But Fielding's response to Aziz, which points out that nationalism has already grown tired and "drab," instead suggests a profound exhaustion with the very model. European nationalism, the novel suggests as it investigated Islam and Hinduism, needed to be left behind to make way for alternative models of community. So too, in Joyce's *Ulysses,* Bloom encounters the aptly named and narrow-minded Citizen in the Cyclops chapter. Exposing the anti-Semitism and xenophobia that characterized European nationalist movements, Bloom responds to the Citizen's rant on Ireland, which suggested that Jews are not Irish, with the retort: "A nation? says Bloom. A nation is the same people living in the same place."[61] So too, as noted earlier, in her pamphlet *Three Guineas,* Virginia Woolf, witnessing the escalation of racialized nationalism and fascist sentiments that co-opted women's bodies, rejected this frame as the basis of community, preferring instead to imagine the world as her community.

If, as I have argued, European nationalism is about turning the accident of birth into destiny as it lays claims to unveiled women's bodies in the production of its racialized citizens, Vaka challenged the forceful imposition of this model on the Ottoman world by foregrounding the *accident* of her birth and upbringing. *Unveiled Ladies* opens with a dedication to Prince Sabaheddine, who was living in Paris to escape the wrath of his uncle, Sultan Abdülhamid II. The prince had worked with the Young Turk movement, which angered the Sultan, but he nevertheless shared Vaka's hope that the cosmopolitanism of the Ottoman Empire would survive the restructuring of Turkey. In her public address to him, Vaka wrote: "we came together, not as a Turk and a Greek, but as two Ottomans, loving the Ottoman Empire."[62] Stressing the co-mingling of the ethnic and religious populations that they both respected, she continued: "I felt you to be the man who might save what was left of the empire, because you believed that all Ottomans, be they Turks or Arabs, Greeks or Armenians, Syrians or Jews, be they Mohammedans or Christians, should look upon one another as compatriots, sharing in the government of their country and its benefits, shouldering its responsibilities, its burdens, its labors, and loving each other in the sharing."[63]

The narrator in *Unveiled Ladies*, herself forcefully resists any naturalized version of national identity and occupies a dizzying number of often transgressive and contradictory positions. At the mosques, this Christian behaves like a "good mussulman" and later claims to be the only woman to pray among the men.[64] In one photo she appears veiled and in another she is "Mrs Kenneth Brown" on a golf green. She variously identifies as American, Ottoman, Greek, European, Eastern, the "child of the orient," and "rip van winkle" in her writings. She is sometimes the "we" or "us" of Turkey and sometimes the "we" and "us" of America or Europe. This confusion of identities is in part about ensuring multiple markets for her work, as Lewis argues. She had to position herself as both a legitimate and authentic "insider" and "outsider." In Turkey, her audience is a difficult one: Vaka needed to be accepted as a friend of the Turks, an insider who understood and could represent their uniqueness, but she also needed to be perceived as enough of an outsider that Americans would accept her interventions on behalf of Turks as legitimate. For her American audience, she needed to be enough of an outsider so as not to be the target of orientalism and western prejudices, but also enough of an insider or native informant to claim unique access and insight into the workings of Turkish culture and the harem, a knowledge unavailable to the average tourist or traveller.

Yet she also holds these multiple and liminal positions in the hopes of fostering a dialogue across the East/West divide. Vaka was writing to a past that she had experienced growing up in Istanbul as much as she was addressing her present life in America, where segregation and ethnic and racial hierarchies competed (and continue to compete) with the immigrant's dream of inclusivity. The cosmopolitanism of Turkey, in her view, had much to teach America and Europe. Moreover, she suggests that had this Ottoman model prevailed, Turkey would not have become the focus of international discord and "commercial rivalry," but rather would have taken its rightful place as an intermediary: "the artery through which the civilization of the West should pass into the East, the contemplative spirit of the East should pass into the West."[65] The fruitful possibilities of this exchange were foreclosed, however, as the Turkish Republic, under the leadership of the Kemalists, adopted the idea of the nation as a monoculture.

In the face of the virulent racialized nationalisms that had sparked the First World War and left her beloved city in ruins, Vaka began her narrative with the hope of keeping alive an alternative modernity that might continue to embrace cosmopolitanism. Her narrative ends, however, with the definitive failure of this model as Turkey "unveiled" women, following Europe and America, and "foreigners" were invented as the problem. Vaka notes that the Kemalists had the "same light in their eyes" as those who participated in the Hamidian massacres of Armenians (1894–6), which were prompted by the empire's pan-Islamism and violent attempts to shore up its territorial boundaries.[66] An aide-de-camp to the Grand Vizier confronts Vaka with the pithy and cynical observation that Turkey was now embracing the American model, asking: "What do you do to the Negroes when they become obstreperous in America? Your government fans race prejudice and instigates riots to kill them off. Well, we can imitate progressive America. Our salvation lies in leaving no living Christian in our lands."[67] So too, the western colonial strategy was now being embraced in the fledgling Republic: "We shall be ruthless, like the English in India," announced one American-educated Turkish girl.[68] Vaka reluctantly concluded: "Some day 'we' may borrow from each other, but that day is not yet near."[69] The hope of a productive dialogue between East and West had ended, at least for a time.

As the model offered by the Ottoman Empire vanished and the various nation states emerged from its ruins, North America, Europe, and the Middle East were left struggling to figure out how to accommodate diversity. The homogenous nation – be it religious, racial, or ethnic – has increasingly proved itself untenable in the twentieth and twenty-first centuries as we continue to witness "cleansing" of various sorts, where women's bodies are claimed, raped, veiled, unveiled, and policed in order to secure national borders. It is in this climate that cosmopolitanism has emerged as a hotly debated post-nationalist version of community, but whether embraced or opposed, contemporary theorists tend to discuss it as a product of western imperialism, globalization, and modernity. For instance, arguing against the trend, Timothy Brennan posits that the turn towards cosmopolitanism disadvantages non-western states that are still in the process of developing a national identity and understands cosmopolitanism as a response to the "new material" reality of globalization, which encourages the interaction between nations and transnational corporations.[70] Arguing in favour of cosmopolitanism, Martha Nussbaum suggests that communities must move beyond nationalism and she focuses, in particular, on the destructive legacy of American patriotism.[71] Kwame Anthony Appiah, on the other hand, suggests the importance of fostering both national and global connections.[72]

Yet the western-centric frame of these debates ignores the cosmopolitanism that proliferated prior to the division of the globe into racialized nations and before the rise of transnational corporations, a version that, as Vaka and others have suggested, was interrupted by western imperialism. Roxanne Euben has convincingly argued that the Islamic cosmopolitanism, which structured various Muslim societies at different historical moments, offers "resources for the reworking of contemporary culture," countering the "presentism," provincialism, and Eurocentrism that has monopolized recent discussions of cosmopolitanism – both pro and anti – that make nationalism their focal point.[73] The Ottoman world with its "Levantine" populations, which Vaka and others describe, offers a useful check to the current resurgence of ahistorical religious and national fundamentalisms that are erupting as anxious responses to the most recent waves of globalization and currently sweeping Europe, America, Africa, Asia, and the Middle East.

Chapter Five

The Burqa and the Bikini: Veiling and Unveiling at the Turn of the Twenty-first Century

Laden with the different meanings and names that have adhered to it over the centuries, the veil, despite predating Islam, has nevertheless become one of the most visible signs of Muslim faith. The global resurgence of veiling in the latter half of the twentieth century has inflamed discussions about the nature of secularism, freedom, tradition, imperialism, patriarchy, race, rights, sexuality, religion, community, and social justice, while the figure of the (un)veiled woman underlies and links a number of disparate events, from the Salman Rushdie affair to the First Gulf War to the attacks on the World Trade Centre and the Pentagon to the ongoing War on Terror to the bombings in London, Bagdad, Istanbul, Kabul, and Madrid to the murder of Theo Van Gogh, to name a few. The clash of civilizations rhetoric – modernity versus Islam – that so often frames these discussions has grown even more entrenched, replaying, with a difference, anxieties about women's veiled and unveiled bodies that first emerged in the eighteenth century.

A popular cartoon by Catherine Beaunez encapsulates the current view of these tensions between Islam and the West. It features a woman in a bikini standing beside a woman in a burqa; the same thought bubble emanates from both of them: "Je ne voudrais pas être à sa place [I would not want to be in her place]." The woman draped in the burqa views the Western woman as oppressed by the dead end of a secularist materialist modernity. Hypersexualized and fetishized, the unveiled woman is symptomatic of a spiritually and morally bankrupt world. By covering her body, the veiled woman retains her honour, self-respect, mystery, privacy, and faith; she avoids being judged and scrutinized by a neoliberal logic that renders her an object of consumption. Alternately, the woman in the bikini views the Muslim woman as oppressed by a backward, patriarchal religion that views women's bodies as sinful and that seeks to confine and control them. Enjoying her uncovered body and sexual freedom, she refuses to be circumscribed and inhibited by unfair gender codes that do not subject male bodies to the same level of surveillance. In a similar vein, Lil' Kim, the hip-hop artist, posed on the cover of an issue of *One World* magazine (2003) in a designer burgundy string bikini and a matching stylish burqa that covered her face but that was defiantly thrown back over her shoulders to reveal her body in order to protest the forced veiling of Afghani women. Similarly, in 2010, the "Niqabitches" video featured two young French women strolling the streets of Paris in mini niqābs, hotpants, and high heels to protest the hypocrisy of the anti-veiling laws in France (see fig. 5.1). Both the video and the magazine cover criticized the global policing of women's bodies, whether forced to veil or unveil.

One extreme of this policing finds educated and politically articulate young women who have grown up in cosmopolitan cities who choose to veil pitted against political leaders like the former presidents of France, Nicolas Sarkozy (2007–12), and Italy, Silvio Berlusconi (1994–5, 2001–6, 2008–11). Both have made face veiling illegal in the name of women's equality and global security even though both men are known womanizers, with the latter explaining "women are natural exhibitionists"; (in his seventies, he was also convicted for paying to have sex with an underage girl in 2013). So, too, factions of the Dutch government have argued that veiled women in the streets are "foreign" and a threat to Dutch culture; however, the scantily clad women for sale in the windows of the red light district in Amsterdam, imported from poorer countries to fill the jobs Dutch women do not want to do, are considered to be signs of liberal Dutch attitudes. In these examples, the exposed bodies of women are taken as the norm, whereas their covered bodies are considered a threat to the social order.

The other extreme of this policing pits the rise of conservative interpretations of Islam that invest in a patriarchal version of "honour," which pressures or forces women to wear the veil or be subjected to violence, against equally articulate women who protest living under this constant threat of masculine aggression. Riverbend, a pseudonym for the young Iraqi woman who started blogging after the American invasion, wrote about having to adopt the hijab in 2006: "For me, June marked the first month I don't dare leave the house without a hijab, or headscarf. I don't wear a hijab usually, but it's no longer possible to drive around Baghdad without one ... There are no laws that say we have to wear a

Figure 5.1. Niqabitches (still image from video).

hijab (yet), but there are the men in head-to-toe black and the turbans, the extremists and fanatics who were liberated by the occupation, and at some point, you tire of the defiance ... If you're a female, you don't want the attention – you don't want it from Iraqi police, you don't want it from the black-clad militia man, you don't want it from the American soldier. You don't want to be noticed or seen."[1] In a more subtle vein, the rise of veiling – a now over-determined sign of being an "authentic" Muslim – is evident in the plethora of online sites and magazines that promote modest fashion, from headscarves to niqābs, the latter upping the ante for the most pious or "Islamic" dress. In these examples, the covered bodies of women are viewed as the norm, whereas exposed bodies are considered a threat to the social order.

Yet an analysis of the representation of women's bodies in the media at the height of the wars in Afghanistan and Iraq suggests that the divide – between the western bikini and the eastern burqa – is not as absolute as it might at first appear. In the case of Afghanistan, Muslim women were portrayed as sexually oppressed in comparison to their American counterparts, but a very different scenario played out in Iraq, where the roles were reversed and it was American women who were cast as modest. If the obsession with women's bodies and dress fuelled both these wars, this next section suggests that it is the problematic maintenance and manipulation of this divide that itself usurps women's agency.

Rescuing Women from Afghanistan to Iraq

At the outset of the war in Afghanistan, images of burqa-clad figures, framed as ghostly and silent victims, filled the front pages of North American and British newspapers. In England, Cherie Blair pronounced that: "Nothing more symbolises the oppression of women than the burqa, which is a very visible sign of the role of women in Afghanistan,"[2] while some at the White House started wearing burqa patches as a sign of their solidarity with Afghani women. Laura Bush, not opposed to the US administration's mandate that American military women don the head to toe abaya and refrain from driving when off the bases in Saudi Arabia as a sign of "cultural tolerance," also emerged as a champion of the veiled Afghani woman. In the First Lady's public radio broadcast from the White House, she insisted: "The fight against terrorism is also a fight for the rights and dignity of women."[3] The vocal protests of prominent Afghani women who were both opposed to the war and had long fought for women's rights in their country were drowned out by the deluge of voices and images emanating from the West, casting Afghani women as helpless and in need of rescue.

When the Taliban regime fell in November 2001, British and North American newspapers and TV stations were there, ready to catch the moment when Afghani women, now "liberated" from their "prisons," shed their burqas on the streets of Kabul. Encouraging them to join the "modern" world and the sexual revolution, L'Oréal, Vogue, and Revlon were also there, ready to introduce them to the pleasures of consumption and the freedom of lipstick, nail polish, and lingerie.[4] But Afghani women continued to resist the logic of this unveiling as the expression of feminine sexuality. Nelofer Pazira writes of her encounter with one young woman, Gulolay from Niatack, whom she was trying to recruit for her film about the life of women after the Taliban. When Gulolay requested a burqa instead of money in exchange for her participation, the distressed filmmaker asked her why, and the young woman explained that she wanted it for her wedding night as it made a woman "'more mysterious and desirable.'"[5] Providing the needed context for these comments, Pazira goes on to explain the history of the burqa in Afghanistan, which was a cloak adopted by rural women when they started to travel beyond the familiar limits of their communities. The burqa provided anonymity and privacy, but it also signalled social mobility as not all women could afford to travel; hence rural women continue to wear this traditional dress even when not travelling as a mark of prestige. Burqa-clad women in the cities, however, were read as unsophisticated villagers; city dwellers adopted the more "modern" and urban look of scarves. Even within local contexts, the veil has no fixed meaning or single history, a point that has consistently been elided in western attempts to rescue women from it.

As we have seen in the previous chapters, the desire to "save" the Eastern woman from her own culture, a gesture that inevitably involves unveiling her, has a long history in the West, a history that has little to do with women's freedom or rights. Leila Ahmed, discussing nineteenth-century colonialism in Egypt, writes: "Veiling – to *Western* eyes, the most visible marker of the differentness and inferiority of Islamic societies – became the symbol now of both the oppression of women (or, in the language of the day, Islam's degradation of women) and the backwardness of Islam, and it became the open target of colonial attack and the spearhead of the assault on Muslim societies."[6] A concern for women's rights was used by colonialists to decry the barbarism of the native culture while at the same time women's rights were actively discouraged on the home front; and colonialist policies, despite the rhetoric of liberation, were detrimental for Muslim women. Ahmed points to Lord Cromer, the consul-general of Egypt, as an example. Adopting a "feminist" rhetoric, he condemned the "Oriental" for his treatment of women – particularly veiling and segregation – but he also restricted access to education for girls in Egypt, was opposed to the tradition of female doctors in Muslim cultures, and was the founder of the anti-suffragist league in England.

Frantz Fanon also notes how the veil in Algeria became one of the major symbols for colonialists to rally around, a symbol that "enabled the colonial administration to define a precise political doctrine: 'If we want to destroy the structure of Algerian society, its capacity for resistance, we must first of all conquer the women: we must go and find them behind the veil where they hide themselves and in the houses where the men keep them out of sight' ... The dominant administration solemnly undertook to defend this woman, pictured as humiliated, sequestered, cloistered ... It described the immense possibilities of woman, unfortunately transformed by the Algerian man into an inert, demonized, indeed dehumanized object."[7] Naively assuming that beneath the veil was a silent, absent, helpless woman, the French occupiers remained mystified by the Algerian woman's resistance to being "saved." Fanon notes that women veiled, deveiled, and reveiled as the situation at borders demanded it, smuggling both arms and money across checkpoints, as they joined the struggle for Algerian independence. This particular moment that Fanon identifies of female agency, however, was usurped, as it was in many revolutionary struggles, by the claiming of women as symbols to secure the nation. More recently, women have played key roles in the uprisings spreading through the Middle East that began in Tunisia, but the jury is still out on how they will fare in the post-revolutionary climate. The rise in brutal rapes against Egyptian women – veiled and unveiled – both during and since the 2012 revolution in Tahrir Square points to the violent opposition to displays of women's agency. But, in the wake of these attacks, feminist activists have also insisted on exposing this horrendous climate, forcing a public debate about sexual violence.[8]

The western desire to save "helpless" women from their culture also inevitably involves the emasculation of native men, evident in the examples cited by Fanon and Ahmed, where the unveiling of women was inseparable from the denigration of Egyptian and Algerian men. So too in the recent war in Afghanistan, loudspeakers on top of an American Humvee blasted out: "The Taliban are women! They're bitches! If they were real men, they'd stop hiding under their burkas and they'd come out and fight!"[9] Part of a vicious cycle, the response of "emasculated" men is often then to redouble their efforts to reclaim and dominate "their" women in the name of "masculinity," so that after the fall of the Taliban, sexual violence against women has been on the rise. An NGO worker told Amnesty International: "During the Taliban era, if a woman went to market and showed an inch of flesh she would have been flogged; now she's raped."[10] Nevertheless, Laura Bush, optimistically, and prematurely, given the ongoing violence, concluded in her radio address that American military men had successfully liberated burqa-clad women: "Because of our recent military gains in much of

Afghanistan, women are no longer imprisoned in their homes. They can listen to music and teach their daughters without fear of punishment."[11]

Patriotic Porn

If the war in Afghanistan was fought in the name of liberating "helpless" women, the American military was all about heroic "manly" men. American military women got little attention in the mainstream media during this war and they were hardly mentioned in the news reports, normalizing Western men as the saviours of veiled women. Rather than American women in combat, it was Western women who took off their clothes as a sign of their support for the troops who were applauded. During the First Gulf War, General Norman Schwarzkopf referred to the "bunnies" who participated in "Operation Playmate," sending autographed photos of themselves and personal letters to the army, as the "true patriots." The "operation" was launched again during the war in Afghanistan and many media outlets reported that the men's magazine was hoping "to boost the morale of the US military by offering a free pen-pal program that lets soldiers communicate with its nude models." Playboy's founder Hugh Hefner said "he felt compelled to aid the war against terror in Afghanistan."[12] An article in *The Globe and Mail* about "Operation Playmate" was titled: "They also serve who only strip and write."

During this war, it seemed it was Western women's patriotic duty to assert their liberty by stripping off their clothes, unveiling their bodies to encourage men to fight. In my spam email, I received advertisements for "Exclusive Quality Lingerie – Look So ... Sexy!" and with every order the buyer was promised "a free link to 'blast bin Laden'" (see fig. 5.2). Spam email also included invitations to look at nude pictures of a nursing student who announced that she "enjoys taking care of people and making friends" and then added "Hey Osama!! There is a picture of my nice butt on my page. You can only wish that you would be allowed to kiss it!! I want to see your butt ... in JAIL!!"Another woman offering up pictures of herself wrote on her website: "for all you darling soldiers out there keeping us safe I want to give you my very best" and invited men in the military to download desktop-sized signed pictures of herself in various states of undress, adding, "Please, I only have a small computer with limited bandwidth so if you are not in the military let the soldier boys get the pictures ok? Be patriotic."

Taunting their enemies, American women were encouraged to bare all with bravado, their sexualized and commodified bodies held up as

Strictly For Pleasure
(Presented by FoxC Sensations)
Grand Opening!!
New Online Lingerie Store
Top quality lingerie for both men and women. The store is shopping cart enabled with secure credit card processing, so you can shop with privacy, confidence, and ease. Wide selection of styles and sizes to fit everyone.
Click Here To Start Shopping Now!
Shop from the comfort and privacy of your own home!
With every order you will be sent a free link to "blast bin Laden".

Figure 5.2. Spam lingerie advertisement.

a sign of freedom and power. In contrast to the women in the burqas who were represented as bodiless and voiceless, these women were all body and voice. This version of female "independence" played out in the larger context of neoliberalism and the marketing of "girl power," which, unlike previous versions of feminism, made money, sold products, and was promoted by the beauty industry. Threatening no existing order, "girl power" was quickly embraced by advertisers, Hollywood, and mainstream media alike. Women's bodies were unveiled in order to be further veiled as ornaments, packaged, and sold as sexual clout in an updated version of Freud's narcissistic woman. If war encouraged men to adopt a militarized metallic sense-less body, women were encouraged to invest narcissistically in their bodies and put them on display to offset their genital "lack." This woman did not fight but rather turned herself into the desired object of the armed man, gaining access to phallic power by inspiring and rewarding his heroic feats. This enforcing of the relentless heteronormative model – American military men "saving" veiled women from "emasculated" Afghani men, while unveiled Western women strip for them as a reward – was carried out in the name of the nation and patriotism as the figure of the unveiled woman remained pivotal in the construction of the American nation.

Rescuing the "veiled woman" as the very logic for the war, however, did not have any validity in Iraq, where the literacy rates among women were among the highest in the Middle East, and where women represented almost half the workforce prior to the UN sanctions. After initially responding with disbelief to a Palestinian lawyer's 1991 description of Saddam Hussein as both a "ruthless tyrant" and as someone who had "done more for women's rights than any leader in the Arab world," Elizabeth Warnock Fernea travelled to Iraq and wrote: "I had come to the reluctant conclusion that she was more or less right: Saddam Hussein, despite his horrendous reputation in the West, had the best record on women's rights in the Arab world."[13] However, the trade and financial embargo imposed on Iraq following Iraq's invasion of Kuwait in 1990, which was extended at the end of the First Gulf War, severely damaged women's rights in Iraq. In the post-sanction economically depressed "emasculated" Iraq, women began to lose the gains they had fought hard for. The rhetoric of liberating and unveiling the Iraqi woman and introducing her to the "modern world," although trotted out half-heartedly by the western media at the start of the war, could not be mobilized effectively given this history and quickly petered out. Western intervention had made the lives of Iraqi women demonstrably worse and the war further accelerated this decline; post-invasion, violence against women dramatically increased. Riverbend, the blogger from Iraq, wrote in August 2003: "Before the war, around 50% of the college students were females, and over 50% of the working force was composed of women. Not so anymore. We are seeing an increase of fundamentalism in Iraq which is terrifying."[14]

Rather than "helpless" women draped in burqas, photos and footage of militarized Iraqi women protesting the invasion – with bombs strapped to their bodies and brandishing guns – were more likely to make media headlines. In stark contrast to the Iraqi women fighters portrayed in the headlines, American women in the forces, despite rigorous military training, were represented as young, helpless, and virginal. When two American soldiers – Jessica Lynch and Shoshana Johnson – went missing in Iraq, the news reports turned their attention to the question of the sexual vulnerability of women serving in an Arab country. Referring to them by their first names, the columnist Margaret Wente described women in the military as "giddy, apple-cheeked girls" who still sleep with stuffed animals, adding: "Call me sexist. But I confess I'm troubled by the thoughts of girls like Jessica and single mothers like Shoshana being rounded up by gunpoint by fedayeen and other men who have never heard of the Geneva Conventions."[15] Another reporter wrote: "Nearly every soldier interviewed here, as well as many civilians and military experts, said the first thing they thought of upon seeing Shoshana's picture was sexual torture."[16] American men, in contrast, were represented as paternal and protective of their "helpless" army mates. A columnist in the *National Review* speculated: "I do not believe American men in the military are capable of pretending that a young woman in their company is exactly the same as a young 18-year-old man ... I think we can expect he will act differently in the interest of trying to protect that young woman. I'm fairly certain she wouldn't mind."[17] No longer represented as full of bravado, strength, and sexual independence, this time it was the American woman who needed saving and the pervasive orientalist stereotype of the "fair" Western woman held captive by "lascivious" and "ruthless" Arab man was activated.

Statistics, however, suggest that American women in the military have far more to fear from their male counterparts as they are more likely to be raped by American soldiers than killed (or raped) in combat. Vastly under-reported, when the small percentage of reported cases are brought to trial, they are often dismissed: "Despite the estimated 150 cases of rape over the past decade, only one male cadet has been court-marshalled on such a charge during that time, and he was acquitted. Even the most flagrant cases usually result only in discharge from the academy. In some cases, attackers have been given such 'punishments' as writing a paper."[18] Another colonel reported that attacks on women drastically escalated during the war: "By April 2004, rapes and assaults of American female soldiers were epidemic in the Middle East. But even after more than 83 incidents were reported during a six-month period in Iraq and Kuwait, the 24-hour rape hotline in Kuwait was still being answered by a machine advising callers to leave a phone number where they could be reached,"[19] and again these reports were consistently ignored. While Arab men were imagined as threatening and violent sexual predators, American men who raped were treated with a "boys will be boys attitude" and American women who reported rape faced a "what did you expect" response; most suffered sexual trauma in silence, betrayed, as they had been, by men who were not supposed to be the "enemy" and a system that was supposed to support them.[20]

Stories also emerged of the brutal rapes of Iraqi girls and women by American soldiers, including the rape and murder of the fourteen-year-old Abeer Qasim Hamza which took place after the murder of her mother, Fakhriyah Taha Muhsin, father, Qasim Hamza Raheem, and six-year-old sister, Hadeel Qasim Hamza. The five American soldiers responsible tried to blame it on Sunni insurgents. Riverbend wrote in her 11 July 2006 blog: "It's gotten so that I dread sleeping because the morning always brings so much bad news ... Rape. The latest of American atrocities. Though it's not really the latest – it's just the one that's being publicized the most. The poor girl Abeer was neither the first to be raped by American troops, nor will she be the last. The only reason this rape was brought to light and publicized is that her whole immediate family were killed along with her ... The naiveté of Americans who can't believe their 'heroes' are committing such atrocities is ridiculous. Who ever heard of an occupying army committing rape??? You raped the country, why not the people?"[21] As if in punishment for their assertiveness, defiance, and resistance to the invasion, Iraqi women were dehumanized. The American porn spam email that I received during this period turned its attention to Iraqi women and turned hardcore, promising pictures of American military men "gang banging" Iraqi women.[22]

It was in this climate that the Jessica Lynch story emerged as front page news. The dramatic headlines initially reported that Lynch had shot her way through an Iraqi ambush, and had been shot, stabbed, beaten, held captive in an Iraqi hospital, and somewhere along the way raped and sodomized. Her rescue by US Special Forces was staged, recorded, packaged, and distributed to the media and an American public anxious for a cause, in a war that increasingly did not seem to have one, to rally around. But Lynch had not been shot or stabbed; she had been badly injured when her truck rolled after taking a wrong turn. The Iraqis had already tried to give Lynch back to the Americans, but they shot at the ambulance carrying her, forcing it to turn back. Lynch reported that she received good care and suffered no abuse at the hospital, and that a nurse had sung to her and others had donated blood. There were no Iraqi troops guarding the hospital and there was no resistance to her being taken from its care. Trying to deflect attention from the discrepancies in her story, the American government then released a report that Lynch was suffering from amnesia, although her parents reported that her memory was fine. NBC, nevertheless, went ahead, without her cooperation, with a quickly assembled TV movie called *Saving Jessica Lynch* (2003).

In a biography, *I am A Soldier, Too: The Jessica Lynch Story*, the author claims Lynch was sodomized during the three hours between being pulled from the truck and being deposited unconscious at a hospital.

The biography is written by the controversial former *New York Times* journalist Rick Bragg, who split the one million dollar advance with Lynch. He claimed in the book that "everyone knew what Saddam's soldiers did to women captives."[23] Despite the fact that the Iraqi doctors reported that there was no evidence of sexual trauma, despite the fact that all the other claims about her capture were false, and despite the fact that Lynch "has no memory of the rape," Bragg asks readers of the biography: "to fill in the blanks of what Jessi lived through" in her unconscious state. Numerous sensationalist headlines generated by the book appeared in popular rags: "Jessica's Rape Horror" and "Fiends Raped Jessica."[24]

While American women during the Afghan war were celebrated for stripping off as a sign of their freedom and power, during the Iraq war they were portrayed as vulnerable and virginal. I did not receive any spam email during this war inviting me to buy lingerie and "blast" the enemy or watch women strip off in the name of patriotism. Larry Flynt, the publisher of *Hustler*, paid large sums of money for pictures of Lynch posing nude for some of her fellow soldiers and planned to feature them in his magazine. In an article that refers to him as the "smut czar," he reported that he had decided against publishing them and instead locked them in a vault, following the public outcry: "'I'm getting so much heat for this is it's unbelievable," he said, "I'm going to take [the photos] out of circulation.'"[25] "Patriotic porn" was out in this war. Western women were no longer being lauded for taunting the enemy while flaunting their tough displays of sexual "freedom" for soldiers, but were now portrayed as sexually innocent and in need of protection by American soldiers against the lascivious Arab "fiends." "Operation Playmate" extended to Iraq, but this time *Playboy* was vocal about the fact that only head shots or photos of clothed "bunnies" were being sent to the troops. A spokesman for the company announced that: "'The decision not to send out any nudes into a region populated mostly by conservative Muslim nations was also due to the fact that there are *far more women in the US armed forces* than ever before'" (emphasis mine). He added: "'Not that we're trying to be PC (politically correct), far from it, but the object of 'Operation Playmate' is to boost morale so we certainly wouldn't want to offend anyone within the services.'"[26] Even in such unlikely venues as *Playboy*, the focus was on modesty and female troops in America. During the Iraq war, the in-your-face sexuality of American "girl power" was displaced by vulnerable and virginal American "girls" in combat.

Shoshana Johnson, however, quietly challenged the pervasive orientalist narrative of the predatory Arab man. Unlike the blue-eyed, blonde, petite Lynch, Johnson was shot in both legs and taken prisoner, but she got very little attention after the initial headlines that focused on her "likely" sexual torture at the hands of the Iraqis. First mistaken for the enemy by rescuing troops who didn't recognize this black, single mother as "American," she said in a comment that got no headline play that after she was taken prisoner: "'They opened my NBC [nuclear biological, chemical] suit and noticed I was female' and after that she said they treated her 'very well.'"[27] The sensationalist accounts of her impending rape that first dominated the media reports at the time of her capture were generated by a western imaginary long fed on stereotypes of despotic and abusive Muslim men, which were then strategically deployed to feed the war. No longer useful, her story quietly faded into the background: there was no dramatic footage of her rescue, no movie of the week, no lucrative book contract, and she received a smaller disability pension from the military than Lynch.

The orientalist fantasy of "violent" Arab men lusting after Western women, however, persisted. Male prisoners at Abu Ghraib, as one of the many abuses they underwent, were forced to simulate sex while American women taunted them. Hayder Sabbar Abd, one of the hooded men in the photos that circulated around the world, recounts that "he and six other inmates were beaten, stripped naked ... forced to pile on top of one another, to straddle one another's backs naked, to simulate oral sex. American guards wrote words like "rapist" on their skin with Magic Marker ... [H]e recalled being forced against a wall and ordered via an Arabic translator to masturbate as he looked at one of the female guards. 'She was laughing, and she put her hands on her breasts,' Mr. Abd said. 'Of course, I couldn't do it. I told them that I couldn't, so they beat me in the stomach, and I fell to the ground. The translator said, 'Do it! Do it! It's better than being beaten.' I said, 'How can I do it?' So I put my hand on my penis, just pretending.'"[28] Playing out at a microcosmic level the larger fiction of this war (the invasion of Iraq was justified on the faulty premise of the country's supposed nuclear weapon stash), the abuser wrote "rapist" on his victim, forcing him to perform an "otherness" that had been scripted for him when he refused to conform to the orientalist stereotype. The fantastical fear of the other – the tyrannical dark-skinned Arab man who preys on vulnerable women (Eastern or Western) – that fuelled both the war in Afghanistan and Iraq imploded in this prison scandal.

The Fallacy of the Divide

The divisions between war and terrorism, between freedom fighters and criminals, between liberators and occupiers that structured these invasions do not hold as both sides have been supported by a military, cultural, industrial complex and empowered by a similar network of interests. The divide between a neoliberal secular modernity and a traditional conservative Islam – secured by the figure of the (un)veiled woman – collapses under closer scrutiny as the two are thoroughly entwined.

In the first part of the twentieth century, the British, interested in securing access to ports and land in Arabia, negotiated with various local tribes and paid them to fight against the Ottomans. One of the poorest countries until the discovery of oil by Americans in 1938, the Kingdom of Saudi Arabia was founded in 1932, the result of an alliance between the descendant of the founder of Wahhabism/Salafism and the royal family. In the second half of the century, the United States joined forces with Saudi Arabia after the Soviet invasion of Afghanistan in 1979 and funded Islamists to fight against the perceived threats from the left. Both imperial powers thus furthered the influence of Saudi Wahhabism, the marginal and radical sect of Islam that had first emerged in the eighteenth century. Wealth from petrodollars combined with western support allowed this obscure sect to effectively gain legitimacy and export its brand of Islam, greatly increasing its power and influence among Muslims around the world even though it had long been considered heretical by a majority of Muslims.

The subsequent entanglement of western governments with warlords, fundamentalists, and dictators – rendering ironic George Bush's oft-quoted line (from his 20 September 2001 speech to Congress): "Either you are with us, or you are with the terrorists" – belies the East/West divide. All wealthy, the various players – from the multimillionaire Dick Cheney, CEO of Halliburton and vice-president under George W. Bush, to the CIA-funded warlords who bought their way into the parliament in Afghanistan with American dollars to the wealthy Saudi heir, Osama bin Laden – have consistently declared themselves on the side of the "disenfranchised" and have appealed variously to "freedom fighters," the "common man," and the "oppressed." The simplistic "us and them" of their speeches constructs a divide that does not exist any more than the western fantasy of a despotic and perverse East, the role forced on the tortured and twisted bodies of the prisoners in Abu Ghraib.

Osama bin Laden, a strict Wahhabi, called America "Satan" and took credit for blowing up the World Trade Center, killing thousands of people. Yet he and the *mujahideen* got their start with the help of the Saudi and American governments, who supported these religious fundamentalists. They were funded and armed by the CIA and trained in Pakistan to fight a holy war against the Soviets, who had been dubbed the "evil" empire by President Ronald Reagan. Sympathy for the victims of the 11 September 2001 attacks poured in from around the world, but President George Bush retaliated, ignoring American complicity in the creation of the *mujahideen* and bin Laden, and the American populace was further whipped into a state of moral panic by the pictures of heavily veiled women that graced the covers of their newspapers.[29] The war has killed more civilians in Afghanistan (there are no precise numbers as to how many more) than died in the World Trade Centre and the Pentagon attacks in America (where the records are meticulous), and Afghanistan's parliament is now stacked by NATO-backed warlords and criminals. The situation for women in some parts of Afghanistan is no better than under the Taliban. In the words of Malalai Joya: "The United States helped turn Afghanistan into a safe haven for fundamentalist terrorists and now helps prop up a corrupt regime and powerful drug mafia ... Day by day the Afghan people become more frustrated by the foreign troops and by the 'warlord strategy' of the United States."[30]

Iraq was invaded on the false grounds that the secular Saddam Hussein had links to al-Qaeda and had nuclear weapons. The war was fuelled by fears of despotic Arab men and helpless innocent American "girls" that were foregrounded by the mainstream western media. Yet until his invasion of Kuwait, the dictator Saddam Hussein had been fully supported by the American government in his war against Iran. Under Ronald Reagan, Iraq had been removed from Jimmy Carter's 1979 list of countries that supported terrorists in order to enable closer economic ties with the US. In 1986, the British and American governments blocked the UN Security Council from denouncing Iraq's use of chemical weapons which culminated in the Halabja massacre of Kurds in 1988. American companies, among others, were licensed to supply Iraq with equipment, raw materials, and biological and bacterial agents. Donald Rumsfeld, then head of the multinational pharmaceutical company G.D. Searle & Co., and presidential envoy under Reagan, met with Hussein in 1983 in Baghdad and chose to ignore the dictator's use of chemical weapons against Iran. Later, as Secretary of Defense, he condemned Hussein for this deployment, citing the atrocity as one of the rationales for the 2003 invasion of Iraq.

Nevertheless, corporations, while pushing America even further into debt and destroying Iraq's infrastructure, made billions from these wars. Despite a well-trained, highly educated Iraqi workforce, American companies consistently won bids for everything from the post-war clean-up to private security. A few of the top money-makers were Halliburton KBR Inc., Veritas Capital/DynCorp, and Washington Group International. In her blog from August 2003, Riverbend refers to a cousin who worked for a prominent engineering firm in Baghdad that had a great deal of experience building and repairing bridges. She reports that the Iraqi company estimated that the cost of replacing the New Diyala Bridge would be approximately $300,000. But the contract was instead given to an American company that had estimated the costs of rebuilding at $50,000,000. She observed: "People roll their eyes at reconstruction because they know (Iraqis are wily) that these dubious reconstruction projects are going to plunge the country into a national debt only comparable to that of America. A few already rich contractors are going to get richer, Iraqi workers are going to be given a pittance and the unemployed Iraqi public can stand on the sidelines and look at the glamorous buildings being built by foreign companies."[31] Joya is equally scathing about the international aid expended for the reconstruction of Afghanistan that so often lines corrupt pockets.[32]

Reminiscent of nineteenth-century imperialist tactics in the Ottoman Empire, the strategy of divide and conquer was employed by the British and the Americans, who set up "representative" governments in Iraq and Afghanistan that encouraged tribal, ethnic, sectarian, and religious tensions.[33] Again, both Joya and Riverbend are articulate on this point. Riverbend commented on the disastrous post-invasion situation in Iraq in her blog from April 2007: "I remember Baghdad before the war – one could live anywhere. We didn't know what our neighbors were – we didn't care. No one asked about religion or sect. No one bothered with what was considered a trivial topic: are you Sunni or Shia? Our lives revolve around it now. Our existence depends on hiding it or highlighting it – depending on the group of masked men who stop you or raid your home in the middle of the night."[34] Four years earlier, in August 2003, she had written: "We get along with each other – Sunnis and Shi'a, Muslims and Christians and Jews and Sabi'a. We intermarry, we mix and mingle, we live. We build our churches and mosques in the same areas, our children go to the same schools … it was never an issue."[35] While a member of parliament in Afghanistan, Joya refused to accept "support" based on her ethnicity: "Whenever anyone asked me about my 'tribe' I have always answered that I am just Afghan ... The fundamentalists who don't have footing among the people always try and provoke ethnic sentiments so they can exploit them for their own political benefit."[36]

A member of RAWA (Revolutionary Association of the Women of Afghanistan), speaking out of necessity under a pseudonym, said in an interview: "The US and British first ladies tried to project the bombardment of Afghanistan as benefiting Afghan women, but the entire world knew that it was a punishment given to the puppets by the masters and nothing else."[37] Jessica Lynch, meanwhile, vocal about the ways in which the American government used her, described herself as a "symbol," telling Congress in her 2007 testimony: "I am still confused as to why they chose to lie and tried to make me a legend."[38] The bodies of women – veiled and unveiled – have long been claimed to construct and secure the divide between East and West. But it is also veiled and unveiled women who undo this divide, exposing the ways in which they have been used to conceal the entangled interests of these "warring" factions.

The Rise of Veiling in the Twenty-first Century

At the outset of the twentieth century, veiling was on the decline in the former Ottoman territories – Turkey, Egypt, Jordan, Syria, Iraq, among others.[39] The prevailing narrative about unveiling at this time was that it was a sign of modernity and the advancement of women. Unveiling promised to liberate Islam from a "backward" practice that was never integral to it but, rather, common to the three Abrahamic religions, predating them all.[40] Yet, if from the 1920s to the 1960s, unveiling was more the norm among many Muslim women, from the 1970s on both veiling (and the opposition to veiling) have been on the rise in countries where veiling is a choice, from North America to Egypt to Turkey. As with all clothing, "choice" is qualified by a diverse number of factors such as class, community standards, religion, culture, family, patriarchy, advertising, the fashion industry, price, weather, and availability, but the emergence of this new and political veiling has been the focus of a number of books written in the last decade that seek to explain the underlying reasons for its increase. I review the arguments in three of these studies which organize their arguments around the tensions between secularism and Islam and cover a range of countries – Turkey, Egypt, Europe, and America – to demonstrate the persistence of this binary that this book has been challenging.

Leila Ahmed's book *A Quiet Revolution* argues that this resurgence in veiling began with Israel's swift defeat of Egypt in 1967, which was interpreted as a punishment from God, provoking a religious revival. Nilüfer Göle's *Islam in Europe: The Lure of Fundamentalism and the Allure of Cosmopolitanism* considers Islam and veiling in the context of the limits of western modernity, whereas Joan Wallach Scott's *The Politics of the Veil* considers the recent veiling controversies in France both in light of its brutal colonization of Algeria, which Scott argues suggests the limits of secularism, and in light of the dangerous rise of fundamentalist religions in American politics. A brief outline of these arguments will provide an overview of the historical and theoretical context for the global rise of veiling.

Ahmed's book traces the history of the Muslim Brotherhood, founded in Egypt in 1928. One of the earliest manifestations of an Islam that combined a social justice platform with a conservative interpretation of Islam, the Muslim Brothers were dedicated to the eradication of poverty and corruption while at the same time supporting shari'a law, a pan-Islamic anti-nationalist agenda, and veiling and modest dress for women as a visible sign of the movement. Gamal Abdel Nasser (1956–70) had come to power with the help of the Muslim Brotherhood and had pursued a socialist, nationalist, anti-imperialist agenda, but he then attempted to curb the power of the Islamists and resisted their call for an Islamic state. After a failed assassination attempt by an extreme element in the Muslim Brotherhood, Nasser ordered thousands of arrests, pushing many educated and professionally trained Brothers to escape persecution. Many found work in the oil industry in Saudi Arabia. When Anwar Sadat (1970–81) came to power, he capitalized on the religious revival that had unfolded in the aftermath of Egypt's defeat by Israel. He released many of the Muslim Brothers from prison and invited others back from Saudi Arabia and elsewhere; he also supported a pro-American, pro-business, anti-left agenda. By the end of the 1970s, however, tensions emerged with the Islamists, who were opposed to the signing of the peace treaty with Israel. Sadat was assassinated in 1981 by Islamic militants – one of whom, Ayman al-Zawahiri, was allowed into the United States in the 1990s even as he was raising funds for a jihad against America; in 2011, he was named the new leader of al-Qaeda following bin Laden's death. At the time, the American government was more concerned about the threat of socialism and communism than with the rise of religious fundamentalism; hence, it, along with Saudi Arabia, funded the militant *mujahideen* against the Soviet-backed regime in Kabul.

With the large influx of Egyptians in the Gulf, the Muslim Brotherhood was well-funded by Saudi Arabia despite its significant differences with Wahhabism/Salafism. Thus, many of the professional Egyptians who had made money in the Gulf returned to their country in the 1970s, influenced by this sect and its more conservative gender politics and dress laws for women even as they remained committed to a social justice platform and continued to resist America's neoliberal agenda. Although preferring persuasion and education over violence, some of these professionals – teachers, lawyers, doctors – also used coercive tactics and intimidation to impose their particular version of Islam while Mubarak's American-supported government (1981–2011) was increasingly trying to forcefully regulate Islamic practices. In 1994, the government revised the Unification of School Uniform policy and attempted to purge the Islamist influence from state-funded schools, banning the wearing of the hijab in younger grades. But this policy caused a great deal of tension with mainstream Muslims who, by the 1990s, had again adopted veiling as a normative part of their practice.

Ahmed also tracks the rise of veiling in North America, where Islamists and their conservative and Saudi-funded version of Islam came to dominate major Muslim organizations (such as the Council on American-Islamic Relations, the Islamic Society of North America, and the Muslim Student Association), causing a rift with moderate Muslims, who resented being represented and spoken for by more radical factions. For instance, when mainstream media outlets called to inquire whether veiling was required for Muslim women, the response would be an unequivocal "yes" despite the fact that generations of Muslim women had chosen not to veil and did not see the practice as a requirement of the religion. Veiled daughters, schooled in the "correct" version of Islam, would return from their lessons, and scold their unveiled mothers for not adhering to what they had been taught were the tenets of the religion.

At the same time, terrorist attacks in Egypt, the Gulf Wars, the fall of the Soviet Union, the history of orientalist discourse that had long fed Muslim and Arab stereotypes in the American cultural industry, and a slate of sensationalist books published for an American market about the oppression of Muslim women – all contributed to the rise in the discrimination against all Muslims in the 1990s. The 11 September 2001 attacks on the World Trade Towers and the Pentagon brought this simmering anti-Muslim sentiment to a head and also exposed the extent to which an extreme but marginal and Saudi-funded version of Islam had hijacked the agenda in America.

Ahmed argues that it was also this catastrophic event that began to shift the conversations about Islam as the mosques began to open up their doors to non-Muslims in order to stem the backlash and quell charges that Islam was extremist, anti-American, anti-Semitic, and anti-woman. Thus, Muslim organizations and mosques in North America, she argues, were put on the defensive and compelled to adopt a more liberal stance: "to listen, giving courteous reception to views that in ordinary times they would not have even permitted to have uttered in their mosques – views, moreover, articulated by people who ordinarily they would not even have allowed to enter into the sanctum of the upper level of the mosque, an area reserved exclusively for Muslim men."[41] Many Muslim women took up the veil in North America as a visible sign of solidarity with Muslims who were being discriminated against and in defiance of the history of using veiled women's "oppression" to justify imperialism and colonialism. At the same time, however, these women were demanding equal rights in Islamic institutions and offering new interpretations of the Qur'an, forcing more conservative versions of Islam to enter into discussions about social justice and rights for other groups that faced discrimination.

Ahmed thus connects the rise of veiling in Egypt, which was about protesting corruption, to the increase in veiling in North America, which was about challenging discrimination: "In both societies wearing hijab became sign and banner of a call for justice."[42] If in Egypt social injustice meant addressing economic disparities, in the American context social justice meant rights for women and minorities: religious, sexual, and racial. Tracing the veil's transformation in meaning, from its association with patriarchy and oppression to its association with social justice, Ahmed notes: "The American notions of protection of life and liberty for example are blended with the idea of the obligation to 'serve the poor and the weak' that is specific to Islamism."[43]

Though both American-centric, as the values of "life and liberty" are not unique to this country, and Islamic-centric, as the mandate "to serve the poor and the weak" is not specific to this religion, Ahmed's book nevertheless ends on a hopeful note about the connection between social justice and the hijab. Yet since 2000, the increase in niqābs (face veils) has also become the focus of heated debates in Egypt that have little to do with social justice. The Salafi defence of wearing the niqāb holds that the female face can be sexually distracting and that this veil offers women protection from men. The simultaneous rise of face veiling and rates of sexual harassment indicate, not surprisingly, that nothing has been accomplished by insisting on more covered bodies. The Salafi position also defends this article of clothing as a sign of modesty, humility, and religious faith. Yet the Gulf fashion of niqābs and abayas, which signal both wealth and power, has encouraged an increasing number of Muslim women outside Saudi Arabia to adopt the face veil as a mark of their status. Displacing unveiling that had earlier been a mark of sophistication among many Muslims, designer veils and burqa-inspired fashion have become regular features on Paris runways, on the high street, in glossy advertisements, and in haute couture fashion houses. This trend is part of the larger move towards Islamic branding, open markets, and consumption that also speaks to the embrace of neoliberalism.

A year before he died, Muhammad Sayyid Tantawy, Grand Imam of Al-Azhar University, the centre of Islamic learning in Egypt, campaigned in 2009 to ban the wearing of the face veil, arguing that it had no basis in Islam (with Italy and France following his lead). His argument was complicated by the fact that Tantawy had been appointed by the American-supported Mubarak and by his forced unveiling, on a visit to a school, of a young woman wearing a niqāb. His often erratic declarations – for instance, he also opposed female imams because of their distracting bodies – merely confirmed for many Egyptians that the institution he was in charge of was a tool of a repressive government and lacking in any legitimacy. In Egypt, at least prior to the Arab uprisings in 2012, the politics of (un)veiling seemed increasingly to be torn between a Saudi-influenced conservative agenda and a coercive state apparatus. Post the uprisings and the ousting of Mubarak, the situation for women remains very precarious. The many women who took part in and organized demonstrations in the name of democracy, anti-neoliberalism, and freedom were no happier with the authoritarianism of Egypt's first democratically elected president, Mohamed Morsi, a former leading member of the Muslim Brotherhood, who took power in June 2012. By November of that year Morsi had granted himself, as president, unlimited powers. As with secularism, Islam is constantly being refashioned to serve political interests and ruling elites. A combination of a popular revolution and a military coup d'état removed Morsi from power in July 2013. Three years after the revolution, things seem to have come full circle with the "election" of Abdel Fattah el-Sisi, the former army field marshal, who was sworn in as the country's president in June 2014 and has since blocked freedom of speech, imprisoned journalists, and brutally repressed and jailed thousands of protestors.

Observing the general rise in fundamentalist religions, Joan Wallach Scott is less optimistic than Ahmed about reconciling secularism and religion. On the one hand, she considers the ways in which anti-veiling laws in France are complicated by French colonialism in Algeria, questioning whether this intolerance around veiling suggests the limits of the Enlightenment. Yet, also disturbed by the increasing political power of Christian evangelicals in America, who want to organize society on the basis of Christian revelation and abandon democracy, she finds herself at an impasse, writing: "It seems I am caught in an impossible dilemma: for or against secularism? Is the principle too easily corrupted, as the French case suggests? Or does it necessarily protect us from religious absolutism?"[44]

Scott points out that in America, the Bill of Rights protects a person's "natural" rights and limits the government's powers, so that rights are understood as preceding the state and attempts to regulate the citizenry are viewed with suspicion. Secularism, in the American context, thus guarantees the right to practise one's religion, and so there is little opposition to veils and mosques or any other religious expression. In France, however, rights are gained through the state and by participation in a secular universal citizenry. Having struggled to liberate itself from the stronghold of the Catholic Church and its priests, France supports the complete separation of church and state, protects the individual from religion, and is dismissive of America's tolerance for multiculturalism and religious difference.[45] Visible veiling in America is about an individual's freedom to choose and practise one's religion whereas in France veiling in public places like schools is viewed as a dangerous thwarting of the ideals of universalism and a culturally homogeneous citizenship. Membership in the Republic requires that the individual give up any public expression of particular religious or cultural values that are not considered universal and shared in order to prevent social fragmentation and fractionalization.

It is this tension that lies at the heart of the controversies about veiling in France, but Scott also argues that these debates must also consider the history of French imperialism and gender politics. From the expulsion of three veiled girls from their middle school in Creil in 1989 to the headscarf ban in 2004, Scott situates these events in the context of

France's legacy of racism in and colonization of Algeria, which culminated in the War of Independence (1954–62). The French government banned the veil ostensibly to protect schoolgirls from religion, assuming that veiling was being forced on them by oppressive fathers and brothers, and to ensure they would be able to participate in and were not excluded from "universal" secular values. Several of the girls, however, were vocal about the fact that wearing a hijab was their choice and not forced on them. Rather, they had adopted it as a defiant response to the generations of racism and discrimination that, since the French occupation of Algeria, had branded them "backward" and "other," forcing them to suppress or disguise their own historically situated identity. In other words, they veiled to reclaim their dignity, assert their cultural "difference," and join an international community of Muslims that promised to welcome them and respect them, unlike France, which had forced them to a literal and metaphorical periphery despite their supposed "equality" within the nation.

These tensions replay the unresolved debates about giving women the vote in France, which did not happen until 1944 and only when suffrage was understood in terms of the "universal" difference between men and women (Muslim women in French Algeria were not granted the right to vote until 1958). As Scott argues, French citizenship depends on the idea of abstract individualism, where the individual is divorced from the particulars of identity (class, religion and ethnicity) and rendered the same as and equal to his fellow humans. Women, it was finally determined, were different – but as this difference was "universal" and "natural" (not culturally specific) – they were finally granted suffrage. Yet gender difference continues to complicate matters and is uneasily accommodated in French political life, which is built on the philosophy of sameness. Although the use of the universal "he" suggests men can be divorced from their sex, "she" is never taken as universal, suggesting women are always defined by theirs.

One of the most recent examples of this inequity involved Cécile Duflot, the housing minister. Duflot wore a dress as she addressed France's National Assembly in July 2012 and was almost drowned out by catcalls and heckling. Not at all an isolated incident but symptomatic of a larger problem, the men in the Assembly defended their behaviour with the claim that it was "natural" for them to express their appreciation of female beauty; hence the limits of France's political system, based on the equal but different model. The paradox of French equality, Scott argues, is exposed by the practice of veiling which openly acknowledges the disruptive force of sexual difference in the public sphere. The attempts to keep questions of this "difference" from erupting explain in part the vocal protests against the veil.

Scott thus finds herself trapped, wary of the religious right in America but also aware of the limits of secular modernity. If the discrimination and racism that are exposed in the veiling case in France point to the limits of secularism on the one hand, on the other the increasing political clout of evangelical Christians who want to impose their moral values on the rest of American society proves the need for a forceful secularism. Scott, referring to this religious surge, writes: "If as a result the right-to-life trumps the right-to-choose, they say, then democracy as we have known it is lost. This is an argument I agree with."[46]

Yet while Scott's argument rests on a divide between secularism and religion, Jean-François Lyotard suggests that the French Republic itself was founded on the confusion between the two as the members of the Constituent Assembly had "hallucinated humanity within the nation."[47] Thus, there is no possibility of reconciling the rights of universal man, which are authorized by a transcendent Ideal (the Supreme Being), with the rights of man as authorized by the nation, which relies on the authority of a necessarily historical/temporal narrative. Because of this double and irreconcilable authorization, Lyotard writes, after the French Revolution, "It will no longer be known whether the law thereby declared is French or human, whether the war conducted in the name of rights is one of conquest or liberation, whether the violence exerted under the title of freedom is repressive or pedagogical (progressive), whether those nations which are not French ought to become French or become human by endowing themselves with Constitutions that conform to the Declaration, be they anti-French."[48] In other words, secularism that is based in universalism cannot but be religious in nature. Ironically, France's secularism shares Islam's gender politics – both are rooted in a binary way of thinking, where men and women are considered fundamentally and naturally different but also complementary. The French vociferously announce their difference from Islamic gender politics, repressing this similarity.[49]

Nilüfer Göle's *Islam in Europe* also tracks the increasing visibility of Islam in Turkey and Europe, from veiling to mosques. Like Ahmed, Göle is more optimistic than Scott about reconciling religion and secularism and argues that religion offers necessary checks to the Enlightenment and vice versa. Again, the figure of the (un)veiled women is at the heart of this tension – both the place of discord and of reconciliation.

On the one hand, the violent quest of Islamic fundamentalists requires both the rejection of western modernity and the oppression of women's bodies. Yet while the veil "preserves the difference between men and women, private and public, Islam and modernity," Muslim women, enabled by the European tradition of a rights-based discourse and freedom of choice, are also "investing in the spaces of modernity, acquiring visibility, mingling with men in mixed places" so that "Islamic modernity can only be written in the feminine."[50] Göle argues that the very announcement of Islamists' separation from the West and their narrative of "return" only proves how completely interconnected the two are as the "actors of Islamism" are "shaped far less by religion than by modernity."[51] On the other hand, Göle observes, Europe has been trying to keep its secularism "pure" from religion by methods such as banning burqas (France and Belgium) and minarets (Switzerland), rendering Islam Europe's constitutive other.[52] Yet the revival of religion in public spaces serves as a useful check to the extremes of modernity as acts like veiling suggest surrender to a higher order: "They privilege a certain dose of humility over the secular, individualistic, all-powerful will of the modern subject."[53]

Göle concludes that contemporary veiling suggests the creative dynamic energy between Europe and Islam, much like Ahmed claims that it signals the constructive and complementary merging of the Islamic obligation to care for the poor and the American emphasis on individual rights. Göle also shares with Scott the view that the veiling controversies expose the limits and intolerance of secularism, but, unlike Scott, she is not concerned about the rise of religiosity. All three books argue that, in any case, the late-twentieth-century resurgence of visible and public veiling is not so much about a "return" to some foundational moment of Islam, but is shaped by recent historical events – an argument I very much agree with, but I would also challenge the secular/religion binary that lies at the heart of these three studies.

Contemporary controversies around veiling and unveiling emerge out of the convergence of many factors: neoliberalism, identity politics, race, capitalism, consumerism, multiculturalism, feminisms, patriarchy, social justice, state coercion, faith, fashion, and cosmopolitanism. But none of these factors fall neatly on one or the other side of the East/West divide. This book has argued that a longer historical view undoes the claim that Islam has ever stood in opposition to secularism or modernity, returning us full circle to the eighteenth century and Lady Mary's insights with which I began. While Gibbon described Islam as the most "rational" of religions, Locke, as one of the leading Enlightenment philosophers, argued for the continuity between man and God and reason and the divine, grounding reason in an absolute and universal truth. The West's claim to secularism and reason is therefore founded in religion even as it announces its separation from faith. Islam, on the other hand, acknowledged from the outset the interconnectedness of secularism and religion, but also the rupture between the human and the divine, making it impossible for humans to claim absolute knowledge and instead insisting on an attentiveness to negotiating differences that emerge from "being in the world." The foundational rhetoric of early Enlightenment philosophers, however, was matched by Wahhabism, a radical and marginal sect of Islam that had first emerged in the eighteenth century. Strengthened by western imperialism and petrodollars, Wahhabism gained global influence in the twentieth century and has encouraged the reading of Islam as non-modern. Desiring to return to the "fundamentals" of the religion, even as it ignores Islam's basis in secularism and reason, Wahhabism claims unmediated access to the divine, a fundamentalist version that bears no resemblance to Islam's long history of inclusion.

Twenty-first-century versions of the East/West divide – most visibly played out on the body of the (un)veiled woman – only further expose the fallacy at the heart of this divide as these "sides" grow more and more entwined, even as they announce, ever more loudly, their difference from each other. Yet continuities between uprisings in such places as Egypt, Turkey, America, Canada, and England – to name a few – also suggest that this East/West divide may be on the verge of imploding as protests against state coercion, regulatory edicts, and global imperialism which encourage and profit from these binary identities (terrorist versus freedom fighter; citizen versus non-citizen; believer versus non-believer; man versus woman; burqa versus bikini) is giving way to the understanding of a subject not as entrenched but as "an active and transitive set of relations"[54] – an identity that resists foundational logic or, in Lady Mary's words, involves a "perpetual masquerade."

Epilogue: The Spectres of Orientalism

In the spring of 2013, a small group of environmentalists, academics, and architects camped out in Gezi Park to peacefully protest the proposed commercial development in Taksim of one of the last remaining public green spaces in this area of Istanbul.[1] Their violent eviction from the park sparked nationwide strikes and protests that encompassed a range of issues, including police brutality, the attack on human rights, the jailing of writers, the curtailing of the right of citizens to assemble, the censorship of the media, the takeover of public spaces by corporate interests, the authoritarianism, and the cronyism and corruption of the ruling Islamic party – the AKP (The Justice and Development Party).[2] Recep Tayyip Erdoğan, the former prime minister of Turkey (2003–14) and president of Turkey since 2014, the most powerful political leader since Mustafa Kemal Atatürk, accused the main opposition, the CHP (Republican People's Party), of helping to orchestrate the demonstrations, condemned the crowds as anti-Muslim and anti-Turkish, and tried to ignite tensions and rally his conservative Muslim supporters by claiming, among other things, that veiled women were being attacked by the protesting crowds. Over the next few months, the brutal repression by riot police of the protesters resulted in thousands of injuries from tear gas, rubber bullets, and water cannons; thousands were imprisoned, including journalists who covered the demonstrations, lawyers who documented the abuses, and the nurses and doctors who helped the wounded.[3]

The park lies adjacent to Taksim Square, which houses the Monument of the Republic (Cumhuriyet Aniti) celebrating the 1923 formation of Turkey that prominently features Atatürk, as both a soldier and a leader, who commissioned it. The proposal to construct an

Ottoman-style shopping mall was meant as a challenge to the secularist legacy of the Republic. Based on a replica of the Taksim Military Barracks, completed in 1806, this mixed-used commercial space was supposed to harken back to "the golden days" of the empire, reversing the Kemalist turn against Ottoman history and culture, which the AKP has been intent on reclaiming. For over a decade, "Ottomania" has been sweeping the country, from a revival of the rich cuisine to movies like the 2012 blockbuster *Fetih 1453* (*The Conquest 1453*) to Ottoman-inspired airline outfits. As the economy thrived, the AKP cooled on the proposal to join the European Union with its falling euro and economic trouble (Europe, of course, has also long been reluctant to include this Muslim country) and looked mostly East for new markets, wanting to situate itself once again as a global power by rekindling Turkey's influence in the former regions of the Empire. But if Kemalism had accepted the "sick-man-of-Europe" thesis and had distanced itself from all things Ottoman, Erdoğan's reclaiming of all things Ottoman has been no less shaped by orientalism.

For instance, *Fetih 1453*, the most expensive and most watched Turkish film in history, counts Erdoğan among its fans. In the film, Sultan Mehmet leads an ethnically homogeneous Turkish Muslim army whereas the Ottoman army would have been intraethnic and multireligious, as was the general population. The neo-Ottomanism that Turkey has embraced under Erdoğan continues the racialized and militarized nationalism of the Kemalists and refuses the earlier cosmopolitanism of the Empire. Eliding the historically porous East/West borders, this production presents as firmly entrenched the divide between Christians and Muslims[4] that this book has been arguing was inaugurated by the shift in the balance of power in the eighteenth century and the rise of orientalism in Europe.

The AKP, however, has been more critical of *Muhteşem Yüzyıl* (*The Magnificent Century*) which first aired in 2011 even though this hugely popular Turkish soap opera also seems to play into Ottomania. Based on the life of Sultan Süleyman, who reigned from 1520 to 1566, the drama focuses on the legendary Roxlena (Hürrem), the politically ambitious Christian slave who married the sultan. In the characterization of the harem and Roxlena, a woman who has long fascinated the West, the makers of this series used many European sources. One scene, which was subject to a state fine for being historically inaccurate, was that of slave girls undergoing virginity checks.[5] According to Elif Batuman, the researcher working on the series cited a seventeenth-century European painting of a girl being inspected at a slave market as evidence (though it was more likely Jean-Léon Gérôme's nineteenth-century *The Slave Market*, 1867).[6] This series, as TV entertainment interested in sales and markets, is not primarily concerned with historical accuracy any more than period dramas like the steamy *The Tudors*, based on Henry VIII and his wives, with which it is often compared.

The government was right to suggest that these orientalist sources did not accurately portray the complexities of the harem.[7] Yet, the source of tension also seems to be once again women's bodies – and the degree of their covering – that is the twenty-first-century manifestation (burqa versus bikini) of the East/West divide. This soap has been criticized by the AKP and the Radio and Television Supreme Council in Turkey for being too hedonistic and for depicting too many harem scenes and not enough victorious Ottoman battle scenes.[8] The producers, worried about displeasing the government, promptly responded by introducing more modestly dressed women, more piety, and less cleavage. But if the TV show, in its orientalist depictions of an exoticized harem, is about selling one version of the East, the AKP's response is about marketing another version: from modest dress to non-alcoholic beverages to the service sector to the culture industry, Islamic branding caters to Muslim consumers around the globe in perfect keeping with the western liberalization of economic markets and privatization.[9] As was the case with Egypt, supporting religious ideology and the Muslim bourgeoisie, and opening Turkey, another American ally, to global markets was seen by western powers, who had been focused on the Cold War, as a way of shutting down the socialist and communist politics that were challenging the right in Turkey in the 1970s, culminating in the 1980 military coup that eventually paved the way for the success of Erdoğan's Islamic party.

The proposed plan for a mall based on the Taksim barracks, which triggered the protests, itself encapsulates an interconnected history that refuses the neat divide between East/West and secularism/Islamism. In 1918, soldiers recruited from Senegal into the French army were stationed there during the occupation of Istanbul by the Allies in 1918, and in 1909 the barracks were the site of a mutiny against the Committee of Union and Progress (CUP), the predecessors of the nationalists who founded the Turkish Republic. This anti-nationalist mutiny was in turn used to justify the exile of Abdülhamid II. Originally, the Armenian architect Kirkor Balyan was commissioned to build the barracks under the reign of the French-influenced Sultan Selim III (1789–1807), who wanted to bring European-style reforms to the military, and was in turn deposed and imprisoned by the Janissaries, then assassinated. The latest proposed reincarnation of this historic building – as a shopping complex – speaks to a post-1980s neoliberalist agenda spliced into Islam, where Ottomania is exposed as being more about markets and consumption than about reviving the history of the empire.

For centuries, the figure of the (un)veiled woman has been held hostage in the "clash of civilizations" argument. In the eighteenth century, this figure was used to inaugurate the divisions between secularism and Islam; in the nineteenth, she was central in the debates about militarized and racialized nations; in the late twentieth century, she has been used to secure global neoliberal interests. The increasing divide between East and West has contributed to the rise of religious and nationalist fundamentalisms, greater financial inequity, and growing sectarian violence – all in the name of "secure" borders. If the destructive division between secularists and Muslims that Erdoğan was trying to inflame in his mobilization of an imperialist Turkish nationalism when he denounced the protestors as – "foreigners," "unfaithful," "marginal," "hooligans," "terrorists," and faux Turks – the diverse crowds in Gezi Park better reflected the cosmopolitan community of the former empire, though reworked for the twenty-first century: Young, old, singles, families, Kurdish, LGBT activists, veiled and unveiled women, Marxists, anarchists, environmentalists, devout Muslims, academics, conservatives, Alevis, and 1990s youth, among others, were all protesting the divide and conquer strategies of their government as they cared for one another, respectful of differences.[10] Challenging the policy of "securing" borders, this study has attempted to restore the continuities between Islam and the West and release the figure of the un(veiled) woman that has been used in the construction of this division, in all its guises, to revive the, albeit differently conceived, inclusivity that operated prior to the rise of Orientalism in order to find the glimmer of an alternative dialogue that Edward Said had hoped was possible.

Notes

Introduction

1 See, for instance, Jennifer Heath's edited and wide-ranging collection on veiling in its many forms, which includes an article on male veiling. *The Veil: Women Writers on Its History, Lore, and Politics* (Berkeley: University of California Press, 2008).

2 Pnina Werbner, "The Veil and the Public Sphere," *Current Anthropology* 54. 2 (2013): 195.

3 Anjum Alvi, "Concealment and Revealment: The Muslim Veil in Context," *Current Anthropology* 54. 2 (2013): 177–99.

4 See Leila Ahmed's *Women and Gender in Islam* (New Haven: Yale University Press, 1992): 14–15; and Fatima Mernissi's *The Veil and the Male Elite: A Feminist Interpretation of Women's Rights in Islam*, translated by Mary Jo Lakeland (Reading: Addison-Wesley Publishing Company, 1991): 180–1.

5 See Letters 31 and 42 in Lady Mary Wortley Montagu's *The Turkish Embassy Letters*, eds. Teresa Heffernan and Daniel O'Quinn (Peterborough: Broadview Press, 2013). Lady Mary reports that the requirement of a "Turkish veil" deterred many travellers, including the French Ambassadress, from seeing Constantinople. Lady Mary, however, reports that this heavier veil is both "very easy" and "agreeable" (164).

6 Halidé Edib, *The Turkish Ordeal* (London: John Murray, 1928), 71. Though the *çarsaf* itself was a recent garment that had replaced the *ferece* in late-nineteenth-century Turkey, Edib is likely referring to it as "old fashioned" as it was in turn modernized to adapt to European fashions. See Nora Şeni's "Fashion and Women's Clothing in the Satirical Press of Istanbul at the End of the Nineteenth-Century," in *Women in Modern Turkish Society*, ed. Sirin Tekeli (London: Zed Books, 1991): 30–1.

7 See, for instance, Margot Badran's "Competing Agenda: Feminists, Islam and the State in Nineteenth- and Twentieth-Century Egypt" in *Women, Islam and the State*, ed. Deniz Kandiyoti (Philadelphia: Temple University Press, 1991), 203.
8 Nelofer Pazira, *A Bed of Red Flowers: In Search of My Afghanistan* (New York: Random House, 2005), 311.
9 See Edward Said's *Culture and Imperialism* (New York: Vintage Books, 1994). Said argues in this work that cultural production worked in tandem with the political agenda of the Empire to produce a "consolidated vision" that left unquestioned the exceptional goodness of Britain and its right to rule the rest of the globe.
10 Edward Said, *Orientalism* (New York: Vintage Books, 1979), 46.
11 For several decades Islam faded into the background as communism took its place as the central "threat" to western modernity; after the fall of the Iron Curtain, Islam as the "other" returned with a vengeance, as evident in the renewed debates about veiling.

1 Islam, the Enlightenment, and the Veil

1 James Porter, *Observations on the Religion, Law, Government, and Manners of the Turks*, 2nd ed. (London: J. Nourse, 1771), xiii.
2 Richard Chandler, *Travels in Asia Minor* (Oxford: Clarendon Press, 1775), ix.
3 Elias Habesci, *The Present State of the Ottoman Empire* (London, 1784), viii.
4 Ibid., ii.
5 Thomas Thornton, *The Present State of Turkey, or, A description of the political, civil and religious constitution, government and laws of the Ottoman Empire* (London: Printed for Joseph Mawman, 1807), iii.
6 Ibid., ix.
7 Ian Watt, *The Rise of the Novel: Studies in Defoe, Richardson and Fielding* (Berkeley: University of California, 1957).
8 See also Michael McKeon's *The Origins of the English Novel 1600–1740*. Discussing eighteenth-century travel literature, McKeon notes: "The fundamental trope of this anti-rhetorical style is the self-reflexive insistence on its own documentary candor, as well as on the historicity of the narrative it transparently mediates" (London: The Johns Hopkins University Press, 1987), 105.
9 Sir Paul Rycaut, *The History of the Present State of the Ottoman Empire*, 5th ed. (London, 1682). See Linda Darling's "Ottoman Politics through British Eyes: Paul Rycaut's 'The Present State of the Ottoman Empire,'" *Journal of World History*, 5.1 (1994): 71–97. Darling reviews this work chapter by

chapter and points to the political interests, shaped by prejudice, that informed this history. She argues: "Behind the facade of contrasting political rhetoric, however, there were certain similarities in the direction of development of the Ottoman Empire and England that have gone almost unnoticed through the centuries. Rycaut's images of loathsome Ottoman tyranny both stemmed from and reinforced an orientalism founded on the contrary assumption of a vast distinction, even alienation, between East and West" (95).

10 See for instance, Ezel Kural Shaw's "The Double Veil: Travelers' Views of the Ottoman Empire, Sixteenth through Eighteenth Centuries" in *English and Continental Views of the Ottoman Empire, 1500 – 1800* (Los Angeles: William Andrews Clark Memorial Library, 1972), 17.

11 George Sandys, *Relation of a Journey begun An. Dom. 1610. Foure Bookes. Containing a description of the Turkish Empire, of Ægypt, of the Holy Land, of the remote parts of Italy, and Ilands adjoyning* (London: W. Barrett, 1615), 80.

12 Aaron Hill, *A full and just account of the present state of the Ottoman Empire in all its branches ... faithfully related from a serious observation taken in many years travels thro' those countries* (London, 1709), 175.

13 See for instance, page 32 in Sandys, *Relation*, and page 147 in Hill, *A full and just account*.

14 Mohja Kahf notes that it was not until the late sixteenth century, according to the Oxford English Dictionary, that the words "seraglio" (1581) and "harem" (1624) surfaced in English (1581). "The veil and the harem do not exist in medieval representations of the Muslim woman and are barely present in the Renaissance" (6–7). *Western Representations of the Muslim Woman: From Termagant to Odalisque* (Austin: University of Texas Press, 1999).

15 See for instance, Nancy Armstrong in *Desire and Domestic Fiction: A Political History of the Novel* (New York: Oxford University Press, 1987): 3. Armstrong discusses "the rise of the domestic woman" and the new gendering of public and private space in the eighteenth century as "a major political event."

16 Jean de Thevenot, *The travels of Monsieur de Thevenot into the Levant: in three parts, viz. into I. Turkey, II. Persia, III. The East-Indies / newly done out of French* (London: Printed by H. Clark for H. Faithorne, 1687), 56–7.

17 William Hunter, *Travels through France, Turkey, and Hungary, to Vienna, in 1792* (London, 1803), 37.

18 Stanley Lane-Poole, *The People of Turkey /Stanley Lane Poole* (London: John Murray, 1878), xxiii.

19 Mary Riddell, "Why I Want to See the Veil Gone from Britain" [interview with Harriet Harman], *New Statesman*, 16 October 2006, 12.

20 Humberto Garcia has argued that Said's theory of orientalism cannot account for Islamic Republicanism or the ways in which "radical Protestants in eighteenth-century England self-consciously recast Islam in constitutional-nationalist terms" (1). His book offers a fascinating reading of how Islam shapes versions of English nationalism. Yet, while I agree with his thesis that the teleological – religion to secular – narrative of the West is problematic and Eurocentric, I do not think his argument adequately accounts for the very different understandings of secularism in Islamic and European modernity, nor does it account for the emergence of the (un)veiled woman, a pivotal figure in the construction of an East/West divide as the balance of world power shifts with the rise of the British Empire. *Islam and the English Enlightenment, 1670–1840* (Baltimore: The Johns Hopkins University Press, 2012).

21 Hill, *A full and just account*, 42.

22 Ibid., 97.

23 Ibid., 111.

24 Ibid., 166.

25 Edward Gibbon, *The Private Letters of Edward Gibbon*, ed. Rowland E. Prothero, 2 vols. (London: John Murray, 1896), 1:53, 83.

26 Lisa Lowe, *Critical Terrains: French and British Orientalisms* (Ithaca: Cornell University Press, 1991), 51.

27 Meyda Yegenoglu, "Supplementing the Orientalist Lack: European Ladies in the Harem," *Inscriptions* 6 (1992): 45–80.

28 Cynthia Lowenthal, *Lady Mary Wortley Montagu and the Eighteenth-Century Familiar Letter* (London: The University of Georgia Press, 1994), 81–2.

29 Srinivas Aravamudan, "Lady Mary Wortley Montagu in the Hammam: Masquerade, Womanliness, and Levantinization," *ELH* 62.1 (95): 69–104.

30 Morris, Marilyn, "Transgendered Perspectives on Premodern Sexualities," *SEL Studies in English Literature 1500–1900* 46.3 (2006): 585–600.

31 Anna Secor, for instance, argues that the main issue in Lady Mary's letters is not feminism or orientalism, but rather class, writing that: "Montagu's letters reproduce dominant discourses which naturalize class inequality, even and especially in moments when she subverts aspects of Orientalist or gendered expectations" ("Orientalism, Gender and Class in Lady Mary Wortley Montagu's *Turkish Embassy Letters: To Persons of Distinction, Men of Letters and C.*," *ECUMENE* 6.4 [1999]: 394). While there is no doubt that Lady Mary is thoroughly invested in rank, which is clearly evident in her denigration of the Tunisian women she encounters, the British class system, based on blood and title, finds no parallel in the Ottoman Empire, where some of the most powerful positions were held by former slaves.

32 Anita Desai, Introduction, *The Turkish Embassy Letters* (London: Virago Press, 1994), xxix.

33 Robert Halsband, ed., *The Complete Letters of Lady Mary Wortley Lady Mary*, 3 vols. (Oxford: Clarendon Press, 1965–7), 314.

34 Ibid., 407.

35 Thanks to Maria Koundoura, who pointed to this tendency in English travel writing, at "Snapshots from Abroad: A Conference on American and British Travel Writers and Writing" (University of Minnesota, November 1997).

36 Halsband, *Complete Letters*, 406.

37 Miguel de Cervantes, *Don Quixote de la Mancha*, trans. J.M. Cohen (London: Penguin Books, 1950), 338.

38 Ibid., 359.

39 Mohja Kahf, reading this tale in the context of the expulsion of the Moors from Spain in 1609 and the banning of Arabic and the erasure of Islamic influences, suggests it marks a significant shift in Western representations of Muslim women. For the first time dress – the veil – becomes a sartorial marker of the difference between Islam and Christianity, and while in previous literature the Muslim woman is represented as aggressive and powerful, here she is rendered passive and an object of pity. *Western Representations of the Muslim Woman from Termagant to Odalisque* (Austin: University of Texas Press, 1999).

40 Ibid., 375.

41 The divide between Christians and Muslims was not always as neat as this reading might suggest. At different points, Catholics were seen as a greater threat and as bizarre, if not more so, in their practices than Muslims. Lady Mary is certainly much harder on Catholicism, with its "popish miracles" and talking crucifixes, than she is on Islam. David Hume in his "The Natural History of Religion" (1757), for instance, recounts the tale of a Russian who takes a Turk captive. While recovering from his wounds in Paris, the doctors convince the Turk (meaning Muslim) to convert to Catholicism as they promise him "plenty of good wine in this world, and paradise in the next." Following his baptism, renaming, and receiving of the sacraments, the convert is then asked by the priest "How many Gods are there?" to which the convert replies "None at all ... " You have told me all along that there is but one God: And yesterday I eat him." David Hume, *Four Dissertations and Essays on Suicide and the Immortality of the Soul* (Bristol, UK: Thoemmes Press, 1992), 74. Turks and Catholic clergy occupy the same space as enemies and infidels of the Reformation in early modern German woodcuts c. 1548 (see, for

instance, Palmira Brummett's "Imagining the early modern Ottoman space, from World History to Piri Reis" [Goffman and Aksan: 15–58], 26). Brummett's persuasive thesis is that in early modern representations and maps of the Ottoman Empire, there are no clear borders between the Ottoman Empire and Christian Europe. The designations of "Turkey in Europe" and "Turkey in Asia" were later additions to maps, and it was not until the eighteenth century that "the state had become the standard by which lands were divided and demarcated" (35). An exhibition at the Metropolitan Museum of Art in New York also showcased the fluid boundaries between Christians and Muslims in the seventh century. The newly rising religion of Islam not only accommodated but adopted many of the secular and religious traditions of Orthodox, Coptic, and Syriac Christians, and Jewish communities in the area, suggesting that the rhetoric of clashing civilizations is a later invention ("Byzantium and Islam: Age of Transition," 14 March–8 July 2012).

42 Nabil Matar's *Islam in Britain 1558–1685* argues that twentieth-century scholars have ignored the superior military, intellectual, and economic power of the Islamic Empire, from the medieval period through to the eighteenth century, as they insist on viewing East/West relations through the lens of postcolonialism. Matar cites the thousands of men and women who were taken captive in Britain and the large number who converted to Islam (attracted as they were by the opportunity for social and economic advancement) as evidence of both the power and allure of Ottoman civilization. The strength of the Ottoman Empire thus foreclosed any imperial or colonial fantasies on the part of the British about dominating or taking possession of Islamic domains. Matar further argues that in the early modern period Muslims had the power of "self-representation" and that it was only post-Napoleonic Europe, having witnessed the decline of the Ottoman Empire, that was able to imagine "Muslims the way they liked" and that only then did "the lands of Islam become material for orientalist 'construction' and for continental and British colonization" (11). These earlier representations of the Muslim woman and the relationship between this representation and subsequent imperial conquests suggests, however, that the shift between Britain's early modern deference to Islam and its post-Napoleonic fantasies about it are not as absolute as Matar suggests (Nabil Matar, *Islam in Britain 1558–1685;* Cambridge: Cambridge University Press, 1998).

Bernadette Andrea agrees with Matar about the importance of the Ottoman Empire in Europe, but suggests he has largely ignored women writers and questions of gender. In writing about Lady Wroth's *Urania,*

Andrea argues that the work "dramatizes the suppression, not of a subdued colonial Other, but of an immensely powerful Other" by effacing the history of the Ottoman's control of Cyprus, which they had captured in 1571 ("Pamphilia's Cabinet," 349; see also, *Women and Islam in Early Modern Literature* [Cambridge University Press, 2007], 4). As with Cervantes's tale, the literary representation of Ottoman powerlessness is at odds with the historical reality of its dominance. Yet, as this orientalist image of the "veiled" woman awaiting liberty from a foreign saviour is key to later European and American imperialism, England's dream of global imperialism can be glimpsed in works that date from the late sixteenth century.

43 Virginia Aksan and Daniel Goffman, "Introduction: Situating the Early Modern Ottoman World," in *The Early Modern Ottomans: Remapping the Empire*, eds. Virginia Aksan and Daniel Goffman (Cambridge: Cambridge University Press, 2007).

44 Edward Said, *Orientalism* (New York: Vintage Books, 1979), 206.

45 Thomas Dallam in *Early Voyages and Travels in the Levant.*

46 John Covel in *Early Voyages and Travels in the Levant.*

47 Ottaviano Bon, *The Sultan's Seraglio, An Intimate Portrait of Life at the Ottoman Court* (from the seventeenth-century edition of John Withers) (London: Saqi Books, 1996), 57.

48 Jean Dumont, *A New Voyage to the Levant: containing an account of the most remarkable curiosities in Germany, France, Italy ... and Turkey. ... Done into English and adorn'd with figures. The second edition* (London, 1696), 167.

49 Habesci, *The present state*, 170.

50 Jean Baptiste, Tavernier, *Collections of Travels through Turkey into Persia and the East-Indies. Giving an account of the present state of those countries* (London, 1684), 86.

51 F.C.H.L Pouqueville, *Travels Through Morea, Albania, and Several Other Parts of the Ottoman Empire to Constantinople*, translated from the French (London: Phillips, 1806), 97.

52 Theodore Bent, Introduction, *Early Voyages and Travels in the Levant*, ed. J. Theodore Bent (New York: Burt Franklin, n.d.), ii.

53 Gayatri Spivak, "Can the Subaltern Speak?" in *Marxism and the Interpretation of Culture*, eds. Cary Nelson and Laurence Grossberg (Urbana: University of Illinois Press, 1988), 241.

54 Jean Dumont, *A New Voyage*, 261.

55 Mary Wollstonecraft, *A Vindication of the Rights of Woman* (London: Penguin, 1975), 80.

56 Joyce Zonana, "The Sultan and the Slave: Feminist Orientalism and the Structure of *Jane Eyre*," *Signs* 18 (1993): 594.

57 From the correspondences between Queen Elizabeth I and Safiye, the Ottoman Valide Sultan, during the last decade of the sixteenth-century, which emphasized the legitimacy of women's right to rule, interrupting the patriarchal structures of both Ottoman and English society, to some of the early Quaker women, who travelled in the Mediterranean, to the early modern playwrights such as Delarivier Manley, Bernadette Andrea suggests that even as feminist orientalism was emerging and embracing western imperialism, there were other early modern women who provided an alternative to this model and "sought to engage the Islamic world on its terms." Andrea, *Women and Islam*, 130.

58 Naila Minai, *Women in Islam: Tradition and Transition in the Middle East* (New York: Seaview, 1981), 64–5. Discussions of Turkey, modernisation and veiling are discussed at length by Meyda Yeğenoğlu in *Colonial Fantasies* (Cambridge, 1998); by Deniz Kandiyoti in, among other essays, "End of Empire: Islam, Nationalism, and Women in Turkey" in *Women, Islam and the State*, ed. Deniz Kandiyoti (Philadelphia: Temple University Press, 1991); and by Nilüfer Göle in *The Forbidden Modern* (Ann Arbour: The University of Michigan Press, 1996).

59 Ayşe Düzkan, *Feminism on Turkey in the 1980s: An Interview with Ayşe Düzkan by Meltem Ahiska* (Grabels, France: Women Living Under Muslim Law, 1994).

60 Gayatri Spivak, "Reading the *Satanic Verses*" in *Outside in the Teaching Machine* (New York: Routledge, 1993), 240.

61 Halsband, *Complete Letters*, 368.

62 Ibid., 406.

63 Ibid., 317.

64 Ibid., 364.

65 The first coffee houses in London, a concept imported from Istanbul, opened in 1637.

66 See Emile Bernard's harem paintings. Chapter 3 discusses his painting "The Three Races."

67 Halsband, *Complete Letters*, 318.

68 Billie Melman, *Women's Orients: English Women and the Middle East, 1718–1918* (Ann Arbor: The University of Michigan Press, 1992), 80.

69 Katherine S.H. Turner, "From Classical to Imperial: Changing Visions of Turkey in the Eighteenth Century," in *Travel Writing and Empire: Postcolonial Theory in Transit*, ed. Steve Clark (London: Zed Books, 1999), 113.

70 See also John Locke's *Reasonableness of Christianity: As Delivered in the Scriptures*, ed. George W. Ewing (Washington: Regnery Gateway, 1965).

71 John Locke, *An Essay Concerning Human Understanding*, ed. Peter H. Nidditch (Oxford: Clarendon Press, 1979), 704.

72 Ibid., 698.

73 Ibid., 704.

74 Ibid., 708.

75 The pervasiveness of this view in the eighteenth century is evident, for instance, in a sermon that is reproduced in Laurence Sterne's *The Life and Opinions of Tristram Shandy, Gentleman* (Boston: Riverside, 1965), 106: "God and reason made the law, and have placed conscience within you to determine; – not like an *Asiatick Cadi* [an Arabic or Persian judge], according to the ebbs and flows of his own passions, – but like a *British* judge in the land of liberty and good sense, who makes no new law, but faithfully declares that law which he knows already written." This passage inadvertently highlights the different understanding of reason in the West and East: the "rational" British judge has access to an unchanging and absolute truth – the Law; whereas the Arabic or Persian judge – ruling by temporal law – is grounded in the secular.

76 Barbara Herrnstein-Smith explicates the problem of universal value in both Hume and Kant in *Contingencies of Value: Alternative Perspectives for Critical Theory* (Cambridge: Harvard University Press, 1988).

77 David Hume, "Of the Standard of Taste," *Essays, Moral, Political and Literary* (Oxford: Oxford University Press, 1963), 232–3.

78 Rycaut, *History*, 13.

79 Fatima Mernissi, *The Veil and the Male Elite: A Feminist Interpretation of Women's Rights in Islam*, trans. Mary Jo Lakeland (Reading: Addison-Wesley Publishing Company, 1991), 26.

80 See Rycaut, *History*, 17.

81 Locke, *Human Understanding*, 94.

82 Edward Gibbon, *The History of the Decline and Fall of the Roman Empire*, ed. David Womersley (London: Allen Lane, Penguin Press, 1994), vol. 3, 230.

83 Matar rightly notes that western historians (such as Bernard Lewis, who claimed that Muslims exhibited no curiosity about Europeans) have failed to acknowledge that "fear was the most powerful deterrent to travel into the lands of Christians," whose "legacy was not only of warfare but of religious persecution" (Introduction, *In the Lands of the Christians: Arabic Travel Writing in the Seventeenth Century*, ed. and trans. Nabil Matar [New York: Routledge, 2003], xxvii). However, Matar's claim that Arab travellers were more likely to describe "what they saw, carefully and without projecting unfounded fantasies" and that they wrote "empirical

accounts about Europe" is more problematic given that, as we have seen, this claim of transparency is also in the works of English travellers (Introduction, xxxi–ii). Rather, I would suggest that the variance between Arabic and English accounts stems from the different understanding of reason that I have been outlining – the first grounded in the temporal and the other in the absolute.

84 John Macdonald Kinneir, *Journey through Asia Minor, Armenia, and Koordistan in the years 1813 and 1814. With remarks on the Marches of Alexander, and Retreat of the Ten Thousand* (London, 1818), 47.

85 Rycaut, *History*, 184.

86 Gibbon, *The Decline and Fall of the Roman Empire*, 215.

87 Edward Said, *The World, the Text, and the Critic* (Cambridge: Harvard University Press, 1983), 281.

88 Spivak, "Reading *The Satanic Verses*," 233.

89 Hussein Ahmad Amin, "The Present State of the Muslim *Umma*," *Muslim World* 79 (1989): 222.

90 See for instance, Wael Hallaq, *The Origins and Evolution of Islamic Law* (Cambridge University Press, 2005); Mohammad Hashim Kamali, *Freedom, Equality and Justice in Islam* (Cambridge, UK: Islamic Texts Society, 2002); and also Indira Falk Gesink, who points to the problematic emphasis on *ijtihad* in the late twentieth century in "'Chaos on the Earth': Subjective Truths versus Communal Unity in Islamic Law and the Rise of Militant Islam," *The American Historical Review* 108.3 (2003): 710–33. Gesink argues that a "rigid" version of Islam was invented by nineteenth-century, largely conservative, Muslim legal scholars and reformers who asserted that the "gate of ijtihad" was closed. Imposing an unchanging and monolithic version of shari'a on their followers, they hoped to guard against western imperialism and solidify the community. The reactive twentieth-century embrace of *ijtihad* by lay people, Gesink cautions, "contributed to the rise of many divergent sects, from secularists to relativists to militant groups," which in turn led to a paradox for religious leaders: For instance, the Muslim Brotherhood, who turned against the authority of Islamic scholars, wanted their followers both to embrace *ijtihad* and to arrive at the same interpretation of faith as their leaders (731).

91 Spivak, "Can the Subaltern Speak?" 242.

92 Halsband, *Complete Letters*, 318.

93 Ibid., 319.

94 Ibid., 314.

95 Ibid., 406.
96 Pouqueville, *Travels Through Morea*, 166.
97 James Dallaway, *Memoir, The Works of the Right Hon. Lady Mary Wortley Montagu*, 5 volumes, ed. Dallaway (London: R. Phillips, 1803), 11.
98 Ibid., 34.
99 William Eton, *A Survey of the Turkish Empire* (London: T. Cadell and W. Davies, 1798), 242.
100 Thornton, *The Present State of Turkey*, 338.
101 Peter Brooks, *Body Works: Objects of Desire in Modern Narrative* (Cambridge: Harvard University Press, 1993), 12–13.
102 John Locke, *Second Treatise of Government*, ed. C.B. Macpherson (Indianapolis: Hackett Publishing, 1980), 44.
103 Halsband, *Complete Letters*, 322.
104 Ibid., 54.
105 Ibid., 64.
106 See Gayatri Spivak for her detailed analysis of the "clitoridectomy" of women in political, economic, and legal exchanges in "French Feminism in an International Frame" in *In Other Worlds: Essays in Cultural Politics* (New York: Routledge, 1988), 151.
107 See Carole Pateman's excellent commentary on the co-option of the "origin" in social contract theory to which this section is indebted: "The Fraternal and Social Contract" in *Civil Society and the State: New European Perspectives*, ed. John Keane (London: Verso, 1988): 101–27. Also see Pateman's *The Sexual Contract* (Cambridge: Polity Press, 1988). I return to Pateman in Chapter 4.
108 Halsband, *Complete Letters*, 328.
109 Ibid., 329.
110 Fatima Mernissi, *Islam and Democracy: Fear of the Modern World*, trans. Mary Jo Lakeland (Reading, Massachusetts: Addison-Wesley Publishing Company, 1992), 128.
111 Halsband, *Complete Letters*, 425.
112 Ibid., 330.
113 Ibid., 427.
114 Lady Elizabeth Craven, *A Journey through the Crimea to Constantinople* (London: Printed by A.J. Valpy, 1814), 102.
115 Ibid., 205.
116 Ibid., 234.
117 Ibid., 188–9.
118 Jonathan Curling, *Edward Wortley Montagu 1713–1776: The Man in the Iron Wig* (London: Andrew Melrose, 1954), 34.

119 Ibid., 217.
120 Ibid.

2 The Great Whore of Babylon: Cosmopolitanism and Racialized Nationalism

1 Jean-Baptiste Tavernier, *Collections of Travels Through Turkey into Persia, and the East-Indies* (London, 1688).
2 Lady Mary Wortley Montagu, *The Turkish Embassy Letters* (Peterborough: Broadview Press, 2013), 117.
3 Jean de Thevenot, *The Travels of Monsieur de Thevenot into the Levant*, trans. A. Lovell, (London, 1686), 1.
4 Charles Macfarlane, *Constantinople in 1828. A residence of sixteen months in the Turkish Capital and Provinces, with an account of the present state of the naval and military power, and of the resources of the Ottoman Empire* (London: Saunders & Otley, 1829), xvii–xviii.
5 "Foreign Affairs," *The Levant Herald and Daily Express*, 5 August 1890.
6 W.H. Davenport Adams, *Celebrated Women Travellers of the Nineteenth Century* (London: W.S. Sonnenschein & Co., 1883), 341.
7 Ibid., 372.
8 Alexander William Kinglake, *Eothen* (Evanston: The Marlboro Press, 1996), 147.
9 Ibid.
10 Ibid., 151.
11 Kinglake, *Eothen*, 24.
12 Frances Elliot, *Diary of an Idle Woman in Constantinople* (London: John Murray, 1893), 5.
13 Ibid., 41.
14 Ibid., 44.
15 Ibid.
16 Stanley Lane-Poole, *Turkey* ([S.l.]: T. Fisher Unwin, 1888), 339.
17 "Crete and the Eastern Question," *The Levant Herald*, 25 Feb. 1867.
18 Duke of Argyll, *Our Responsibilities for Turkey: Facts and Memories of Forty Years* (London: John Murray, 1896), 20.
19 Stanley Lane-Poole, *Turkey* ([S.l.]: T. Fisher Unwin, 1888), 339, 341–2.
20 Lane-Poole, *Turkey*, 343.
21 Elie Kedourie, *England and the Middle East: The Destruction of the Ottoman Empire, 1914–1921* (London: Bowes & Bowes, 1956), 15.
22 Ibid., 3.
23 Rycaut, *History*, 17.

24 Ibid., 152.
25 Leslie Pierce, *The Imperial Harem: Women and Sovereignty in the Ottoman Empire* (New York: Oxford University Press, 1993), 37.
26 Lady Mary Wortley Montagu, *The Turkish Embassy Letters*, 174.
27 Ibid., 163.
28 Jean de Thevenot, *The travels of Monsieur de Thevenot into the Levant: in three parts, viz. into I. Turkey, II. Persia, III. The East-Indies / newly done out of French*, 63.
29 James Porter, *Observations on the religion, law, government, and manners of the Turks. The second edition, corrected and enlarged ... To which is added, the state of the Turkey trade, from its origin to the present time*, 255.
30 *Murray's Handbook for Travellers in Constantinople, Brusa, and the Troad* (London: John Murray, 1900), 6.
31 Charles Eliot, *Turkey in Europe* (London: Edward Arnold, 1900), 97.
32 Benedict Anderson, *Imagined Communities: Reflections of the Origin and Spread of Nationalism* (London: Verso, 1983), 19.
33 Michael Hardt and Antonio Negri, *Empire* (Cambridge: Harvard University Press, 2000), 102.
34 Vasant Kaiwar and Sucheta Mazumdar, "Race, Orient, Nation in the Time-Space of Modernity," in *Antinomies of Modernity: Essays on Race, Orient, Nation*, eds. Vasant Kaiwar and Sucheta Mazumdar (Durham and London: Duke University Press, 2003), 265.
35 David Theo Goldberg, *The Racial State* (Oxford: Blackwell, 2002), 49.
36 Daniel Goffman, *Britons in the Ottoman Empire, 1642–1660* (Washington: University of Washington, 1998), 20.
37 Stanford J. Shaw, *History of the Ottoman Empire and Modern Turkey: Volume 1, Empire of the Gazis: The Rise and Decline of the Ottoman Empire 1280–1808* (Cambridge: Cambridge University Press, 1976), 262.
38 Broughton, John Cam Hobhouse, Baron , *A Journey through Albania and other provinces of Turkey in Europe and Asia, to Constantinople, during the years 1809 and 1810* (London: 1813), 596.
39 See Ayse Gül Altinay, *The Myth of the Military Nation: Militarism, Gender, and Education in Turkey* (New York: Palgrave Macmillan, 2004), 17.
40 Halidé Adivar Edib, *Memoirs of Halidé Edib* (Piscataway, NJ: Gorgias Press, 2004), 22.
41 Ibid., 37.
42 Ibid., 23.
43 Ibid., 187.
44 Ibid., 287.
45 Melek Hamin, *Thirty Years in a Turkish Harem* (Piscataway, NJ: Gorgias Press, 2007), 37.

46 Ibid., 51.
47 "A Romance of Stamboul," *Levant Herald*, 22 January 1871: 954.
48 Thomas Thornton, *The Present State of Turkey*, 4.
49 J.C. Nott, "The Mulatto a Hybrid—Probable extermination of the two races if the Whites and Blacks are allowed to intermarry," *American Journal of the Medical Sciences* 6 (July 1843): 252–6. Reprinted in the *Boston Medical and Surgical Journal* 29 (16 August 1843): 29–32.
50 Robert Knox, *The Races of Man: A Philosophical Enquiry into the influence of Race over the Destinies of Nations*, 2nd ed. (London: Henry Renshaw, 1862).
51 Arthur de Gobineau, *The Inequality of Races*, trans. Adrian Collins (New York: G.P. Putnam's Sons, 1915).
52 Julia Pardoe, *The City of the Sultan; and Domestic Manners of the Turks* (London: Henry Colburn, 1837), 57.
53 Charles Macfarlane, *Constantinople in 1828.* (London: Saunders & Otley, 1829), 14–15.
54 Lucy Garnett, *Turkey of the Ottomans* (London: Isaac Pitman, 1911), 3.
55 Lucy Garnett, *The Women of Turkey and their Folklore* (London: David Nutt, 1891), 414.
56 Robert Young skillfully lays out this history in his book *Colonial Desire: Hybridity in Theory, Race and Culture* (London: Routledge, 1995).
57 J.C. Nott, *Two lectures, on the natural history of the Caucasian and Negro races* (Mobile, AL: Dade and Thompson, 1844), 14.
58 *The Near East*, 22 Jan. 1920: 115.
59 Ibid., 117.
60 *The Near East*, 5 Feb. 1920: 177.
61 See, for instance, Jill Didur's *Unsettling Partition: Literature, Gender, Memory* (Toronto: University of Toronto Press, 2006) for a discussion of the violence, in particular violence against women, that erupts with "the two-nation solution" in South Asia.
62 See for instance: Kwame Anthony Appiah, *Cosmopolitanism: Ethics in a World of Strangers* (New York: Norton, 2006); Gita Rajan and Shailja Sharma, eds., *New Cosmopolitanisms: South Asians in the US* (Stanford, CA: Stanford University Press, 2006); Timothy Brennan, *At Home in the World: Cosmopolitanism Now* (Cambridge: Harvard University Press, 1997). Peng Cheah and Bruce Robbins, eds., *Cosmopolitics: Thinking and Feeling Beyond the Nation* (Minneapolis: University of Minnesota, 1998). This list represents only a handful of the many recent works on cosmopolitanism.
63 Roxanne Euben has convincingly argued that an Islamic cosmopolitanism, which has structured various Muslim societies at different historical moments, offers "resources for the reworking of

contemporary culture," countering the "presentism," provincialism, and eurocentrism of some of the recent discussions of cosmopolitanism – both pro and anti – that make nationalism the focal point. See her *Journey to the Other Shore: Muslim and Western Travelers in Search of Knowledge* (Princeton and Oxford: Princeton University Press, 2006). I return to this argument in chapter 4.

64 Richard Burton, *Five Footsteps in East Africa; or, an An Exploration of Harar* (London: Longman, 1856), 26.

65 See Fatima Mernissi's *The Veil and the Male Elite: A Feminist Interpretation of Islam*, trans. Mary Jo Lakeland (New York: Addison-Wesley, 1991) and *Scheherazade Goes West: Different Cultures, Different Harems* (New York: Washington Square Press, 2001).

66 *Les mille et une nuits, tome premier* (1704), translated by Antoine Galland (Project Gutenberg, 2005), http://www.gutenberg.org/ebooks/15371, accessed 10 June 2012, 3.

67 *The Book of The Thousand Nights and a Night*, Volume 1 (1885), trans. Richard Burton (Project Gutenberg, 2003), http://www.gutenberg.org/ebooks/3435accessed 10 June 2012, 12.

68 Ibid.

69 Ibid., footnote #7.

70 Robert Irwin, *The Arabian Nights: A Companion* (London: Allen Lane, 1994), 24.

71 *The Thousand and One Nights, Vol. I.* (1840), trans. Edward William Lane (Project Gutenberg), http://www.gutenberg.org/files/34206/34206-h/34206-h.htm, accessed 10 June 2012, 27.

72 Bernard Lewis, *Race and Color in Islam* (New York: Harper Torchbooks, 1971), 4.

73 "*Hadjira. A Turkish Love Story*. By 'Adalet.' New York: Edward Arnold. $1.50," *The New York Times*, 17 May 1896: 27.

74 Lucy Garnett, *Women of Turkey*, 471.

75 "*Hadjira*," 27.

76 Adalet, "A Voice from a Harem: Some Words about the Turkish Woman of Our Day," *The Nineteenth Century*, Aug. 1890, 186.

77 Adalet, "Life in the Harem," *The Nineteenth Century*, Dec. 1890, 959.

78 Adalet, "A Voice from a Harem," Aug. 1890, 186.

79 Ibid., 190.

80 Adalet, "Life in the Harem," *The Nineteenth Century*," Dec. 1890: 965.

81 Adalet, *Hadjira* (London: Edward Arnold, 1896).

82 Ibid., 164.

83 Ibid., 170.

84 Ibid., 217.
85 Reina Lewis, "'Oriental' Femininity as Cultural Commodity: Authorship, Authority and Authenticity" in *Edges of Empire: Orientalism and Visual Culture*, eds. Jos Hackforth-Jones and Mary Roberts (London: Blackwell Publishing, 2005), 116.
86 Adalet, *Hadjira*, 95–6.

3 Two Western Women Venture East: Lady Annie Brassey and Anna Bowman Dodd

1 W.H. Davenport Adams, *Celebrated Women Travellers*.
2 For a discussion of Lady Brassey's photography, please see Nancy Micklewright, *A Victorian Traveler in the Middle East: The Photography and Travel Writing of Annie Lady Brassey* (Burlington VT: Ashgate, 2003).
3 Lady Annie Brassey, *Sunshine and Storm in the East, or Cruises to Cyprus and Constantinople* (Piscataway, NJ: Gorgias Press, 2005), 102.
4 Ibid., 387. See Ottaviano Bon and his 1625 account of the Ottoman Court, mentioned in chapter 1.
5 Ibid., 117.
6 Lord Thomas Brassey, Introduction to *Outlines of British Colonisation* by William Greswell (London: Percival and Co., 1893), iv.
7 Ibid., ix.
8 Ibid., 164.
9 Ibid., 301.
10 Ibid., 136.
11 Ibid., 159–60.
12 Ibid., 360.
13 Lady Annie Brassey, *A Voyage in the "Sunbeam": Our Home on the Ocean for Eleven Months* (London: Longmans, Green, and Co., 1880), 57.
14 Ibid., 59–60.
15 Lady Annie Brassey, *Sunshine and Storm*, 117–18; 72 (emphasis mine).
16 Ibid., 427.
17 Ibid., 169.
18 Ibid., 431.
19 Ibid., 438–9.
20 Ibid., 86–7.
21 Lord Brassey, Introduction, xi.
22 Ibid., xi.
23 Lady Annie Brassey, *Sunshine and Storm*, 87.
24 Ibid., 387.

25 Ibid., 57.
26 Lady Annie Brassey, *A Voyage in the "Sunbeam,"* 469.
27 See Homi Bhabha, *Location of Culture* (London: Routledge, 1995).
28 Benjamin Disraeli, *Tancred, or the New Crusade*, Vol. II (London: Henry Colburn, 1847), 181.
29 Ibid., 157.
30 Lady Annie Brassey, *Sunshine and Storm*, 377.
31 Although there are several references to Brassey taking photos in Istanbul and though she had a dark room on board the Sunbeam, most of the photos in this album are from the studios of photographers, such as Pascal Sabah. Nevertheless, the way Brassey chooses to represent Turkey and the photos she selects for the album suggest some of her preoccupations.
32 Ibid., 91.
33 Ibid., 375.
34 Ibid., 297.
35 Ibid., 385.
36 It is difficult to know whether the woman in the photo is Lady Brassey or not. Nancy Micklewright observes that this is such a common type of image that either scenario might be possible: people might have purchased a generic photo in the shop to remind them of their own experience or photographers onsite might have captured images of specific climbs, which people could then purchase in the shop.
37 Frantz Fanon, *Black Skin, White Masks* (New York: Grove, 1967), 86.
38 "Turkish Palaces." Review, *The New York Times* 5 Dec. 1903: BR47.
39 Anna Bowman Dodd, *In the Palaces of the Sultan* (Piscataway, NJ: Gorgias Press, 2005), 94.
40 Ibid., 4.
41 Billie Melman, *Women's Orients—English Women and the Middle East, 1718–1918: Sexuality, Religion, and Work* (Ann Arbor: University of Michigan Press, 1995), 101.
42 See for instance, Holly Edwards, *Noble Dreams, Wicked Pleasures: Orientalism in America, 1870–1930* (Princeton: Princeton University Press in association with the Sterling and Francine Clark Art Institute, 2000).
43 Ibid., 143.
44 Ibid., 191.
45 Anna Bowman Dodd, *In the Palaces*, 210.
46 Ibid., 255.
47 Ibid., 421.
48 Ibid., 448.

49 Ibid., 449.
50 Ibid., 431.
51 Ibid., 463.
52 Ibid., 63.
53 Selim Deringil writes humorously of Abdülhamid's penchant for bestowing these awards: "The fact that the decorations usually came with an award of money meant that they were solicited by some rather dubious characters. Such was the case of one Professor Adolf Strauss, who wrote to Yildiz claiming that his articles in the Hungarian Press had created such positive feeling towards the sultan that when they were read aloud in the Hungarian parliament the deputies spontaneously leapt to their feet shouting: 'eligien a sultan!' (long live the sultan). The good professor actually went on to recommend that several of his colleagues be awarded specific decorations." *The Well-Protected Domains: Ideology and the Legitimation of Power in the Ottoman Empire 1876–1909* (London: I.B. Taurus, 1998), 36.
54 Anna Bowman Dodd, *In the Palaces*, 50. This is the same sultan that Lady Brassey refers to as "cadaverous."
55 Edward Gibbon, *The Decline and Fall of the Roman Empire*, 653.
56 Carolyn Goffman, in her Introduction to Hester Donaldson Jenkins's *Behind Turkish Lattices: The Story of a Turkish Woman's Life* (Piscataway, NJ: Gorgias Press, 2004), xviii.
57 Anna Bowman Dodd, *In the Palaces*, 479.
58 Ibid., 490. More recently, Britain and America have condemned Islamist homegrown "revolutionaries," who have taken advantage of western institutions to spread propaganda and encourage violent attacks against western targets.
59 Anna Bowman Dodd, *In the Palaces*, 19.
60 William Eleroy Curtis, *The Turk and His Lost Provinces* (Chicago: Fleming Revell Co., 1903), 9.
61 Although America, in the late nineteenth and early twentieth centuries, following Britain's lead, was initially outraged by Muslims killing Christians, by the thirties the whole question of the Armenian massacres was gradually displaced by the more pragmatic interests of America's economic ties with Turkey.
62 Ibid., 476.
63 See for instance, Hülya Adak in her introduction to Halidé Edib's *The Turkish Ordeal*, where she discusses the souring of Edib's relationship with the nationalist party, The Committee of Union and Progress (CUP),

following the massacres; also see Edib's *Memoirs* (387) for a criticism of the 1915–16 massacres.

64 Anna Bowman Dodd, *In the Palaces*, 422.

65 Ibid., 6.

66 Ibid., 41 (emphasis mine).

67 The legacy of these policies and the fear of miscegenation are still active in America: "Interracial marriages are still relatively rare in the US, but the number is growing. In 1970, just three years after the US Supreme Court struck down laws across the country that prohibited interracial marriages, less than 2 percent of marriages in the United States were interracial. Today, that number is almost 6 percent." Katia Riddle, "Minnesota Girl, Sri Lankan Guy Still Turn Heads," *National Public Radio*, 11 July 2010.

68 Ibid., 169.

69 David Theo Goldberg, *The Racial State*, 189.

70 Anna Bowman Dodd, *In the Palaces*, 487.

71 Ibid., 428.

72 Ibid., 237.

73 Ibid., 492.

74 Albert Howe Lybyer, *The Government of the Ottoman Empire in the Time of Suleiman the Magnificent* (Cambridge: Harvard University Press, 1913), 4.

75 Ibid., 15.

76 Ibid.

4 The Great War and Its Aftermath: Militarized Citizens, (Un)Veiled Bodies, and the Nation

1 Naila Minai, *Women in Islam: Tradition and Transition in the Middle East* (New York: Seaview, 1981), 64–5.

2 Grace Ellison, *Turkey To-day* (London: Hutchinson, 1928), 8.

3 Ibid., 8.

4 Ibid., 23. See also Reina Lewis's article on Grace Ellison and Zeyneb Hanim, which begins with the same question and arrives at quite a different analysis. Focusing on photographic representations and the coding of women's dress in both oriental and occidental contexts, Lewis examines the implications of racialized identities as they relate to the cross-dressing that Ellison and Zeyneb participate in. Ellison is not above employing the tropes of the genre as a way of engaging her audience (in this quote, invoking both the conventions of the nineteenth-century picturesque travel narrative with "woman as

landscape" and the conventions of the eroticized oriental women with the "flirty" reference to veils as "becoming"), but this "hook" is often quickly subverted, I will suggest, by a more in-depth and serious discussion of the issues of modernization. Lewis also comments on the ways in which Ellison's work both promises and then refuses to fulfill the orientalist expectations of her audience as British and American travel writing of the period often indulges in a nostalgia for the "romance" of a "disappearing" Orient ("On Veiling," 507). Lewis includes in this camp Demetra Vaka Brown and her romanticization of veiling and polygamy: "In contrast to the pro-Westernism of many progressives, Vaka Brown's need to commodify the East as a recognizable Orient for her Western readers in conjunction with her own mainly conservative politics works against the recognition of the value of social and political change" ("Writing," 72). But my chapter will argue that Ellison's simultaneous favouring of the veil *and* modernization and Vaka's progressive understanding of cosmopolitanism suggest that the literary conventions, racial cross-dressing, and nostalgia that Lewis discusses also play themselves out in the bigger context of militarized nationalism.

5 Zeyneb Hanim, *A Turkish Woman's European Impressions* (Piscataway, NJ: Gorgias Press, 2005), xvi.

6 See for instance, Leila Ahmed (*Women and Gender*) on the assimilation of the veil into Islam and the centrality of debates about the veil in the struggles for political power in Egypt at the end of the nineteenth century. Also see Hamideh Sedghi's *Women and Politics in Iran: Veiling, Unveiling, Reveiling* (Cambridge: Cambridge University Press, 2007); Ahmed argues that by claiming women's bodies and unveiling and reveiling them, "states draw upon gender to define and redefine their domestic and global objectives" (279). See also Deniz Kandiyoti, who argues that the new woman of the Turkish Republic became one of the key symbols signalling the break with the Ottoman past in "End of Empire: Islam, Nationalism, and Women in Turkey," in *Women, Islam and the State*, ed. Deniz Kandiyoti (Philadelphia: Temple University Press, 1991). Also, Nilüfer Göle on Kemalism, secularism, and the changing dress codes in the Turkish Republic in *The Forbidden Modern*; Frantz Fanon's "Algeria Unveiled"; and Meyda Yegenoglu's work on nationalism, feminism, and veiling in Turkey and Algeria in chapter 5 of her *Colonial Fantasies Towards a Feminist Reading of Orientalism* (Cambridge, UK: Cambridge University Press, 1998), where she writes: "However, although the veiling and unveiling of women appear to

be reverse strategies of responding to Western hegemony they are both in fact conditioned by and therefore the products of Orientalist hegemony."

7 Nilüfer Göle, *The Forbidden Modern: Civilization and Veiling* (Ann Arbor: University of Michigan Press, 1999), 93.

8 Fatima Mernissi, *Islam and Democracy: Fear of the Modern World*, trans. Mary Jo Lakeland (Reading: Addison-Wesley, 1992), 127.

9 Carole Pateman, "The Fraternal and Social Contract," *Civil Society and the State: New European Perspectives*, ed. John Keane (London: Verso, 1988), 102.

10 See for instance, Elizabeth Thompson, "Public and Private in Middle Eastern Women's History," *Journal of Women's History* 15.1 (2003): 52–69.

11 Nancy Armstrong, *Desire and Domestic Fiction: A Political History of the Novel* (New York: Oxford University Press, 1987), 3–27.

12 See Alev Çınar, "Subversion and Subjugation in the Public Sphere: Secularism and the Islamic Headscarf," *Signs* 33. 4 (2008): 891–913.

13 Leslie Pierce, *The Imperial Harem: Women and Sovereignty in the Ottoman Empire* (Oxford: Oxford University Press, 1993), 6–9.

14 Fadwa El Guindi, *Veil: Modesty, Privacy, Resistance* (Oxford, New York: Berg Publishers, 1999), 81.

15 See also Cynthia Nelson's "Public and Private Politics: Women in the Middle Eastern World," *American Ethnologist* 1.3 (1974): 551–63, which considers the nuances of women's political and social capital in segregated societies.

16 See Nilüfer Göle, "Islamic Visibilities and Public Sphere," eds. Nilüfer Göle and Ammann Ludwig in *Islam in Public: Turkey, Iran and Europe* (İstanbul: İstanbul Bilgi University Press, 2006), 3–43. In her argument, Göle (and others in the collection) discusses the ways in which the rise of the visibility of Islam post-1980 challenges secular public life by introducing notions of interiority, boundaries, and privacy into these spaces.

17 Selma Ekrem in *Unveiled: The Autobiography of a Turkish Girl* (Piscataway, NJ: Gorgias Press, 2005), similarly imagined American women "as free as the wind"; in contrast, she sees herself "as shackled and bound" (270–1) and has a "horror of veils," a "black prison" that signalled resignation (178–80). Ekrem was born in 1902 and suffered through the First World War in Istanbul before moving to America.

18 Zeyneb Hanim, *A Turkish Woman's European Impressions*, 214.

19 Ibid., 157.

20 Elaine Showalter, *Sexual Anarchy: Gender and Culture at the Fin de Siècle* (New York: Viking, 1990), 144.

21 I borrow this term from Marcia Pointon's study on the female nude in the nineteenth century (*Naked Authority: The Body in Western Painting 1830–1906* [Cambridge: Cambridge University Press, 1990], 30). See also Peter Brooks's work; Brooks argues that whereas the male nude dominates Greek and Renaissance art, by the end of the nineteenth century "the female emerges as the very definition of the nude, and the censorship of the fully unclothed male body becomes nearly total" (*Body Work: Objects of Desire in Modern Narrative* [Cambridge: Harvard University Press, 1993], 16). Whereas in the modern nation, the male body is armoured, the female body is exposed.

22 Angela Carter, "A Well-Hung Hang Up," *Nothing Sacred* (London: New Virago, 1982), 103.

23 Oscar Wilde, *The Picture of Dorian Gray* (Harmondsworth: Penguin, 1971), 98.

24 Friedrich Nietzsche, *The Gay Science*, trans. Walter Kaufmann (New York: Random House, 1974), 317.

25 Friedrich Nietzsche, *Beyond Good and Evil: Prelude to a Philosophy of the Future*, trans. Walter Kaufmann (New York: Vintage, 1966), 163. This denial of women as differently sexed subjects prevails. Jacques Derrida, concurring with Nietzsche, writes: "Feminism is nothing but the operation of a woman who aspires to be like a man." *Spurs*, trans. Barbara Harlow (Chicago: University of Chicago Press), 64. Jean Baudrillard recounts the myth of Tiresias, who experiences sex as a woman and as a man and concludes that a woman's experience is nine times more pleasurable than a man's; for this response he is blinded by Hera. Baudrillard writes that Tiresias is blinded not for "betray[ing] the secret (?) of the feminine orgasm, for the latter does not exist: the multiplication by nine of feminine *jouissance* is only the ironic multiplication of the man's desire. It bears witness to the fact that the woman is only the ironic ecstasy of man's desire." *Fatal Strategies*, trans. Philip Beitchman and W.G.J. Niesluchowski (New York: Semiotext(e)/Pluto, 1990), 126–7.

26 Gayatri Spivak, "Displacement and the Discourse of Woman," *Displacement: Derrida and After* (Bloomington: Indiana University Press, 1983), 170.

27 Spivak argues in this essay that "male and female sexuality are asymmetrical" because, unlike "male orgasmic pleasure," which involves male reproduction as insemination, "the clitoris escapes reproductive framing"; thus any attempt to read male and female sexuality as symmetrical, which would include representations of the female solely as an object of male desire, participates in clitoral effacement. "French

Feminism," *In Other Worlds: Essays in Cultural Politics* (New York: Routledge, 1988), 151.

28 See Fatima Mernissi's argument about *fitna* as disrupting the *umma* in *Beyond the Veil.*

29 Leila Ahmed, *Gender in Islam: Historical Roots of a Modern Debate* (New Haven: Yale University Press, 1992), 180.

30 See for instance, Ahmed, who discusses the veiled women on campuses in Cairo; traditional dress is adopted with the belief that it will protect them from "vivid inequalities, consumerism and materialism, and foreign mores" that plague the West (*Gender in Islam*, 222). See also Nadiya Takolia, "The Hijab Has Liberated Me from Society's Expectations of Women," *The Guardian*, 28 May 2012. http://www.theguardian.com/commentisfree/2012/may/28/hijab-society-women-religious-political (accessed 30 June 2012). In this article, Takolia explains her reasons for adopting the veil as a political – about not being "a pawn in the beauty game" – rather than a religious statement. "It is me telling the world that my femininity is not available for public consumption," she writes. The rise of lad magazines in the 1990s, like *Maxime, Gear,* and *Stuff,* where the assertion of male identity depends on the collapsing of scantily clad women's bodies with the "gear" and "stuff" laid out for consumption, is one of the more notable trends of this objectification and commodification of women's bodies in the West. See also Reina Lewis's edited collection, *Modest Fashion: Styling Bodies, Mediating Faith* (London: I.B. Taurus, 2013).

31 Albert V. Dicey, *Letters to a Friend on Votes for Women* (London: John Murray, 1909), 7.

32 Ibid., 8.

33 Ibid., 91.

34 Ibid., 93.

35 Rossiter Johnson, *The Blank-Cartridge Ballot* (New York: n.d.), 11.

36 Ibid., 12.

37 Ibid., 13.

38 Ibid., 14.

39 Susan Buck-Morss, "Aesthetics and Anaesthetics: Walter Benjamin's Artwork Essay Reconsidered," *October* 62 (Fall 1992): 8.

40 Ibid.

41 Sigmund Freud, "Fetishism" (1927), *The Standard Edition of the Complete Psychological Works of Sigmund Freud*, ed. and trans. James Strachey et al., 24 vols. (London: Hogarth, 1953–74), 21:154.

42 Sigmund Freud, "Narcissism," *Standard Edition,* 14: 88.

43 Sigmund Freud, "Fetishism," 21:155.

44 J.K. Huysmans, *Against Nature*, trans. Robert Baldick (London: Penguin, 1959), 68 (emphasis mine).
45 Grace Ellison, *The Disadvantages of Being A Woman* (London, 1922), 70.
46 Ibid., 50.
47 Grace Ellison, *Turkey To-Day*, 75.
48 Ibid., 106.
49 Frances Power Cobbe, "Introduction," *The Woman Question in Europe*, ed. Theodore Stanton (New York: G.P. Putman's Sons, 1884), xvi.
50 Jenny White points to the Wealth Tax of 1942–44 which ruined the lives of many non-Muslims; the attacks against Greeks and other minorities, which had the backing of the Turkish State in 1955; and the pogrom against the Jews in Thrace in 1934 – as among the many examples of the ways in which the Republic violently asserted its national boundaries. Jenny White, *Muslim Nationalism and the New Turks* (Princeton: Princeton University Press, 2013), 107–8. Cosmopolitanism as a way of life, however, was not instantly eradicated despite the racialization of the Republic. Many Jews left for France after the Great War, but were rescued and welcomed back "as citizens" during the Second World War whereas Britain, America, and Canada were all turning them away from their shores. Behiç Erkin, the Turkish ambassador in Paris (when France was under Nazi occupation) and Necdet Kent, who served as Turkey's consul-general (1941–4), resisted the pressures of the Nazis and intervened, saving many Turkish Jews from the trains heading to the death camps in Germany. See, for instance, Arnold Reisman, *Shoah: Turkey, the US and the UK* (Charleston, SC: BookSurge Publishing, 2009).
51 Zeyneb Hanim, *A Turkish Woman's European Impressions*, 246.
52 Grace Ellison, *Turkey To-Day*, 120.
53 In *Turkey To-day*, Ellison comments, referring to herself: "For a cosmopolitan, war is tragedy" (142).
54 Ibid., 119.
55 Virginia Woolf, *Three Guineas*, ed. Jane Marcus (New York: Harcourt, Inc., 2006), 125.
56 Demetra Vaka Brown, *The Unveiled Ladies of Istanbul* (Piscataway, NJ: Gorgias Press, 2005), 10.
57 Reina Lewis, *Rethinking Orientalism*, 36.
58 Frederick Nietzsche, *The Gay Science*, 242.
59 E.M. Forster, *Passage to India* (London: Penguin, 1979), 289.
60 Edward Said, *Culture and Imperialism* (New York: Vintage, 1994), 205.
61 James Joyce, *Ulysses*, ed. Hans Walter Gabler (Harmondsworth: Penguin, 1986), 12:1419.

62 Demetra Vaka Brown, *The Unveiled Ladies*, v.
63 Ibid.
64 Ibid., 12.
65 Ibid.
66 Ibid., 260
67 Ibid.
68 Ibid.
69 Ibid., 21.
70 Timothy Brennan, "Cosmo-Theory," *The South Atlantic Quarterly* 100.3 (2001).
71 Martha Nussbaum et al., "Patriotism or Cosmopolitanism," *Boston Review* 19.5 (October–November 1994).
72 Kwame Anthony Appiah, *Cosmopolitanism: Ethics in a World of Strangers* (New York: W.W. Norton and Co., 2006).
73 Roxanne Euben, *Journey to the Other Shore: Muslim and Western Travelers in Search of Knowledge* (Princeton and Oxford: Princeton University Press, 2006).

5 The Burqa and the Bikini: Veiling and Unveiling at the Turn of the Twenty-first Century

1 Riverbend, "Summer of Goodbyes," 5 August 2006, http://riverbendblog.blogspot.ca.
2 *Independent*, 20 November 2001.
3 Laura Bush, "George W. Bush: Radio Address by Mrs. Bush," The American Presidency Project, 17 November 2001, http://www.presidency.ucsb.edu/ws/?pid=24992, accessed 15 April 2011.
4 See for instance, Ellen McLarney, "The Burqa in Vogue: Fashioning Afghanistan," *Journal of Middle East Women's Studies* 5.1 (Winter 2009): 1–20.
5 Nelofer Pazira, *A Bed of Red Flowers: In Search of My Afghanistan* (New York: Random House, 2005), 311.
6 Leila Ahmed, *Women and Gender in Islam: Historical Roots of a Modern Debate* (New Haven: Yale University Press, 1992), 152.
7 Frantz Fanon, *A Dying Colonialism*, trans. Haakon Chevaliar (New York: Grove Press, 1965), 57–8.
8 http://nazra.org/en/2013/02/position-paper-sexual-violence-against-women-and-increasing-frequency-gang-rape-tahrir.
9 Mark McDonald, "A War of Words in Afghanistan," *The Seattle Times*, 13 September 2004.

10 Nicholas D. Kristof, "Afghan Women, Still in Chains," *The New York Times*, 14 February 2004.
11 Laura Bush, "Radio Address by Mrs. Bush."
12 "Playboy Centerfolds become Pen-Pets," *Associated Press*, 23 November 2001.
13 Elizabeth Warnock Fernea, *In Search of Islamic Feminism: One Woman's Global Journey* (New York: Doubleday, 1997).
14 Riverbend, *Baghdad Burning: Girl Blog from Iraq II* (New York: The Feminist Press at CUNY, 2006), 17.
15 Margaret Wente, "Women at War: Should We Think Again?" *The Globe and Mail*, 29 March 2003: A2.
16 Jodi Wilgoren, "Women in Combat," *The New York Times*, Saturday, 29 March 2003.
17 See Kate O'Beirne, qtd in "Women in Combat."
18 Patrick Martin, "US Air Force Academy Chiefs Removed Over Rape Scandal," 29 March 2003, http://www.wsws.org/en/articles/2003/03/acad_m29.html, accessed 27 Oct. 2015.
19 David H. Hackworth, "Other Priorities," *DefenseWatch*, SFTT.org, 20 September 2004, http://www.sftt.org/cgi-bin/csNews/csNews.cgi?database=Hacks%20Target%20Homepage.db&command=viewone&op=t&id=84&rnd=399.25183065658893. See also Lisa Broadbent, "Rape in the US Military: America's Dirty Little Secret," *The Guardian*, 9 December 2011.
20 See http://www.cnn.com/2013/06/16/us/military-recruitment.
21 Riverbend, "Atrocities," 11 July 2006, http://riverbendblog.blogspot.ca.
22 See, for instance, Susan J. Briston's article on the similarities between American porn sites that featured Iraqi women and the photos from Abu Ghraib: http://mediagovernance.univie.ac.at/fileadmin/user_upload/p_mediagovernance_industriesresearchgroup/Ressourcen/Good_Old_American_Pornography.pdf.
23 Rick Bragg, *I am a Soldier Too: The Jessica Lynch Story* (New York: Knopf, 2003).
24 Paul Colford and Corky Siemaszko, "Fiends Raped Jessica," *Daily News*, 6 November 2003, and "Jessica's Rape Horror," *Western Daily Press*, 7 November 2003. See also Susan Faludi for a more extensive account of the manufacturing of Jessica Lynch: *The Terror Dream: Myth and Misogyny in an Insecure America* (New York: Metropolitan Books, 2007).
25 George Rush and Bill Hutchinson, "Smut Czar Nixes Nudes of Jessica," *The Daily News*, 12 November 2003.
26 "Playboy Launches 'Operation Playmate,'" *Agence France-Presse*, 21 September 2004.

27 Colin Freeze, "PoWs Fought Despair, US Army Cook Says," *The Globe and Mail*, 15 April 2003: A8.

28 Ian Fisher, "Iraqi Recounts Hours of Abuse by US Troops, *The New York Times*, 5 May 2004.

29 Compare George Bush's response to 9/11 with the prime minister of Norway Jens Stoltenberg's response to the 2011 massacre of Norwegians carried out by Anders Behring Breivik. Breivik, inspired by al-Qaeda's tactics, attacked "Muslims" and "multiculturalism," killing 77 people. Whereas the US president announced that America was "open for business" and advised Americans to "get down to Disney World in Florida" and "enjoy life" in the wake of the devastating loss of life after the collapse of the Towers, as if entertainment and consumption were the end goals of a democratic society, the prime minister of Norway announced that in the face of intolerance, Norway would be more tolerant, more open, more democratic. Bush's government met intolerance with intolerance, promoted a culture of fear, stripped Americans of basic rights, encouraged spending and debt, engaged in a "war on terror" that further bankrupted America, and bombed civilian populations in the name of freedom.

30 Malalai Joya, *A Woman Among Warlords* (New York: Scribner, 2009), 209.

31 Riverbend, "The Promise and the Threat," 28 August 2003.

32 Joya, *A Woman Among Warlords*, 214.

33 The rise of ISIS and the disaster of contemporary Iraq, which has been destroyed by the sectarian violence that has long been fuelled by American and British oil interests in the Middle East, has been well documented by Nafeez Ahmed in his "Iraq Blowback: Isis Rise Manufactured by Insatiable Oil Addiction," *The Guardian*, 16 June 2014.

34 Riverbend, "The Great Wall of Segregation," 26 April 2007.

35 Riverbend, "We've Only Just Begun," 23 August 2003.

36 Joya, *A Woman Among Warlords*, 128.

37 Ra Ravishankar, "Afghanistan: The Liberation that Isn't. An Interview with 'Miriam' from RAWA," *CounterPunch*. 2 March 2004, http://www.rawa.org/punch.htm, accessed 12 July 2011.

38 Sam Jones, "US Military's History of Backtracking on Initial Reports," *The Guardian*, 4 May 2011.

39 See Albert Hourani, "The Vanishing Veil: A Challenge to the Old Order," *UNESCO Courier*, January 1956: 35–7. Also see Leila Ahmed and her discussion of Hourani in *A Quiet Revolution: The Veil's Resurgence, from the Middle East to America* (New Haven: Yale University Press, 2011): 43–5.

40 For instance, textual and artistic references suggest it was likely that elite women covered their face and hair in ancient Greece. For more on veiling practices in ancient Greece, see Lloyd Llewellyn-Jones, *Aphrodite's Tortoise: The Veiled Woman of Ancient Greece.* (Swansea: The Classical Press of Wales, 2003).

41 Leila Ahmed, *A Quiet Revolution* (New Haven: Yale University Press, 2011), 203.

42 Ibid., 210.

43 Ibid., 235.

44 Joan Wallach Scott, *The Politics of the Veil* (Princeton: Princeton University Press, 2007), 93.

45 For many feminists, veiling in Quebec is also reminiscent of the oppressive legacy of the Catholic Church, which is one of the reasons the issue of headscarves and veiling has been much more explosive in Quebec than the rest of Canada. Women in Quebec were the last in Canada to gain the right to vote, which did not happen til 1940 (women in Manitoba were the first, winning the right to vote in 1916).

46 Joan Wallach Scott, *Politics of the Veil*, 93.

47 Jean-François Lyotard, *The Differend: Phrases in Dispute*, trans. Georges Van Den Abbeele (Minneapolis: University of Minnesota Press, 1988), 147.

48 Ibid.

49 Judith Butler considers the "secular" French state's discrimination against same-sex relationships and enforcement of heterosexuality on the grounds that it is "natural" and its race discrimination against Muslims based on their "unnatural" and "problematic" family structures as analogous "to the papal arguments that condemn gay parenting and Islamic practice." *Frames of War: When Is Life Grievable*? (London: Verso, 2010), 116.

50 Nilüfer Göle, *Islam and Europe: the Lure of Fundamentalism and the Allure of Cosmopolitanism*, trans. Steven Rendall (Princeton, NJ: Markus Wiener Publishers, 2011), 61.

51 Ibid., 85.

52 For more on the veil in Europe, see *Politics, Religion and Gender: Framing and Regulating the Veil*, eds. Sieglinde Rosenberger and Birgit Sauer, (London: Routledge, 2012). The essays in this edited collection consider the national, cultural, political, and religious systems that frame the debates about and policies around veiling in a broad selection of countries, including Germany, United Kingdom, Denmark, Austria, Netherlands, France, Turkey, and Bulgaria. These essays compare the different levels of accommodation and regulation of Muslim women's

dress in each country in the context of its liberal principles, moral values, and commitment to universal rights.

53 Ibid., 148.

54 Judith Butler, *Frames of War*, 147.

Epilogue: The Spectres of Orientalism

1 Istanbul has faced rapid gentrification under Recep Tayyip Erdoğan's government. Minorities and the poor have been evicted as areas of the city have been bulldozed to make way for luxury hotels and shopping malls; harsh laws, top-down aggression, and police force have been used to silence any dissent.

2 From Occupy to the Arab Spring to anti-G8 demonstrations, people around the globe have shared many of the same concerns.

3 See the report from Amnesty International, https://www.amnestyusa.org/sites/default/files/eur440222013en.pdf, and also the lawsuit that has been launched on behalf of the dead animals, "Activists Sue Turkey Over Animal Deaths During Gezi Protests," *Hürriyet* (20 November 2013).

4 Fiachra Gibbons, "Turkish Delight in Epic Film *Fetih 1453*," *The Guardian* (12 March 2012).

5 Despite the concern in many cultures for the intactness of the hymen as a guarantee of paternity and bloodline, early Islam did not put any emphasis on marrying virgins. Only one of Muhammad's wives was a virgin; the rest were widows and divorcées many years older than he (his first wife, Khadija bint Khuwaylid, was forty and he was twenty-five when they married; they had a monogamous marriage til her death at sixty-five).

6 Elif Batuman, "Letter from Istanbul: Ottomania," *The New Yorker* (17 & 24 February 2014). Batuman lays out the complexities of the series and the production, including interviews with the directors and the Ottoman historian Leslie Peirce, against the backdrop of the history and politics of Turkey.

7 Also see the discussion in chapter 1 of eastern representations of the harem: "Rayhana, Daughter of Ka'b ibn Malik, Neglected by her Husband" (1594–95) and "Women Reading," from the Mughal Empire in India (c.1600).

8 Jenny White has suggested that "the image of scantily-clad women cavorting with these men and having power, even if it's in this limited sphere, is just too much for them (AKP)" and that their view is that women "shouldn't be in [the] public space whatsoever because they

should be at home having children." See Alexander Christie-Miller, "Turkey: Television Drama Generates Official Angst," *EurasiaNet.org*, 11 January 2013.

9 See Nilüfer Göle's "Islamic Visibilities and Public Sphere," *Islam in Public: Turkey, Iran, and Europe* (Istanbul: Istanbul Biligi University Press, 2006, 3–43). In this essay, Göle discusses the ways in which the public visibility of Islam – from headscarves to Islamic resorts to mass media – challenges the modern secular definitions of the public sphere. However, I would argue that the rise in Islamic branding and markets is also continuous with the rise of neoliberalism.

10 See Tayfun Atay's "The Clash of 'Nations' in Turkey: Reflections on the Gezi Park Incident," *Insight Turkey* 15.3 (2013): 39–44, and Yeşim Arat's "Violence, Resistance, and Gezi Park," *International Journal of Middle East Studies* 45 (2013): 807–9 for more on these demonstrations and the diversity of the crowd. Atay notes the attempts of youth to create a safe zone from the attacks of the police force for Muslims wanting to pray and Arat comments on the crowd's resistance to the simplistic orientalism / occidentalism narrative.

Bibliography

"A Romance of Stamboul." *Levant Herald*, 22 January 1871: 954.

Adak, Hülya. Introduction to Halidé Edib's *The Turkish Ordeal*. London: John Murray, 1928. http://culturesindialogue.com/main/images/the-turkish-ordeal-with-intro.pdf.

Adalet. *Hadjira*. London: Edward Arnold, 1896.

– "Life in the Harem." *The Nineteenth Century* 28: 959–66, December 1890.

– "A Voice from a Harem: Some Words About the Turkish Woman of our Day." *Nineteenth Century* 28: 186–90, August 1890.

Adams, W.H. Davenport. *Celebrated Women Travellers of the Nineteenth Century*. London: W.S. Sonnenschein & Co., 1883.

Ahmed, Leila. *A Quiet Revolution: The Veil's Resurgence, from the Middle East to America*. New Haven: Yale University Press, 2011.

– *Women and Gender in Islam: Historical Roots of a Modern Debate*. New Haven: Yale University Press, 1992.

Ahmed, Nafeez. "Iraq Blowback: Isis Rise Manufactured by Insatiable Oil Addiction." *The Guardian*, 16 June 2014.

Aksan, Virginia and Daniel Goffman. "Introduction: Situating the Early Modern Ottoman World." In *The Early Modern Ottomans: Remapping the Empire*, edited by Virginia Aksan and Daniel Goffman. Cambridge: Cambridge University Press, 2007.

Alvi, Anjum. "Concealment and Revealment: The Muslim Veil in Context." *Current Anthropology* 54. 2 (2013): 177–99.

Altinay, Ayse Gül. *The Myth of the Military-Nation: Militarism, Gender, and Education in Turkey*. New York: Palgrave Macmillan, 2004.

Amin, Hussein Ahmad. "The Present State of the Muslim Umma." *Muslim World* 79 (1989): 222.

Anderson, Benedict. *Imagined Communities: Reflections of the Origin and Spread of Nationalism*. London: Verso, 1983.

Andrea, Bernadette. "Pamphilia's Cabinet: Gendered Authorship and Empire in Lady Mary Wroth's 'Urania.'" *ELH* 68.2 (2001): 335–58.

– *Women and Islam in Early Modern Literature*. Cambridge: Cambridge University Press, 2007.

Anonymous. *The Book of the Thousand Nights and a Night*. Vol. 1. Translated by Richard Burton. 1885. Project Gutenberg, 2003. http://www.gutenberg.org/ebooks/3435.

– *Les mille et une nuits, tome premier*. Translated by Antoine Galland. 1704. Project Gutenberg, 2005. http://www.gutenberg.org/ebooks/15371.

– *The Thousand and One Nights*. Vol. I. Translated by Edward William Lane. 1840. Project Gutenberg, 2010. http://www.gutenberg.org/files/34206/34206-h/34206-h.htm.

Appiah, Kwame Anthony. *Cosmopolitanism: Ethics in a World of Strangers*. New York: Norton, 2006.

Arat, Yeşim "Violence, Resistance, and Gezi Park." *International Journal of Middle East Studies* 45 (2013): 807–9.

Aravamudan, Srinivas. "Lady Mary Wortley Lady Mary in the Hammam: Masquerade, Womanliness, and Levantinization." *ELH* 62.1 (95): 69–104.

Argyll, George Douglas Campbell. *Our Responsibilities for Turkey: Facts and Memories of Forty Years*. London: John Murray, 1896.

Armstrong, Nancy. *Desire and Domestic Fiction: A Political History of the Novel*. New York: Oxford University Press, 1987.

Atay, Tayfun. "The Clash of 'Nations' in Turkey: Reflections on the Gezi Park Incident," *Insight Turkey* 15.3 (2013): 39–44.

Badran, Margot. "Competing Agenda: Feminists, Islam and the State in Nineteenth- and Twentieth-Century Egypt." In *Women, Islam and the State*, edited by Deniz Kandiyoti, 201–36. Philadelphia: Temple University Press, 1991.

Batuman, Elif. "Letter from Istanbul: Ottomania." *The New Yorker*, 17 February 2014.

Baudrillard, Jean. *Fatal Strategies*. Translated by Philip Beitchman and W.G.J. Niesluchowski. New York: Semiotext(e)/Pluto, 1990.

Bhabha, Homi. *Location of Culture*. London: Routledge, 1995.

Bon, Ottaviano. *The Sultan's Seraglio: An Intimate Portrait of Life at the Ottoman Court: (from the seventeenth-century edition of John Withers)*. London: Saqi Books, 1996.

Bragg, Rick. *I Am a Soldier Too: The Jessica Lynch Story*. New York: Knopf, 2003.

Brassey, Lady Annie. *Sunshine and Storm in the East, or Cruises to Cyprus and Constantinople.* Piscataway, NJ: Gorgias Press, 2005.

– *A Voyage in the "Sunbeam": Our Home on the Ocean for Eleven Months.* London: Longmans, Green, and Co., 1880.

Brassey, Lord Thomas. Introduction to *Outlines of British Colonisation* by William Greswell, V–XI. London: Percival and Co., 1893.

Brennan, Timothy. *At Home in the World: Cosmopolitanism Now.* Cambridge: Harvard University Press, 1997.

– "Cosmo-Theory," *The South Atlantic Quarterly* 100.3: 2001.

Broadbent, Lisa. "Rape in the US Military: America's Dirty Little Secret." *The Guardian*, 9 December 2011.

Brooks, Peter. *Body Works: Objects of Desire in Modern Narrative.* Cambridge: Harvard University Press, 1993.

Broughton, John Cam Hobhouse, Baron. *A Journey Through Albania and Other Provinces of Turkey in Europe and Asia, to Constantinople, During the Years 1809 and 1810.* London: 1813.

Brummet, Palmira. "Imagining the Early Modern Ottoman Space from Piri Reis to World History." In *The Early Modern Ottomans: Remapping the Empire*, edited by Virginia Aksan and Daniel Goffman, 15–58. Cambridge: Cambridge University Press, 2007.

Buck-Morss, Susan. "Aesthetics and Anaesthetics: Walter Benjamin's Artwork Essay Reconsidered." *October* 62 Fall: 1992.

Burton, Richard. Trans. *The Book of The Thousand Nights and a Night*, Volume one (1885): 12. Project Gutenberg, 2003. Accessed 2 September 2015. http://www.gutenberg.org/ebooks/3435.

– *Five Footsteps in East Africa; or, An Exploration of Harar.* London: Longman, Brown, Green, and Longmans, 1856.

Bush, Laura. "George W. Bush: Radio Address by Mrs. Bush." *The American Presidency Project.* 17 November 2001. Accessed 15 April 2011. http://www.presidency.ucsb.edu/ws/?pid=24992.

Butler, Judith. *Frames of War: When is Life Grievable*? London: Verso, 2010.

Carter, Angela. "A Well-Hung Hang Up." *Nothing Sacred.* London: New Virago, 1982.

Cervantes, Miguel de. *Don Quixote.* Translated by J.M. Cohen. London: Penguin Books, 1950.

Chandler, Richard. *Travels in Asia Minor: or, an Account of a tour made at the expense of the Society of Dilettanti.* Oxford: Clarendon Press, 1775.

Cheah, Peng, and Bruce Robbins, eds. *Cosmopolitics: Thinking and Feeling Beyond the Nation.* Minneapolis: University of Minnesota, 1998.

Christie-Miller, Alexander. "Turkey: Television Drama Generates Official Angst," *EurasiaNet.org*, 11 January 2013.

Çinar, Alev. "Subversion and Subjugation in the Public Sphere: Secularism and the Islamic Headscarf." *Signs* 33. 4 (2008): 891–913.

Cobbe, Frances Power. "Introduction." *The Woman Question in Europe*. Edited by Theodore Stanton. New York: G.P. Putnam's Sons, 1884.

Colford, Paul, and Corky Siemaszko. "Fiends Raped Jessica." *Daily News*. 6 November 2003.

– "Jessica's Rape Horror." *Western Daily Press*. 7 November 2003.

Craven, Lady Elizabeth. *A Journey Through the Crimea to Constantinople*. London: Printed by A.J. Valpy, 1814.

"Crete and the Eastern Question." *The Levant Herald*, 25 February 1867.

Curling, Jonathan. *Edward Wortley Montagu 1713–1776: The Man in the Iron Wig*. London: Andrew Melrose, 1954.

Curtis, William Eleroy. *The Turk and his Lost Provinces*. Chicago: Fleming Revell Co., 1903.

Dallam, Thomas, James Theodore Bent, and John Covel. *Early Voyages and Travels in the Levant*. New York: Burt Franklin, n.d.

Dallaway, James. *Memoir, The Works of the Right Hon. Lady Mary Wortley Montagu*. Edited by James Dallaway. 5 vols. London: R. Phillips, 1803.

Darling, Linda T. "Ottoman Politics Through British Eyes: Paul Rycaut's "The Present State of the Ottoman Empire." *Journal of World History* 5. 1 (1994): 71–97.

Deringil, Selim. *The Well-Protected Domains: Ideology and the Legitimation of Power in the Ottoman Empire 1876–1909*. London: I.B. Taurus, 1998.

Desai, Anita. *The Turkish Embassy Letters*, by Lady Mary Wortley Montagu. Annotated and edited by Malcolm Jack. London: Virago Press, 1994.

Dicey, Albert V. *Letters to a Friend on Votes for Women*. London: John Murray, 1909.

Didur, Jill. *Unsettling Partition: Literature, Gender, Memory*. Toronto: University of Toronto Press, 2006.

Disraeli, Benjamin. *Tancred, or the New Crusade*. Vol. 2. London: Henry Colburn, 1847.

Dodd, Anna Bowman. *In the Palaces of the Sultan*. Piscataway, NJ: Gorgias Press, 2005.

Dumont, Jean. *A New Voyage to the Levant: containing an account of the most remarkable curiosities in Germany, France, Italy ... and Turkey. ... Done into English and adorn'd with figures. The second edition*. London, 1696.

Düzkan, Ayşe. *Feminism in Turkey in the 1980's: An Interview with Ayşe Düzkan by Meltem Ahiska*. Grabels, France: Women Living Under Muslim Law, 1994.

Edib, Halidé Adivar. *Memoirs of Halidé Edib*. Piscataway, NJ: Gorgias Press, 2004.
– *The Turkish Ordeal*. London: John Murray, 1928.
Edwards, Holly. *Noble Dreams, Wicked Pleasures: Orientalism in America, 1870–1930*. Princeton: Princeton University Press in association with the Sterling and Francine Clark Art Institute, 2000.
Ekrem, Selma. Unveiled: The Autobiography of a Turkish Girl. Piscataway, NJ: Gorgias Press, 2005.
Eliot, Charles. *Turkey in Europe*. London: Edward Arnold, 1900.
Elliot, Frances. *Diary of an Idle Woman in Constantinople*. London: John Murray, 1893.
Ellison, Grace. *The Disadvantages of Being a Woman*. London, 1922.
– *Turkey To-day*. London: Hutchinson, 1928.
Eton, William. *A Survey of the Turkish Empire*. London: T. Cadell and W. Davies, 1798.
Euben, Roxanne. *Journey to the Other Shore: Muslim and Western Travelers in Search of Knowledge*. Princeton and Oxford: Princeton University Press, 2006.
Faludi, Susan. *The Terror Dream: Myth and Misogyny in an Insecure America*. Metropolitan Books, 2007.
Fanon, Frantz. *Black Skin, White Masks*. New York: Grove Press, 1967.
– *A Dying Colonialism*. Translated by Haakon Chevaliar. New York: Grove Press, 1965.
– "Foreign Affairs." *The Levant Herald and Daily Express*, 5 August 1890.
Fisher, Ian. "Iraqi Recounts Hours of Abuse by US Troops," *New York Times*, 5 May 2004.
Forster, E.M. *Passage to India*. London: Penguin, 1979.
Freeze, Colin. "PoWs Fought Despair, US Army Cook Says." *The Globe and Mail*, 15 April 2003: A8.
Freud, Sigmund. "Fetishism" (1927). *The Standard Edition of the Complete Psychological Works of Sigmund Freud*. Edited and translated by James Strachey et al. 24 vols. London: Hogarth, 1953–74.
– "Narcissism." *Standard Edition*. London: Hogarth, 1953–74.
Galland, Antoine, trans. *Les mille et une nuits, tome premier* (1704): 3. Project Gutenberg, 2005. Accessed 2 September 2015. http://www.gutenberg.org/ebooks/15371.
Garcia, Humberto. *Islam and the English Enlightenment, 1670–1840*. Baltimore: Johns Hopkins University Press, 2012.
Garnett, Lucy. *Turkey of the Ottomans*. London: Isaac Pitman, 1911.
– *The Women of Turkey and their Folklore*. London: David Nutt, 1891.

Gesink, Indira Falk. "'Chaos on the Earth': Subjective Truths versus Communal Unity in Islamic Law and the Rise of Militant Islam." *The American Historical Review* 108.3 (2003): 710–33.

Gibbon, Edward. *The History of the Decline and Fall of the Roman Empire.* Vol. 3. Edited by David Womersley. London: Allen Lane, Penguin Press, 1994.

– *The Private Letters of Edward Gibbon.* Edited by Rowland E. Prothero. 2 Vols. London: John Murray, 1896.

Gibbons, Fiachra. "Turkish Delight in Epic Film *Fetih 1453.*" *The Guardian,* 12 March 2012.

Gobineau, Arthur de. *The Inequality of Races.* Translated by Adrian Collins. New York: G.P. Putnam's Sons, 1915.

Goffman, Carolyn. Introduction to *Behind Turkish Lattices: The Story of a Turkish Woman's Life* by Hester Donaldson Jenkins. Piscataway, NJ: Gorgias Press, 2004.

Goffman, Daniel. *Britons in the Ottoman Empire, 1642–1660.* Washington: University of Washington, 1998.

Goldberg, David Theo. *The Racial State.* Oxford: Blackwell, 2002.

Göle, Nilüfer. *The Forbidden Modern: Civilization and Veiling.* Ann Arbor: The University of Michigan, 1999.

– *Islam and Europe: The Lure of Fundamentalism and the Allure of Cosmopolitanism.* Translated by Steven Rendall. Princeton, NJ: Markus Wiener Publishers, 2011.

Göle, Nilüfer, and Ludwig Ammann. *Islam in Public: Turkey, Iran and Europe.* Istanbul: Istanbul Bilgi University Press, 2006.

Greswell, William. *Outlines of British Colonization.* London: Percival and Co., 1893.

Guindi, Fadwa El. *Veil: Modesty, Privacy, Resistance.* New York: Berg Publishers, 1999.

Habesci, Elias. *The present state of the Ottoman Empire. Containing a more accurate ... account of the religion, government, customs, and amusements of the Turks than any yet extant.* London, 1784.

Hackworth, David H. "Other Priorities." *Defense Watch,* SFTT.org, 20 September 2004. http://www.sftt.org/cgi-bin/csNews/csNews.cgi?database=Hacks%20Target%20Homepage.db&command=viewone&op=t&id=84&rnd=399.25183065658893.

"*Hadjira. A Turkish Love Story.* By 'Adalet.' New York: Edward Arnold. $1.50." *The New York Times,* 17 May 1896: 27.

Hallaq, Wael. *The Origins and Evolution of Islamic Law.* Cambridge: Cambridge University Press, 2005.

Halsband, Robert, ed. *The Complete Letters of Lady Mary Wortley Lady Mary*. 3 vols. Oxford: Clarendon Press, 1965–7.

Hanim, Melek. *Thirty Years in a Turkish Harem*. Piscataway, NJ: Gorgias Press, 2007.

Hanim, Zeyneb. *A Turkish Woman's European Impressions*, xiv. Piscataway, NJ: Gorgias Press, 2005.

Hardt, Michael, and Antonio Negri. *Empire*. Cambridge: Harvard University Press, 2000.

Heath, Jennifer. *The Veil: Women Writers on Its History, Lore, and Politics*. Berkeley: University of California Press, 2008.

Herrnstein-Smith, Barbara. *Contingencies of Value: Alternative Perspectives for Critical Theory*. Cambridge: Harvard University Press, 1988.

Hill, Aaron. *A full and just account of the present state of the Ottoman Empire in all its branches ... faithfully related from a serious observation taken in many years travels thro' those countries*. London, 1709.

Hourani, Albert. "The Vanishing Veil: A Challenge to the Old Order." *UNESCO Courier*, January 1956: 35–7.

Hume, David. *Four Dissertations and Essays on Suicide and the Immortality of the Soul*. Bristol, UK: Thoemmes Press, 1992.

– "Of the Standard of Taste." In *Essays, Moral, Political and Literary*. Oxford: Oxford University Press, 1963.

Hunter, William. *Travels through France, Turkey, and Hungary, to Vienna, in 1792. To which are added, several tours in Hungary, in 1799 and 1800 ...* 3rd ed. London, 1803.

Huysmans, J.K. *Against Nature*. Translated by Robert Baldick. London: Penguin, 1959.

Irwin, Robert. *The Arabian Nights: A Companion*. London: Allen Lane, 1994.

Johnson, Rossiter. *The Blank-Cartridge Ballot*. New York: n.d.

Jones, Sam. "US Military's History of Backtracking on Initial Reports." *The Guardian* 4 May 2011.

Joya, Malalai. *A Woman Among Warlords*. New York: Scribner, 2009.

Joyce, James. *Ulysses*. Edited by Hans Walter Gabler. Harmondsworth: Penguin, 1986.

Kahf, Mohja. *Western Representations of the Muslim Woman: From Termagant to Odalisque*. Austin: University of Texas Press, 1999.

Kaiwar, Vasant, and Sucheta Mazumdar. "Race, Orient, Nation in the Time-Space of Modernity." In *Antinomies of Modernity: Essays on Race, Orient, Nation*, edited by Vasant Kaiwar and Sucheta Mazumdar. Durham and London: Duke University Press, 2003.

Kamali, Mohammad Hashim. *Freedom, Equality and Justice in Islam*. Cambridge, UK: Islamic Texts Society, 2002.

Kandiyoti, Deniz. "End of Empire: Islam, Nationalism, and Women in Turkey." In *Women, Islam and the State,* edited by Deniz Kandiyoti. Philadelphia: Temple University Press, 1991.

Kedourie, Elie. *England and the Middle East. The Destruction of the Ottoman Empire, 1914–1921*. London: Bowes & Bowes, 1956.

Kinglake, Alexander William. *Eothen*. Evanston: The Marlboro Press, 1996.

Kinneir, John Macdonald. *Journey through Asia Minor, Armenia, and Koordistan in the years 1813 and 1814. With remarks on the Marches of Alexander, and Retreat of the Ten Thousand*. London, 1818.

Knox, Robert. *The Races of Man: A Philosophical Enquiry into the influence of Race over the Destinies of Nations.* 2nd ed. London: Henry Renshaw, 1862.

Koundoura, Maria. "Snapshots from Abroad: A Conference on American and British Travel Writers and Writing." Presented at the University of Minnesota, November 1997.

Kristof, Nicholas D. "Afghan Women, Still in Chains." *The New York Times*, 14 February 2004.

Lane-Poole, Stanley. *The People of Turkey / Stanley Lane Poole.* Vol. 1. London: John Murray, 1878.

– *Turkey*. London: T. Fisher Unwin, 1888.

Lewis, Bernard. *Race and Color in Islam.* New York: Harper Torchbooks, 1971.

Lewis, Reina. ed. *Modest Fashion: Styling Bodies, Mediating Faith*. London: I.B. Tauris, 2013.

– '"Oriental' Femininity as Cultural Commodity: Authorship, Authority and Authenticity." In *Edges of Empire: Orientalism and Visual Culture,* edited by Jos Hackforth-Jones and Mary Roberts. London: Blackwells, 2005.

– *Rethinking Orientalism: Women, Travel and the Ottoman Harem*. London: I.B. Tauris, 2004.

Llewellyn-Jones, Lloyd. *Aphrodite's Tortoise: The Veiled Woman of Ancient Greece.* Swansea: The Classical Press of Wales, 2003.

Locke, John. *An Essay Concerning Human Understanding,* Edited by Peter H. Nidditch. Oxford: Clarendon Press, 1979.

– *Reasonableness of Christianity: As Delivered in the Scriptures*. Edited by George W. Ewing. Washington: Regenery Gateway, 1965.

– *Second Treatise of Government*. Edited by C.B. Macpherson. Indianapolis: Hackett Publishing, 1980.

Lowe, Lisa. *Critical Terrains: French and British Orientalisms.* Ithaca: Cornell University Press, 1991.

Lowenthal, Cynthia. *Lady Mary Wortley Montagu and the Eighteenth-Century Familiar Letter*. London: The University of Georgia Press, 1994.

Lyber, Albert Howe. *The Government of the Ottoman Empire in the time of Suleiman the Magnificent*. Cambridge: Harvard University Press, 1913.

Lyotard, Jean-François. *The Differend: Phrases in Dispute*. Translated by Georges Van Den Abbeele. Minneapolis: University of Minnesota Press, 1988.

Macfarlane, Charles. *Constantinople in 1829. A residence of sixteen months in the Turkish Capital and Provinces, with an account of the present state of the naval and military power, and of the resources of the Ottoman Empire.* London: Saunders & Otley, 1829.

Martin, Patrick. "US Air Force Academy Chiefs Removed Over Rape Scandal," 29 March 2003. Accessed 2 September 2015. http://www.wsws.org/en/articles/2003/03/acad_m29.html.

Martinez, Michael. "Daughters and moms now consider rape before applying to military." *CNN* 17 June, 2013.

Matar, Nabil. *In the Lands of the Christians: Arabic Travel Writing in the Seventeenth Century*. Edited and Translated by Nabil Matar. New York: Routledge, 2003.

– *Islam in Britain 1558–1685*. Cambridge: Cambridge University Press, 1998.

McDonald, Mark. "A War of Words in Afghanistan." *The Seattle Times*, 13 September 2004.

McKeon, Michael. *The Origins of the English Novel 1600–1740*. London: Johns Hopkins University Press, 1987.

McLarney, Ellen. "The Burqa in Vogue: Fashioning Afghanistan." *Journal of Middle East Women's Studies* 5.1 (Winter 2009): 1–20.

Melman, Billie. *Women's Orients: English Women and the Middle East, 1718–1918: Sexuality, Religion, and Work.* Ann Arbor: The University of Michigan Press, 1995.

Mernissi, Fatima. *Islam and Democracy: Fear of the Modern World*. Translated by Mary Jo Lakeland. Reading: Addison-Wesley Publishing Company, 1992.

– *Scheherazade Goes West: Different Cultures, Different Harems.* New York: Washington Square Press, 2001.

– *The Veil and the Male Elite: A Feminist Interpretation of Women's Rights in Islam.* Translated by Mary Jo Lakeland. Reading: Addison-Wesley Publishing Company, 1991.

Micklewright, Nancy. *A Victorian Traveler in the Middle East: The Photography and Travel Writing of Annie Lady Brassey*. Burlington: Ashgate, 2003.

Minai, Naila. *Women in Islam: Tradition and Transition in the Middle East.* New York: Seaview Books, 1981.

Mohammad Hashim Kamali, *Freedom, Equality and Justice in Islam*. Cambridge, UK: Islamic Texts Society, 2002.

Montagu, Lady Mary Wortley. *The Turkish Embassy Letters.* Edited by Teresa Heffernan and Daniel O'Quinn. Peterborough: Broadview Press, 2013.

Morris, Marilyn. 2006. "Transgendered Perspectives on Premodern Sexualities." *SEL: Studies in English Literature.* 46.3.

Murray, John. *Handbook for Travellers in Constantinople, Brûsa, and the Troad: With Maps and Plans.* London: John Murray, 1900.

Naghibi, Nima. *Rethinking Global Sisterhood: Western Feminism and Iran.* Minneapolis: University of Minnesota Press, 2007.

Nelson, Cynthia. "Public and Private Politics: Women in the Middle Eastern World. *American Ethnologist* 1.3 (1974): 551–63.

Nietzsche, Friedrich. *Beyond Good and Evil: Prelude to a Philosophy of the Future.* Translated by Walter Kaufmann. New York: Vintage, 1966.

– *The Gay Science.* Translated by Walter Kaufmann. New York: Random House, 1974.

– *Spurs.* Translated by Barbara Harlow. Chicago: University of Chicago Press, 1981, 64.

Nott, J.C. "The Mulatto a Hybrid-Probable Extermination of the Two Races if the Whites and Blacks are Allowed to Intermarry." *American Journal of the Medical Sciences* (6 July 1843): 252–6.

– *Two lectures, on the Natural History of the Caucasian and Negro races.* Mobile, AL: Dade and Thompson, 1844.

Nussbaum, Martha, et al. "Patriotism or Cosmopolitanism." *Boston Review* 19.5 (October–November 1994).

Pardoe, Julia. *The City of the sultan; and Domestic Manners of the Turks.* London: Henry Colburn, 1837.

Pateman, Carole. "The Fraternal and Social Contract." In *Civil Society and the State: New European Perspectives.* Edited by John Keane. London: Verso, 1988.

– *The Sexual Contract.* Cambridge: Polity Press, 1988.

Pazira, Nelofer. *A Bed of Red Flowers: In Search of My Afghanistan.* New York: Random House, 2005.

Pierce, Leslie. *The Imperial Harem: Women and Sovereignty in the Ottoman Empire.* New York: Oxford University Press, 1993.

"Playboy Centerfolds Become Pen-Pet." *Associated Press,* 23 November 2001.

"Playboy Launches 'Operation Playmate.'" *Agence France-Presse,* 21 September 2004.

Pointon, Marcia. *Naked Authority: The Body in Western Painting 1830–1906.* Cambridge: Cambridge University Press, 1990.

Porter, James. *Observations on the religion, law, government, and manners of the Turks. The second edition, corrected and enlarged ... To which is added, the state of the Turkey trade, from its origin to the present time.* London: J. Nourse, 1771.

Pouqueville, F.C.H.L. *Travels Through Morea, Albania, and Several Other Parts of the Ottoman Empire to Constantinople, translated from the French.* London: Phillips, 1806.

Rajan, Gita, and Shailja Sharma, eds. *New Cosmopolitanisms: South Asians in the US*. Stanford: Stanford University Press, 2006.

Ravishankar, Ra. "Afghanistan: The Liberation That Isn't. An Interview with 'Miriam' from RAWA." *CounterPunch*, 2 March 2004. http://www.rawa.org/punch.htm.

Reisman, Arnold. *Shoah: Turkey, the US and the UK*. Charleston, SC: BookSurge Publishing, 2009.

Riddell, Mary. "Why I Want to See the Veil Gone from Britain: Interview with Harriet Harman." *New Statesman*, 16 October 2006, 12.

Riddle, Katia. "Minnesota Girl, Sri Lankan Guy Still Turn Heads." *National Public Radio*, 11 July 2010.

Riverbend. "Atrocities," 11 July 2006, http://riverbendblog.blogspot.ca.

– *Baghdad Burning: Girl Blog from Iraq II*. New York: The Feminist Press at CUNY, 2006.

– "The Great Wall of Segregation," 26 April 2007.

– "The Promise and the Threat," 28 August 2003.

– "Summer of Goodbyes," 5 August 2006.

– "We've Only Just Begun," 23 August 2003.

Rosenberger, Sieglinde and Sauer, Birgit, eds. *Politics, Religion and Gender: Framing and Regulating the Veil*. London: Routledge, 2012.

Rush, George and Bill Hutchinson. "Smut Czar Nixes Nudes of Jessica." *The Daily News*, 12 November 2003.

Rycaut, Paul, Sir. *The History of the Present State of the Ottoman Empire*. 5th ed. London, 1682.

Said, Edward. *Culture and Imperialism*. New York: Vintage Books, 1994.

– *Orientalism*. New York: Vintage Books, 1979.

– *The World, the Text, and the Critic*. Cambridge: Harvard University Press, 1983.

Sandys, George. *Relation of a Journey begun An. Dom. 1610. Foure Bookes. Containing a description of the Turkish Empire, of Ægypt, of the Holy Land, of the remote parts of Italy, and Ilands adjoining*. London: W. Barrett, 1615.

Scott, Joan Wallach. *The Politics of the Veil*. Princeton: Princeton University Press, 2007.

Secor, Anna. "Orientalism, Gender and Class in Lady Mary Mortley Montagu's *Turkish Embassy Letters*: To Persons of Distinction, Men of Letters and C." *ECUMENE* 6.4 (1999): 375–98.

Şeni, Nora. "Fashion and Women's Clothing in the Satirical Press of Istanbul at the End of the 19th Century." In *Women in Modern Turkish Society*, edited by Şirin Tekeli, 25–45. London: Zed Books, 1991.

Sedghi, Hamideh. *Women and Politics in Iran: Veiling, Unveiling, Reveiling*. Cambridge: Cambridge University Press, 2007.

Shaw, Ezel Kural. "The Double Veil: Travelers' Views of the Ottoman Empire, Sixteenth through Eighteenth Centuries." In *English and Continental Views of the Ottoman Empire, 1500–1800*. Los Angeles: William Andrews Clark Memorial Library, 1972.

Shaw, Stanford J. *History of the Ottoman Empire and Modern Turkey: Volume 1, Empire of the Gazis: The Rise and Decline of the Ottoman Empire 1280–1808*. Cambridge: Cambridge University Press, 1976.

Showalter, Elaine. *Sexual Anarchy: Gender and Culture at the Fin de Siècle*. New York: Viking, 1990.

Spivak, Gayatri. "Can the Subaltern Speak?" In *Marxism and the Interpretation of Culture*. Edited by Cary Nelson and Laurence Grossberg. Urbana: University of Illinois Press, 1988.

– "Displacement and the Discourse of Woman." In *Displacement: Derrida and After*. Bloomington: Indiana University Press, 1983.

– "French Feminism." In *In Other Worlds: Essays in Cultural Politic*. New York: Routledge, 1988.

– *In Other Worlds: Essays in Cultural Politics*. New York: Routledge, 1988.

– "Reading *The Satanic Verses*." In *Outside in the Teaching Machine*. New York: Routledge, 1993.

Sterne, Laurence. *The Life and Opinions of Tristram Shandy, Gentleman*. Edited by Ian Watt. Boston: Riverside, 1965.

Tavernier, Jean Baptiste. *Collections of Travels through Turkey into Persia and the East-Indies. Giving an account of the present state of those countries*. London, 1684.

– *The Near East*. 22 January 1920, 115.

– *The Near East*. 5 February 1920, 177.

Thevenot, Jean de. *The travels of Monsieur de Thevenot into the Levant: in three parts, viz. into I. Turkey, II. Persia, III. The East-Indies / newly done out of French*. London: Printed by H. Clark for H. Faithorne, 1687.

Thompson, Elizabeth. "Public and Private in Middle Eastern Women's History." *Journal of Women's History* 15.1 (2003): 52–69.

Thornton, Thomas. *The present state of Turkey, or, A description of the political, civil and religious constitution, government and laws of the Ottoman Empire ....* London: Printed for Joseph Mawman, 1807.

– "Turkish Palaces." Review. *The New York Times*, 5 December 1903: BR47.

Turner, Katherine S.H. "From Classical to Imperial: Changing Visions of Turkey in the Eighteenth Century." *Travel Writing and Empire: Postcolonial Theory in Transit*. Edited by Steve Clark. London: Zed Books, 1999.

Vaka Brown, Demetra. *The Unveiled Ladies of Istanbul*. Piscataway, NJ: Gorgias Press, 2005.

– *The Unveiled Ladies of Stamboul*. Piscataway, NJ: Gorgias Press, 2005.

Warnock Fernea, Elizabeth. *In Search of Islamic Feminism: One Woman's Global Journey*. New York: Doubleday, 1997.

Watt, Ian. *The Rise of the Novel: Studies in Defoe, Richardson and Fielding*. Berkeley: University of California, 1957.

Wente, Margaret. "Women at War: Should We Think Again?" *The Globe and Mail*, 29 March 2003.

Werbner, Pnina. "The Veil and the Public Sphere." *Current Anthropology* 54.2 (2013): 195–6.

White, Jenny. *Muslim Nationalism and the New Turks*. Princeton University Press, 2013, 107–8.

Wilde, Oscar. *The Picture of Dorian Gray*. Harmondsworth: Penguin, 1971.

Wilgoren, Jodi. "Women in Combat." *The New York Times*, 29 March 2003.

Wollstonecraft, Mary. *A Vindication of the Rights of Woman*. London: Penguin, 1975.

Woolf, Virginia. *Three Guineas*. Edited by Jane Marcus. New York: Harcourt, Inc., 2006.

Yegenoglu, Meyda. *Colonial Fantasies: Towards a Feminist Reading of Orientalism*. Cambridge: Cambridge University Press, 1998.

– "Supplementing the Orientalist Lack: European Ladies in the Harem." *Inscriptions* 6 (1992): 45–80.

Young, Robert. *Colonial Desire: Hybridity in Theory, Race and Culture*. London: Routledge, 1995.

Zonana, Joyce. "The Sultan and the Slave: Feminist Orientalism and the Structure of *Jane Eyre*." *Signs* 18.3 (1993): 594.

Index

www.ingramcontent.com/pod-product-compliance
Lightning Source LLC
LaVergne TN
LVHW090159080826
844660LV00013B/865/J

* 9 7 8 1 4 4 2 6 3 7 2 3 8 *